If you have a home computer with Internet access you may:
- request an item to be placed on hold.
- renew an item that is not overdue or on hold.
- view titles and due dates checked out on your card.
- view and/or pay your outstanding fines online (over $5).

To view your patron record from your home computer click on
Patchogue-Medford Library's homepage: **www.pmlib.org**

A NEW
VOICE
for
ISRAEL

A NEW VOICE for ISRAEL

FIGHTING FOR THE SURVIVAL OF THE JEWISH NATION

JEREMY BEN-AMI

palgrave
macmillan

First published in 2011 by PALGRAVE MACMILLAN® in the United States—
a division of St. Martin's Press LLC, 175 Fifth Avenue, New York, NY 10010.

Where this book is distributed in the UK, Europe and the rest of the world, this is
by Palgrave Macmillan, a division of Macmillan Publishers Limited, registered in
England, company number 785998, of Houndmills, Basingstoke, Hampshire RG21
6XS.

Palgrave Macmillan is the global academic imprint of the above companies and has
companies and representatives throughout the world.

Palgrave® and Macmillan® are registered trademarks in the United States, the
United Kingdom, Europe and other countries.

ISBN: 978-0-230-11274-2

Library of Congress Cataloging-in-Publication Data

Ben-Ami, Jeremy.
   A new voice for Israel : fighting for the survival of the Jewish nation / Jeremy
Ben-Ami.
       p.   cm.
   Includes bibliographical references and index.
   ISBN 978-0-230-11274-2 (hardback)
     1. United States—Foreign relations—Israel.   2. Israel—Foreign relations—
United States.   3. Zionists—Political activity—United States.   4. Lobbying—
United States.   5. J Street (Organization)—Influence.   6. Jews—United
States—Attitudes toward Israel.   7. Jews—United States—Politics and
government—21st century.   8. United States—Ethnic relations.   I. Title.
E183.8.I7B435   2011
327.7305694—dc22

                                                                        2011005456

A catalogue record of the book is available from the British Library.

Design by Letra Libre, Inc.

First edition: July 2011

10 9 8 7 6 5 4 3 2 1

Printed in the United States of America.

For my partner, Alisa,

and for the next generation, Shira and Ari

CONTENTS

ACKNOWLEDGMENTS

About two years ago, my father-in-law called to suggest that I write a book about J Street and what led to this new effort to change the American conversation on Israel in the United States. I told him there was no way I could do it without putting way too much strain on all those around me, from family to colleagues. He assured me that everyone would do their part to help—and he was right.

This book wouldn't have been possible without the assistance of my colleagues, family and friends. Two of J Street's staff assistants, Sarah Turbow and Jeremy Sherer, helped with months of research. My colleagues Dan Kohl, Rachel Lerner, Carinne Luck, Isaac Luria and Hadar Susskind were kind enough to read early drafts. Others in and around J Street provided important feedback, including Jim Gerstein, Matt Dorf and Janette Hillis-Jaffe. I owe a special thanks to Daniel Levy, my partner in launching J Street, a constant source of intellectual inspiration and challenge and the person whose thinking has most deeply influenced my work and this book.

J Street itself wouldn't be possible without the leadership and support of many people—advisers, funders and activists. However, there are a few whose support stands out as essential to everything we're achieving: Bill Benter, Davidi Gilo, Mort Halperin, Victor Kovner, Kathleen Peratis, Deborah Sagner, Alan Sagner and Alexandra Stanton. Our work is only possible in partnership with a number of other terrific leaders and organizations with whom we work closely, including Debra DeLee and her team at Americans for Peace Now and Daniel Sokatch and his colleagues at the New Israel Fund.

I am grateful that a broader circle of friends and associates agreed to read some or all of the book, including Deborah Lewis, Gabrielle and David Fitzgerald, Alan Snitow and Deborah Kaufman, Rabbi Jonathan Roos, Steven M. Cohen and Rafael Medoff. And I know there would be no book without my editor, Emily Carleton, who reached out on her own initiative to express interest in the project, and my agent, Priscilla Gilman, who guided me through the unfamiliar waters of bringing a book idea to fruition.

But the biggest thank-you goes, of course, to my family. My mother-in-law, Paula Biran, gave the project the thorough read it needed and caught every mistake that I had overlooked. After all, that's what mothers-in-law are for, and I'm so grateful for her time and caring. My father-in-law, Ephraim Biran, lived much of the history recounted in the book, from Petah Tikva to the Upper West Side of Manhattan. He was kind enough to read it and give me his feedback and his approval. My sister, Debbie Benami-Rahm, is a powerful source of encouragement in all that I do, and, of course, there wasn't a moment when I was working on this book that my father and mother were not with me in spirit. Their inspiration guides me every day.

My wife, Alisa, made not only this book but really the entire J Street effort possible. She was the first to suggest, nearly a decade ago, that if I found the politics of the Jewish community on Israel so disturbing, then I should stop complaining and do something about it. And she has carried far more of the weight in our parenting partnership, particularly during the months when this book was in the works and I needed time away to write. I love her and cherish our friendship.

In the end, I am inspired and fired up to do the work that I do by my wonderful children, Shira and Ari, who embody a delight in what is good in life that should focus all those in positions of power on the imperative to end conflicts and build a future deserving of their faith in us as parents.

INTRODUCTION

Ten or fifteen years ago, I believed that the arc of conflict involving Israel in the Middle East, though long, ultimately bent toward peace.

Time was on the side of the peace makers. First, Anwar Sadat came to Jerusalem, paving the way for compromise with Egypt. Then there were historic handshakes on the White House lawn hosted by President Bill Clinton. Next, peace with Jordan.

True, terror attacks and assassinations occasionally marred the path to peace, but Martin Luther King had warned that, on the road to justice, "There will still be rocky places of frustration and meandering points of bewilderment. There will be inevitable setbacks here and there. And there will be those moments when the buoyancy of hope will be transformed into the fatigue of despair."[1]

We almost made it. Syria and Israel came within a few hundred meters of resolving their dispute. And Israelis and Palestinians flirted on several occasions with meaningful compromise. All we needed, it seemed, was a different mix of leaders and a dose of courage, and we could get it done.

Today, sadly, time seems to have switched sides, and the arc is bending in the wrong direction. Ideologies are becoming more extreme, gaps between the parties wider, and the technology for killing and destruction ever-more sophisticated.

If things don't change pretty soon, chances are that the two-state solution to the Israeli-Palestinian conflict will slip through our fingers. As that happens, the dream of the Jewish people to be a free people in their own land also slowly disappears.

There will not be one winner in the Israeli-Palestinian conflict. There can be only a win-win compromise or a perpetual, bloody conflict.

For too long, Israel advocacy in the United States has ignored this reality. Pro-Israel advocates have filtered discussion of the Middle East conflict through only one lens—a simple us-versus-them formulation that demands unquestioning support for Israel. Politicians, community leaders, media and academics have been told you're either with Israel or against it, while the Jewish community has turned a blind eye to the moral and ethical implications of occupation and its impact on both the Palestinian people and Israel itself.

On the surface, this kind of advocacy appears to serve the State of Israel well. It's resulted in a generous aid package, the patronage of the world's only superpower and absolute loyalty from friends and family abroad.

However, it has also abetted the failure to resolve the conflict by enabling Israel to avoid taking the tough but necessary steps to end it. And it has had a poisonous impact on the American Jewish community, where debate is stifled and criticism of Israeli policy unwelcome.

In 2008, together with other passionate supporters of Israel, I helped start J Street to give a voice in American politics to those who believe that Israel's future depends on a two-state solution. Believing that active American diplomacy is essential to ending the conflict, our core mission is to change the political dynamics that prevent its resolution, while opening up greater space for debate and discussion on Israel in the Jewish community.

A New Voice for Israel is the personal story of how I've arrived at these views from my roots in a household on the far right of Jewish politics and in a pioneering family that immigrated to the land of Israel in the 1880s.

More importantly, it is a call to arms, imploring friends of Israel in the United States and abroad to sound the alarm—preaching that advocacy for Israel must move boldly and urgently away from its traditional zero-sum paradigm. The time has come to end the peace process as we've known it and to focus relentlessly on getting to a result, not just back to the negotiating table.

And finally, it is a blueprint for how we can make the necessary changes to the conversation—and the policy—while we still have time.

WE NEED A NEW definition of victory for pro-Israel advocacy.

Victory means ensuring the long-term security and survival of Israel as the democratic home of the Jewish people. Victory means defining borders for Israel that the world recognizes and that give Israel enduring legitimacy in the community of nations. And it means helping ensure that Israel is solidly rooted in the values, ethics and principles of the Jewish people.

For too long, the relationship between Israel and the Diaspora has been defined by Israel's requests for assistance from friends abroad. We've been asked to send money. To move to Israel. To lobby. To send our children to visit. And we've responded—some by moving, others by visiting, many more by raising money. Most important, we've established a powerful political base of support for Israel in the United States.

To quote a man I admire, Ami Ayalon (former head of Israel's secret service and commander of its navy), it is now time for friends of Israel to perform the ultimate act of Zionism—to tell Israel the truth. We need to warn that this amazing effort to re-establish a home for the Jewish people after two thousand years is about to go seriously off the tracks.

Israel's very existence is in fact threatened by a progressive, terminal illness. Without defining its borders and ending the occupation, Israel is living on borrowed land and time. And time is no longer on the side of those seeking a peaceful resolution to the Arab-Israeli conflict.

Change is sweeping the Middle East in 2011. The people of the region are rising up to achieve their freedom and dignity and to change a status quo that has been accepted for too long. The status quo between Israel and the Palestinian people is also unsustainable. Israel either needs to change course now or the wave of change will sweep across its shores, possibly with devastating effect. Dramatic action is needed now for the sake of Israel and the Jewish people.

My hope is that this book contributes in some small way to opening up minds and conversation in the American Jewish community and beyond about the need not just for such action but for a whole new approach to Israel advocacy in the United States.

I

FOUR GENERATIONS
OF ZIONISTS

1

THE PIONEERS AND
THE BUILDERS

My great-grandfather was a bootlegger, my grandfather was a card shark and my father was a terrorist.

I've always loved delivering that line when asked about my family history. In reality, I'm just a preppy, private-school kid from the Upper West Side of Manhattan, not exactly the rabble-rousing type. The colorful ancestry has always been the one thing that gives me a bit of an edge. Of course, the story's better if you don't know that my mother's father was actually a European bridge champion, not a hardened gambler—but good comedy does depend on slight exaggeration.

The truth is that my family's story wouldn't be all that different from that of most other Jewish Americans if my father's family hadn't chosen to escape the Russian pogroms in the late nineteenth century by heading south to the land of Israel (then Ottoman Palestine), rather than west to Europe or the United States. We took a sixty-year, three-generation detour on our way from the shtetls of Russia to the shtetl of the Upper West Side.

In fact, of the nearly two million Jews who left Russia from the late nineteenth century through the end of World War I, only 1 or 2 percent actually made their way to Palestine. The rest headed west—and most, at least initially, had little interest or stake in the success or failure of the Zionist enterprise.

The few Jews who went to Israel in those early years were true visionaries. They dreamed of rebuilding a nation for the Jewish people in the ancient homeland of their ancestors.

Three generations of my family devoted their lives to this dream. They were pioneers, builders and ultimately fighters for the cause, for their family and for their people. The work of these first generations of Zionists was valiant, at times miraculous and, of course, controversial. Their story sets the scene for some of the toughest challenges facing the Jewish people today—in Israel, in the United States and throughout the rest of the Diaspora.

As of today, their work remains incomplete. The Israel they founded is still without internationally accepted borders. It is technically at war with several of its neighbors and has yet to be formally recognized by most of the countries in the region. It still struggles to accept that another people live on the same land and that they, too, call it home. Despite over a hundred years of hard work building a secure and democratic Jewish home in the land of Israel, the entire experiment remains at risk.

It falls to the Jewish people of today to complete the work, to bring the dreams of our grandparents and great-grandparents to fruition. This generation must make the decisions and compromises necessary to ensure the future of the Jewish homeland that my great-grandparents envisioned when they arrived by boat in the historic port of Jaffa 130 years ago in the second year of the First Aliyah.

PIONEERS

On March 13, 1881, Tsar Alexander II was killed in St. Petersburg. For my family, as for so many Jews in the Russian Empire, his assassination and the ensuing reprisals against the Jewish community sent a crystal-clear message: Wake up and move to safety.

For nearly one hundred years before that, both sides of my father's family, like half the world's Jews, had lived under Russian authority. They experienced a constantly changing set of rules and regulations governing where and how they lived as the Russian Empire grappled with what they called their "Jewish problem." The problem began when the expanding Russian Empire absorbed hundreds of thousands of Jews as part of its takeover of Poland and Lithuania in the late eighteenth century.

The primary challenge was economic. In the Russian economic system, Jews formed a poor though stable middle class. As craftsmen, merchants and innkeepers, they occupied the economic space between wealthy aristocrats and landless serfs and peasants. Only a small number worked the land—as late as 1897, less than 4 percent of Russia's Jews were farmers, according to the national census.

Economic tensions grew through the nineteenth century. The serfs were freed and needed more opportunity. As the empire expanded, the tsars sought more taxes. The nobility found itself owing more to the tsar, while controlling less land, workers and resources. The lower classes found themselves with greater freedom, but limited opportunities. And the Jews, as the outsiders, served as a convenient scapegoat and focus of anger from all quarters. Their separation from those around them—with their own language, schools, houses of worship and community councils—only reinforced deepening suspicion and hostility among the broader population.

The Russian authorities tried different approaches to managing the challenges posed by this large minority living in their midst. They passed and then rescinded numerous laws on where and how Jews could live and what professions they could pursue. They tried forcing Jews into the army. And they focused particular attention on the Jewish education system—the heart and soul of the community—as the key to integrating the Jews into Russian society. They employed carrots, encouraging Jewish students to enroll in Russian schools, and sticks, requiring that traditional Jewish schools teach in Russian, Polish or German—not in Yiddish or Hebrew.

Owning land was one of the great obstacles facing Jews, not simply in Russia but throughout the Diaspora. Country after country forbade Jewish land ownership. In the Russian Empire, Jews were initially confined to living in certain areas and denied the right to own or work the land. But in the early nineteenth century, Tsar Alexander I—in an effort to move Jews out of the villages and to break up their concentrated pockets of "alien" life—allowed them to settle on lands allocated by the government.

Part of my family took him up on this, moving from their village outside the larger town of Brisk to a farm outside Grodno, today a regional capital in northwest Belarus. There my great-grandparents Ze'ev and Batya made their home and brought up six children—including my grandmother Sara—in the late 1860s and 1870s.

The other part of my father's family made its home near Vitebsk—today in northeast Belarus. This family was part of the Chabad movement, a branch of Hasidic Judaism dating to late eighteenth-century Russia. Chabad is today one of the largest ultra-Orthodox movements, well known for its network of community centers around the world and its active program of Jewish education and outreach. The Jewish community in the Vitebsk area traced its origins back to the sixteenth century, when Jews made their way across Europe from Spain following the Inquisition.

My great-grandparents on this side of the family, Shmuel and Chaya-Frieda Rosin, had eight children, including my grandfather Menahem. It was a source of great pride to my father that he could trace Chaya-Frieda's family directly back to Don Isaac Abravanel, a respected leader, scholar and adviser to the Spanish royal court, who was regarded as the leader of the Jewish community in Spain at the time of the Inquisition.[1]

Abravanel, in an effort to convince the royal family not to expel the Jews from Spain in 1492, famously pleaded the case for the Jewish community to King Ferdinand and Queen Isabella, ultimately losing his argument to the Grand Inquisitor Torquemada. Abravanel fled to Italy, and the family traveled through the Rhineland to Poland. Their route was the same one followed by much of the community that lived for hundreds of years in what I grew up referring to as "Russia-Poland."

By the 1870s and 1880s, my great-grandfather Shmuel was neither an adviser to kings nor a treasurer to empires, but a simple miller with a distillery, turning the grain farmed by peasants into alcohol for the tsar's soldiers.

Families with roots in this age and place are never short of tales of the prejudice and hardship they suffered. Mine is no different. As a boy, my father and his cousins often heard the story of how grandfather Shmuel was kidnapped at age seven and taken to serve in the army of Tsar Nicholas I.

In fact, kidnappings of young Jewish boys for army service had been routine for decades. Local councils were required to meet quotas of boys and men for army service, and they often employed "snatchers" who would seize youngsters and send them off to the army or military school. Particularly during the Crimean War in the early 1850s, when the quotas for conscription were much higher, kidnappings of boys as young as seven were incredibly common.

One night, Shmuel's mother, exhausted and shaken from the grief of her son's disappearance, dreamed that he was at the local train station, ready to be transported to a military camp. Against the will of her husband and family, she insisted on going to the station in the morning. She found little Shmuel there amid a large group of other young boys— guarded by two dozing, drunk soldiers. She snuck up behind him, grabbed him by the arm without waking the soldiers, and quietly spirited him back to their shtetl.

Another time, this same unlucky woman was preparing for the Sabbath. In the midst of making the meal, setting the table, cleaning and other Friday night preparations, she left the house to run some last-minute errands. She returned to find her Shabbat table disturbed and knew immediately that something was wrong.

Checking under the challah (bread) cover, she found a dead fetus that had been hidden there while she was out. Without hesitation, she tossed the bundle in the fire.

Moments later, she heard a knock on the door and a young Russian peasant woman stood outside with the police, accusing Shmuel's mother of stealing her baby. The police searched the house but found no evidence. Outside, an angry mob that had gathered seeking vengeance grumbled but silently returned home, their thirst for violence unfulfilled.

"Blood libel"—the centuries-old accusation that Jews used the blood of Christian children to bake their bread and in other rituals—was a prime source of terror and suffering in the Polish communities of the eighteenth century. It was eventually outlawed by Tsar Alexander I in 1817, but remained a common anti-Semitic rallying cry all through the 1800s.

Needless to say, the stress and tension of such a life is unimaginable for most of us, and Shmuel's mother died when he was still young. Shmuel grew up, married and had his own family during the twenty-six-year reign of Tsar Alexander II in the mid-nineteenth century (1855–1881), which brought enormous changes to the entirety of Jewish life throughout the empire. Perhaps best known for freeing the serfs, Alexander II also allowed Jews to enter far more professions, to engage in secular education and to live outside the towns and rural settlements to which they had been limited.

By granting draft exemptions to those with a Russian secondary-school education, he encouraged Jews to abandon their traditional schooling and join the secular mainstream. Jews gradually entered into the intellectual and cultural life of the country as active participants in political debates, and in theater, literature and music. They quickly emerged as well as distinguished artists, journalists, musicians and academics.

The sparks of the Enlightenment that had earlier swept through Europe now caught fire in the Russian Empire, and a new generation of Jews—including my great-grandparents—was suddenly free not just to dream but to truly plan for life beyond the shtetl. The seeds of revolution were planted as well, as the accelerated exchange of ideas and intellectual ferment led to questions about the justice of the social and economic order.

This relatively sudden integration of Jews into all aspects of Russian life caused inevitable resentment and backlash, given the preceding centuries of prejudice, tension and racism. Opponents of the Jews could be found among both the tsar's loyalists and his most radical opposition.

In fact, many of the revolutionary forces beginning to oppose the tsar blamed at least part of the widespread suffering of the masses on exploitation by the Jews. The competition for land became especially fierce, as the emancipation of the serfs took hold at the same time as the Jewish population doubled from two and a half to five million in the late nineteenth century.

The 1881 assassination of Alexander II threw fuel on this ready fire of resentment and anger. When anti-tsarist revolutionaries tried to foment rebellion among the broader masses, the government pushed back and made the Jews the scapegoat. A wave of pogroms broke out—likely encouraged by the government—in the south of Russia. Many Jewish communities endured looting, rioting and in some cases murder and rape.

The new tsar, Alexander III, took the opportunity to roll back some of the freedoms and privileges accorded by Alexander II, imposing new prohibitions on where Jews could live and limiting the number of Jewish students allowed in Russian schools. The press was overtly anti-Semitic, and a right-wing, ultra-nationalist party, also powered by a strong under-current of anti-Semitism, emerged to fight the more liberal revolutionary tendency.

It was this environment that spawned the most famous anti-Semitic screed of all time—the "Protocols of the Elders of Zion," a tract cited to this day by notoriously anti-Semitic leaders like Iran's Mahmoud Ahmadinejad.

Clearly, this was no place for a generation of more enlightened and more ambitious young Jews to raise their families. The previous generation or two had shown them that a different life was possible. Their long-held aspirations and dreams had been inflamed by these new-found freedoms, and they could not bear to go backward.

Armed with a greater awareness of the world, transferable skills and a deep concern for their children's future, many Jewish families began to consider how to make the most of their lives and, most important, where to raise their children in safety. Some moved within Russia from the more traditionally Jewish areas in the north and west of the Pale of Settlement (today's Belarus, Ukraine, Poland and Lithuania) to the southern part of the empire. Established by Catherine the Great in 1791, the Pale was the part of the Russian Empire where permanent Jewish residency was allowed. Others looked toward Western Europe and the United States.

As many as two million Jews left Russia between Alexander II's assassination and the outbreak of World War I in 1914. And they were right to leave because the future for those who stayed turned out to be darker than their worst nightmares.

A small percentage of Russian Jews began to consider the notion of returning to the promised land of Zion. Motivated by the writings of Leon Pinsker and later by the dreams of Theodore Herzl, they formed organizations like Hovevei Zion and Hibbat Zion in which they worked in small groups to turn those dreams into practical reality. Together, they determined that real freedom for the Jewish people could not come within the society of another people, but only in their own country, on their own terms.

For centuries, Jews had prayed to return to the land promised by God to their ancestors. It was a longing built into the DNA of the Jewish people, a reaction to their history of exile and return through the millennia. But at the dawn of the modern era, there was one key difference. No longer were the younger, educated Jews of Russia content to pray and wait for the Messiah to bring them to the Promised Land. They were ready to take matters into their own hands and bring that Promised Land into being.

My father writes in his autobiography that his grandfather Ze'ev went to see his rebbe, the spiritual leader of the local Chabad community, to ask whether he should go to Palestine, and the rabbi told him no. As my father relates it, the rebbe told Ze'ev, "It isn't time to go to Palestine. We have to be patient. We have to wait. . . . We are to stay here and suffer. Our suffering will make us ready for the Messiah."

Needless to say, Ze'ev and his generation were not convinced. Ready to take their future into their own hands, they launched organizations dedicated to settling in Palestine and groups to prepare their young children. They started newspapers and published pamphlets to promote their ideas. They held clandestine meetings in the evenings to plan what only a generation earlier would have been an improbable, perhaps impossible journey—to reclaim their ancient homeland for themselves.

Only a very small number of pioneers, probably thirty to forty thousand, made the journey to Ottoman Palestine between 1881 and 1904, defying conventional wisdom and the rules of their own rabbis. They are known today as members of the First Aliyah—the first "ascendance" to the land of Israel.

Nearly two million of their friends, neighbors and families headed west to Europe and to America. Millions more argued that the known evil at home was better than the unknown evil abroad.

But, at the vanguard of the pioneers who headed to Palestine were my great-grandparents—Shmuel and Chaya-Frieda Rosin and Ze'ev and Batya Yatkovsky—and the fourteen young children they had between them.

BUILDERS

In the spring of 1878, a small group of young Orthodox families left Jerusalem to start a new agricultural settlement at the source of the Yarkon River, in the heart of the coastal plain between the hills of Jerusalem and the Mediterranean Sea. They called it Petah Tikva—the Gate of Hope.

The area was extraordinarily inhospitable, little more than a malarial swamp. The going was hard, and the settlement was abandoned in 1881.

By the time Ze'ev and Batya arrived by boat in Jaffa in 1882, the settlers were making a second attempt to tame the area. The original group, which included a friend of Ze'ev's from Grodno, was not to be denied—this time they were armed with financial help from Baron Edmund de Rothschild and with reinforcements from the First Aliyah.

When Ze'ev and Batya arrived in Petah Tikva, with all their worldly belongings packed on a cart drawn by a mule, there were only a dozen homes—mostly lean-tos and mud-brick shacks. Without a permit from the sultan, the family could not build a permanent structure of their own, so, for the first few years, they rented a room from another family.

Ze'ev initially raised wheat, as he had in Russia, and the family battled the elements and at times local thieves to establish a permanent foothold on the land. Ze'ev spent most nights in a shack in the field to keep an eye on his land. Only after six years did the family build a permanent home that would become the center of their life for fifty years and the site of many of their happiest celebrations, including my father's bar mitzvah.

Even today when I visit Israel, my older cousins still love to drive through downtown Petah Tikva, now a bustling metropolis of 200,000 people, and recall what the town was like in their youth. We'll drive by the main branch of Bank Leumi at a central intersection downtown, and they'll tell me that's where the family homestead used to be. They also make sure that I know of their gratitude to this day to Baron de Rothschild, whose assistance starting in the late 1880s saved the family and the town as it wobbled frequently on the brink of failure.

With Rothschild's assistance, the farmers of Petah Tikva planted citrus groves, almonds and a vineyard—crops far better suited than wheat to the local environment. They raised cattle, providing their own dairy and meat. Over time, Petah Tikva's success made it an agricultural model for other settlements; they even established a school for newer agricultural pioneers to learn how to make the most of difficult land.

Just as the settlement's roots seemed to be taking a firmer hold, Ze'ev's youngest daughter caught scarlet fever and passed away. Having brought his family thousands of miles against almost everyone's advice, Ze'ev could scarcely handle the guilt. Wracked with despair and self-doubt, his own health deteriorated.

In and out of the hospital in Jaffa, weakened by bouts of raging fever and insomnia, he still insisted on standing guard over his crops in the field. Ze'ev died just months after his little daughter Chaya, partly from the fever, partly from the grief.

My other great-grandfather, Shmuel, and his family made the journey to Palestine in 1891. He had attended Hovevei Zion meetings in Vitebsk but ultimately traveled to Palestine on his own, having sold his possessions and packed up his wife and eight children. They too traveled by boat from Odessa, through Constantinople to Jaffa—a twelve-day journey in a small cargo ship in what my father described as "grimy dungeon-like holds."

Unlike many of those arriving in these first waves of immigration, Shmuel and his family were not part of an organized effort to settle a particular community. The family moved to the Old City of Jerusalem, settling initially on Hebron Street in the Muslim Quarter and then in a small two-room apartment in the Jewish Quarter. He soon established himself in business again, distilling vodka and brandy. Apparently his products gained such repute that when the Russian consul in Jerusalem asked where to buy vodka, he was referred to Shmuel, whose vodka was said to be on a par with the best in all of Russia.

For a brief time, Shmuel lived happily with his family in Jerusalem, following his dream and the Chabad tradition. Tragically, that dream was cut short after only a few years. One day, as he tried to fix a broken valve on his still, the boiler exploded, burning much of his body. He died within days and was buried on the Mount of Olives overlooking the Old City of Jerusalem. His wife, Chaya-Frieda, joined him on the Mount of Olives only a few years later.

I remember going with my father as a young boy after the Israelis gained control over the ancient cemetery in the 1967 war to see his grandparents' graves. The cemetery had suffered nearly two decades of neglect since the Jordanians took control of it in 1948. Rumor had it that the tombstones had been used to pave streets and that large parts of the cemetery had been desecrated.

My father searched the hillside for hours to identify the seventy-year-old headstones. Finally finding them intact gave him a measure of personal peace with the knowledge that his grandparents' long journey to rest in Jerusalem was complete. Today, my parents are also at rest in the Chabad section of the Mount of Olives overlooking the Old City, waiting, as tradition would have it, in front-row seats for the coming of the Messiah.

After the sudden death of the family patriarch, the children—ranging in age from their mid-teens through their twenties—scattered throughout the country to create their own lives in the new land. One son, Meir, stayed in Jerusalem and became an artist. His work was among the first to be displayed at the new Bezalel Academy of Arts and Design and was recently included in a retrospective there of early twentieth-century visions of Jerusalem.

Another son, my grandfather Menahem, took the skilled hands he inherited from Shmuel and moved first to Rehovoth, where he repaired farm machinery, and then to Jaffa, where he apprenticed with the town's leading watchmaker on the main commercial street. He soon opened his own shop on Boustros Street, in the heart of the city. As my father tells it, "Before long the shop developed into a social center. Father was a gregarious man who could tell a story while keeping his eyes fixed unwaveringly on the inside of a watch."

At least to my father's eyes, Menahem was "a tall, handsome young man. Clean-shaven except for twirling mustaches, he had dark hair combed neatly to the side. He wore hard collars, flared ties and a watch-chain across his vest. He had come a long way from the family's lean years in Jerusalem."

The community of Russian Jewish immigrants in Palestine in the early years of the twentieth century still numbered only several thousand. With fewer single young women than men, it wasn't surprising that my grandfather in Jaffa heard about young Sara Yatkovsky in Petah Tikva and had friends arrange an introduction. Three weeks after their first meeting, they married and settled in the small room above Menahem's Jaffa repair shop.

The couple exemplified the burgeoning middle class in the new Jewish community—children of immigrants now earning a reasonable living and trying, as young couples do, to get more room to raise a family and improve their quality of life. Jaffa, as the port of entry for most new arrivals, both legal and illegal, was overcrowded, noisy and dirty. Another wave of pogroms in Russia, particularly following the 1905 Russian revolution, brought tens of thousands of new immigrants to Palestine in the Second Aliyah, from 1904 to 1914.

Jaffa's residents—veterans and newcomers—with the means to do so began to look for alternatives. A group of young families—most with young children or thinking of having them—formed a housing association called

Ahuzat Bait. Their goal: to establish the Jewish community's first "garden suburb."

Sixty families in the group each put 100,000 francs on deposit with the Anglo-Palestine Company, obtained construction loans and together purchased twenty-five acres of land, just northeast of the heart of Jaffa.

In April 1909, the families gathered in their holiday finest on a sand dune just north of Jaffa, and each family drew a seashell from a hat to determine which lot in the new planned community would be their new home. The group photo taken that day remains one of the iconic images of the early creation of the state.

My grandparents drew lot number ten on Herzl Street, and, in 1910, they were one of the first families to move into their new home in the place now officially called Tel Aviv.

My father was born in 1913. Because he arrived nearly twenty years after Menahem and Sara were married, and long after they had come to accept that parenthood was not to be their lot in life, he was greeted as a minor miracle. They named him Yitshaq (Isaac)—in tribute to the biblical Sara, who was also well along in years when she was blessed by her own little Yitshaq.

According to family lore, my father was one of the first boys born in Tel Aviv. Yet, as I found out very quickly on attending a "reunion" in 2009 of the descendants of the city's founding families, almost all the first families of Tel Aviv believe that they have equally strong claims to that distinction!

Among my father's earliest memories is spending the last days of World War I hiding at the family homestead in Petah Tikva after the family fled their home in Tel Aviv, closer to the coast. They had been caught between the artillery blasts of the advancing British and the last-ditch efforts of the Ottomans to hold onto their receding empire. He recounted stories—his memory undoubtedly buffed over the years by other, older relatives—of hiding under the bed with bullets whizzing through windows and of his parents bribing Ottoman soldiers to overlook the extra family members hiding in back rooms.

The British gained the loyalty of the local and global Jewish population by promising, in the 1917 Balfour Declaration, to create a national home for the Jewish people in Palestine, and the end of the Ottoman era was greeted as a triumph for the young Jewish community.

My father's childhood in Tel Aviv revolved around his schooling at the Herzliya Gymnasia, the epicenter of the linguistic and cultural rebirth of the Jewish people. The children found nothing unusual about learning and studying in Hebrew, a language that until twenty years earlier had been functionally dead for thousands of years. As my father would write years later, "Not until I traveled through the Diaspora as an adult did I feel the full thrill of having belonged to the first generation of a re-born nation."

His politics as a young man reflected the dominant Socialist Zionist consensus of the time. He took part in Saturday "Circle" discussion groups sponsored by the socialist youth movement to which he belonged. There, he studied the writings and teachings of the legendary Ahad Ha'am, whose house was just four doors away from my father's and next to the school.

Ahad Ha'am taught that the realization of the dreams of the Jewish people would come through the nourishment and development of a spiritual center where they could act on and carry out their own ethical and spiritual standards. One day, they thought, through this cultural rebirth, a Jewish state might evolve. This was not an active vision of nationalism and certainly not a political vision of Zionism, aimed squarely at creating a state for the Jewish people. Rather, it was a movement grounded in the pursuit of higher values, in Jewish ideals of justice and morality.

My father and his peers in those years did not see themselves as part of a national enterprise working to secure the independence and freedom of the Jews, but as part of a larger movement to improve the lot of all people around the world—working people in particular. Their goal was to build in Palestine a society that was more just and more equitable than any other, and through the righteousness of their cause to give rise to a state.

This philosophy suggested that the only people fit to join the Zionist enterprise were those immigrants who had been properly trained and prepared for such higher pursuits. This ran counter to the vision of political Zionists like Theodore Herzl and Max Nordau and their followers, who sought to create a home for the masses of disenfranchised European Jews and would have welcomed half a million arrivals on the beach of Palestine.

These early idealists also believed that the commonality between Jewish and Arab workers was greater than the national divides between them, and that together they would one day defeat the twin evils of British imperialism and capitalism.

These sentiments were common in Jewish and Zionist thought in the early twentieth century all over the world. In furtherance of their ideals, my father and his classmates spent high-school summers on new kibbutzim, or collective farms, being established around the country as part of the Hanoar Haoved (working youth) movement.

I can only imagine the conversation between my father and his father. Grandfather Menahem apparently could not fathom how—in light of all the education my father had received, all the privileges he'd had, all the forward progress the family had made—he could possibly want to return to living in the fields with next to nothing. Wasn't that exactly what the family had spent forty years trying to move beyond?

They argued, apparently, over higher education—with my father believing that hard work and toil in the fields were the routes to advancing the greater good, and his father wanting him to get the university education that he himself had missed out on. Ultimately, my father agreed to pursue a degree in agriculture so he could bring back skills and knowledge from abroad to further develop the land.

My father's worldview began to change in 1929—sparked by massive riots in the Arab community that grew out of a long-running dispute over

Jewish access to the Western Wall in Jerusalem and fed on simmering tensions between the Arab and Jewish communities in Palestine. Hundreds of Jews were killed and Jewish property was destroyed across the country. The riots claimed the farm belonging to my father's uncle Shraga in the southern outpost of Be'er Tuvia as well as the homes and lives of other friends and family around the country.

My father's belief in class solidarity between the Jewish and Arab populations was shaken to its core as he realized that nationalism could and did override alliances based on class.

His intellectual awakening continued during his studies in Italy the following year when he was introduced to the thinking of Jewish nationalists whose main concern was not global class struggle but the growing threat of fascism to the lives and well-being of the Jews of Europe.

The nationalists had no patience for my father and his idealistic classmates who talked of building the perfect socialist society in Palestine to serve as a model for the broader world. They sought instead the immediate creation of a homeland for the Jewish people in Palestine, where those already suffering and those fearing for their future could find refuge.

As my father learned more about the threat brewing in Europe, he came to understand the need for a haven for the Jewish people in the face of the coming tide of fascism, and to realize that history wasn't going to give his people time to build a workers' paradise. They would need to take control of history.

In just a few years, my father transformed from an idealistic agrarian socialist to a right-of-center political Zionist, believing that the Jewish people had to achieve their independence by force of arms, and that the fate of Europe's Jews hung in the balance.

In the space of just one generation, the Jewish people had built a home in the land of Palestine. They had gone from a few thousand scattered pioneers, barely hanging on, to a community of a couple hundred thousand people with a strong modern city in Tel Aviv and vital outposts all over the country.

They had built a new home and a life for their people from scratch—learning to work a new land in a new climate, revitalizing a language and building a whole new culture of their own.

Now, they would have to fight for the dreams that had brought their parents and grandparents to Palestine, to fight for the right of the "Hebrew Nation," as my father called it, to take its place among the community of nations. It would be not only a battle for independence, but a fight for the survival of Jews everywhere.

2
THE FIGHTERS

fter moving to the right politically in the early 1930s, my father never looked back. He became a devoted follower of Vladimir (Ze'ev) Jabotinsky, the leader of what is called Revisionist Zionism. Jabotinsky and the Revisionists believed that the core problem facing world Jewry in the 1930s was the lack of a state where the Jewish people could go without restriction to find safety. In their view, the situation in Europe was so urgent that, even in the absence of a state, as many Jews as possible should be brought to Palestine by any means, including illegal immigration, to ensure their safety.

The Revisionists broke fully with the mainstream in 1935, contending that the central purpose of Zionism should be the establishment of an independent state of the Jewish people. They believed that the danger was so imminent that they needed to take matters into their own hands, achieving independence by force if necessary. As my father later wrote, "if the British and the League of Nations which had entrusted Palestine to the care of Great Britain would not act, we, the Jewish youth, would have to act alone."[1]

However, the "establishment" voices in the Jewish community—the Socialist Zionists—believed that Jews, as a moral people, were not meant to break laws or start revolutions. They believed that the "Palestine problem" could be resolved through peaceful negotiations and gradual change facilitated by the British. And they believed that the sole legitimate purpose of force was self-defense.

The Revisionists had little patience for either the ideology of the Socialists or their tactics when it came to the local Arabs and the British. In 1931, a breakaway group of commanders from the Socialist self-defense forces formed their own underground militia, the Irgun Zvai Leumi, known in short as the Irgun. If it was going to be necessary to fight for independence with violence, then fight they would. And if that meant disregarding the authority and command of the official structures of the community, so be it.

The Irgun began retaliatory attacks in response to Arab violence against Jews in the mid-1930s. In the 1940s, they did not shy away from using violence to push the British out of Palestine. Perhaps their most notorious act was the bombing of the King David Hotel in Jerusalem, which served as a command center for the British military in Palestine.

They set up their own command structure, amassed their own weapons, issued their own pamphlets and propaganda and fought a three-front running battle for over a decade—with the Zionist establishment, the local Arabs and the British. In the eyes of the British and establishment Jews, they were terrorists. They saw themselves as fighting for their lives and the lives of Jews around the world.

Splits between those who believe that their goals can be accomplished through peaceful negotiations and those who believe that power will only be ceded by force are common in national movements throughout history. In this case, I believe time has proved my father and his comrades right about two things: first, that the urgency of the situation in Europe in the 1930s called for drastic action, and second, that the British were trapped by dueling interests and promises and never fully intended to keep their promise to create a national home for the Jewish people.

My father returned from Italy in 1932, joined Jabotinsky's youth movement (the Betar) and was soon recruited into the Irgun's underground militia. In the coming years, he immersed himself fully in both these endeavors, eventually becoming the commander of Betar's Jerusalem branch. He enrolled in Hebrew University in Jerusalem and switched his line of study from agriculture to politics.

My father's running argument with his father now evolved into a discussion of whether he ought to focus less on politics and more on a career with a future. Ironically, my grandfather—reversing his prior position—tried to lure my father back to productive work on the land (and back to his family home in Petah Tikva), going so far as purchasing for him a small orange grove in the family's old neighborhood. The orange grove didn't succeed at diverting my father from politics, but it did pay off as an investment when he sold it years later and used the proceeds to fund my sister's and my college education.

In June 1937, Jabotinsky's son Eri, who headed the Betar in Palestine, asked my father to go to Vienna to run the Irgun's illegal immigration efforts. Tensions in the 1930s between political and Socialist Zionists focused heavily on the question of immigration to Palestine. Jabotinsky was calling for the immediate evacuation of millions of Jews from Europe to Palestine, warning desperately that the Jews of Poland in particular faced "impending catastrophe" and urging them to wake up to the danger from "the volcano which will soon begin to spew forth its fires of destruction."[2] In a famous speech in Warsaw's Great Synagogue in 1938, he went on to say, "I see a horrible vision. . . . Listen to my words at this, the twelfth hour. For God's Sake: let everyone save himself, so long as there is time to do so, for time is running short."

The Socialists who controlled the Jewish Agency and the World Zionist Organization (WZO) continued to endorse limited and selective immigration and to cooperate with the British in choosing the relatively small numbers that were allowed to immigrate to Palestine legally. The Revisionists, fed up with arguing theory, decided to do what they could to move the largest possible number of Jews out of Europe to Palestine in defiance of British legal restrictions.

So my father headed to Vienna, assumed the name Yitshaq Ben-Menahem and posed as a university student while living in the poorest section of the Jewish ghetto. He spent the next two years traveling throughout eastern Europe, organizing small groups of mostly young immigrants, arranging transport, bribing officials and raising money.

During these and subsequent years, he used a range of names and identities to stay a step ahead of various authorities, primarily the British in Palestine. He was born with the last name Rosin, but the name that endured was Ben-Ami (which means "son of my people" in Hebrew).

He was in Vienna when the Nazis annexed Austria, and he witnessed first-hand the ensuing violence and the shades of ultimate horror to come. In the course of his work, he met personally with Adolf Eichmann and other Nazi officials, who actually encouraged his work to "free the land of Jews." The Gestapo even authorized the opening of an office to manage the emigration efforts and initially paid a small sum per person.

As thousands lined up at the Irgun's offices trying to find their way out of Europe, the Zionist establishment continued to object, concerned that the British would reduce the number of legal certificates controlled by the official Jewish Agency charged with managing immigration.

The efforts of my father and his compatriots saved thousands of Jews in the years leading up to World War II, yet they are hardly mentioned in the museums or history books dedicated to that era. The leaders of the Jewish establishment failed to recognize the coming catastrophe and focused too much of their energy on fighting the Revisionists. On this issue, they were wrong and Jabotinsky was right—and the consequences of that failure of vision are far too painful for many to acknowledge, even to this day.

By 1939, with conditions worsening, funds low and time running out, my father and his Irgun commanders agreed that the time had come to seek support in the United States for their immigration work. He was dispatched to New York in 1939—the first of a small band of Palestinian Jews bringing the Irgun's message to the United States.

He was soon followed by Hillel Kook (also known in the United States as Peter Bergson) who took command of the operation, Sam Merlin, Alex Rafaeli, Eri Jabotinsky and others who came to be known as "the Bergson Group."

Their message was not well received in American Jewish circles. Many parts of the community were still anti-Zionist, and those American Jews who were Zionist, under the leadership of Rabbi Stephen S. Wise, were allied with the worldwide Socialist establishment and were avowed opponents of Jabotinsky and the Revisionists.

Given the centrality of Israel to organized American Jewish life today, it is hard to imagine that significant numbers of American Jews were anti-Zionists right up until the War of Independence in 1948. Their opposition was based in some cases on politics, in some cases on religious beliefs and in others on concerns over the tension between Zionism and American patriotism.

In the early twentieth century, Zionist supporters faced particular opposition from groups and voices on the left. These included the anti-Zionist Workmen's Circle, as well as the Jewish *Daily Forward,* which continued to publish Socialist-driven anti-Zionist commentary until the 1920s.

Although we associate religious anti-Zionism today with some in the ultra-Orthodox world, in the earlier part of the twentieth century, Zionism encountered opposition from the Reform movement, especially from Rabbis Emil G. Hirsch, the editor of the *Reform Advocate* from 1891 to 1923, and

Kaufmann Kohler, who was elected president of Hebrew Union College in Cincinnati in 1903. Among the first opponents of Zionism in America was the Central Conference of American Rabbis, the organization representing Reform rabbis in America. In July 1897, the Conference wrote,

> Such attempts [to establish Israel] do not benefit, but infinitely harm our Jewish brethren where they are still persecuted, by confirming the assertion of their enemies that the Jews are foreigners in the countries in which they are at home, and of which they are everywhere the most loyal and patriotic citizens.
>
> We reaffirm that the object of Judaism is not political nor national, but spiritual, and addresses itself to the continuous growth of peace, justice and love in the human race.[3]

After the British promised a Jewish homeland in Palestine in the 1917 Balfour Declaration, the Reform movement unofficially adopted a position of non-Zionism and, in 1935, began to support a policy of individual choice among its rabbis and adherents.

The potential conflict between loyalty to the United States and loyalty to the Zionist cause was probably the most significant root cause of anti-Zionism. Professor Jerold S. Auerbach, a leading scholar of twentieth-century Jewish history, writes that this question featured prominently in the American Zionist struggle: "[I]f Jews everywhere constituted a single nation (as Zionists boldly proclaimed), then the implications for the undivided loyalty of American Jews to the United States were ominous."[4]

Enthusiastic American Zionists, like Supreme Court Justice Louis Brandeis, found an answer in the ideas of "cultural pluralism, the essence of which is that America is a nation of nations in which different cultures are blended. This theory served to reconcile 'Americanism' with Zionism."[5]

But not everyone felt that the two were so easily reconcilable. The most noteworthy, and perhaps (for today's American Jews) surprising, organization expressing these concerns was the American Jewish Committee (AJC). Today, one of the AJC's key areas of focus is "supporting Israel's quest for peace and security,"[6] but through much of the first half of the twentieth century, it was one of the most significant proponents of anti- and non-Zionist sentiment. Much of its opposition stemmed from fear that Israel would interfere with the "internal affairs" of the American Jewish community and provoke charges of "dual loyalty."[7] Many of the AJC's famous lay leaders saw "Diaspora nationalism" as a threat to their patriotism and platform.

Over time, however, the AJC gradually reconciled itself to Zionism, but remained reserved until a famous agreement in 1950 between then-president Jacob Blaustein and Israeli Prime Minister David Ben-Gurion that was published in the 1952 edition of the *American Jewish Yearbook*:

> (1) that Jews of the United States, as a community and as individuals, have only one political attachment, namely, to the United States of America; (2) that the Government and people of Israel respect the integrity of Jewish life in the democratic countries and the right of the Jewish communities to develop their indigenous social, economic and cultural aspirations, in accordance with their own needs and institutions and (3) that Israel fully accepts the fact that the Jews in the United States do not live "in exile," and that America is home for them.[8]

My father and the Bergson Group ran into walls of opposition from all parts of American Jewry practically from the moment they landed in the States. Forming the advocacy group American Friends of a Jewish Palestine in June 1939, they set about raising funds to support the small trickle of illegal immigration they were still able to coordinate out of central Europe and down the Danube. My father writes,

We had hardly launched our fund-raising campaign in the United States when the "Emergency Committee on Zionist Affairs," a united front of Establishment Zionists from Robert Szold of the mainstream Zionist Organization of America to Haim Greenberg, editor of the Labor-friendly *Jewish Frontier*, issued this statement: "The American Friends of a Jewish Palestine and the 'Tel Hai' fund are appealing to the public for funds for purposes of immigrant transportation, agricultural colonization . . . and other activities. There is no public record by which the claims advanced . . . may be established."[9]

The Zionist establishment flatly denied that all the work that my father and the Irgun and Betar had been doing for several years to save Jews by the thousands had actually taken place. And they barred the door to American support for the work that could have saved thousands or more, with a smear campaign driven by a political agenda blind to the larger interests at stake.

In an ironic twist, seventy years later, another "Emergency Committee" would emerge[10] to launch a campaign against the work that I am doing today, again motivated by politics, though inverted this time. My organization, J Street, is attacked by the modern "Emergency Committee" from the right for being left-wing, while the attacks in the 1930s against the Bergson Group came from the left and called them "fascist."

In both cases, efforts designed to sound the alarm over imminent catastrophe for the Jewish people met stiff opposition from the "establishment" leaders of the American Jewish community. The exact words and the specific charges are different, but the overall strategy and the tactics—defeating opponents with new ideas through smears and personal attacks—are all too familiar.

Few synagogues or rabbis would open their doors and pulpits to my father and the Revisionists. One of the rare exceptions was Congregation Rodeph Sholom on Manhattan's Upper West Side, whose senior rabbi,

Louis I. Newman, was a lone voice in the Reform rabbinate willing to buck the establishment and open doors for the Bergson Group.

Yet Newman, who served as president of the New Zionist Organization of America (NZOA, the U.S. support group for the Revisionists), was not permitted by his board even to meet with Jabotinsky in the synagogue. They had to sit together on a bench in Central Park, across the street. Ultimately, Newman was forced to resign as president of the NZOA in order to keep his job at the synagogue. Not surprisingly, years later Rodeph Sholom would be the synagogue where I became a bar mitzvah and was married.

The efforts to block the group's work went far beyond cutting off financial support for illegal immigration. My father describes in his memoirs how officials of the Jewish Agency in London, in May and June 1939, provided the British with the names and countries of origin of the various transports being coordinated by the Revisionists, so that the boats could be stopped and those escaping deported back to the Nazi-controlled lands from which they had come.[11]

By 1940, with the doors of Europe closing fast, the United Jewish Appeal (UJA) was still supporting the notion that only "selected" immigrants "trained in Europe for productive purposes" would be allowed to enter Palestine. In a letter signed by the UJA's executive director, and with such storied names on the masthead as Stephen S. Wise, Albert Einstein, New York Governor Herbert Lehman and Edward M. Warburg, the UJA reiterated its view of illegal immigration work:

> Sentimental considerations are, of course, vital and everyone would wish to save every single Jew who could be rescued out of the cauldron of Europe. . . . I think it is fair to point out that many who have been brought into Palestine by the Revisionists . . . have been prostitutes and criminals.

The letter goes on to say that my father's group, the American Friends of Jewish Palestine, should stop fund-raising and agree to "selectivity" in immigration.[12] As my father would angrily point out for the rest of his life, "the entire World Zionist Organization managed to bring into Palestine only about 6,200 *ma'apilim* (illegal immigrants), though it had world-wide Jewish financial resources at its disposal. During the same period, we moved about twice that many *ma'apilim*, with hardly any financial means whatsoever."[13] Astoundingly, the UJA—in an effort to stir controversy and to raise money for its own operations—actually ran photos in its material of boats organized by the Irgun.

The American Jewish establishment didn't stop there. The same Emergency Committee that attacked the Revisionists in 1939 for lacking a track record of accomplishment reversed course in 1940—acknowledging the work but attacking the conditions on the boats organized by the Revisionists, saying they resembled "concentration camps."[14] It attacked the ideology of the group as "fascist" and spoke of there being "no room in democratic America for the empty slogans and destructive activities of Revisionism."[15]

Informants were planted in the group's offices, as personal memos from J. Edgar Hoover revealed when they were released decades later. Jewish community leaders urged the government to investigate whether my father and his colleagues should in fact be deported as illegal immigrants or, alternatively, drafted into the army—as my father eventually was.

For years, establishment leaders and organizations worked to convince various arms of the U.S. government that the Bergson Group was trying to undercut the interests of the United States. One arm of the Department of Justice was trying to get my father's Jewish Army Committee to register as foreign agents, basing its conclusion on information that "the N.Z.O. is advocating a sort of Fascist Jewish State."[16] Another arm of Justice was calling the group "thoroughly disreputable Communist Zionists" and having key supporters of the group's work designated as "Communists."[17]

As my father wrote: "Now [the Department of] Justice was faced with a difficult choice: should our 'Fascist' character be stressed, or our 'Communist' character? The idea never occurred to Justice that possibly 'the six Palestinians' were simply agents of Jewish misery all across Europe."[18]

THE STORY OF THE Bergson Group and the work that it did to try to sound the alarm in the United States over the plight of the Jews of Europe is neither well known nor fully appreciated even now. A few books have appeared—notably a wonderful history of the period called *The Abandonment of the Jews: America and the Holocaust, 1941–1945* by David Wyman—that have assessed the lack of response from the established Jewish community in the 1930s and 1940s to the impending and ongoing Holocaust. Others, like my father's autobiography and those of his colleagues, provide a memoir of the time. And a Washington, D.C.–based academic institute called the David S. Wyman Institute for Holocaust Studies (named for the scholar, and on whose board I sit) works to preserve the memory of those who worked to change the history of that era.

For many, however, facing up to the failure of the Jewish establishment to fully gauge the danger is still too daunting a task. Certainly this was true in the early 1980s, when the American Jewish Commission on the Holocaust, under the chairmanship of former Supreme Court Justice Arthur Goldberg, was unable to advance a common, objective assessment of that period or to analyze the lessons learned. In fact, an initial draft, written primarily by my father's close friend Samuel Merlin, was so critical of the Jewish community's leadership and their role in the events of World War II that the report was pulled and the commission shut down.

Even today, efforts to highlight the work of the Bergson Group at the Holocaust Museum in Washington, D.C., or at Yad Vashem in Jerusalem meet with institutional resistance. Recognition of the group's work was recently added as a part of the permanent exhibit at the Washington museum, but only after a five-year fight led by relatives of the Bergson Group's members and the Wyman Institute. Efforts to have the group's work recognized at Yad Vashem have faced similar difficulties but are finally coming to fruition in 2011.

The story of the Bergson Group and its work to open up a broader debate in the Jewish community, to impact national policy and to reverse the thinking of the American Jewish establishment provides an interesting point of reference for the American Jewish community today in the conversation about Israel.

Voices of dissent by definition bring views and ideas to the table that are at times uncomfortable to consider. But they may also have a critical message to convey—a message that can save lives and change history. If the experience of the Bergson Group teaches us anything, it is that the appropriate way to deal with those new voices is not to reflexively shut them down but to engage them on the merits and see what value there may be in what they are trying to say.

FOLLOWING HIS SERVICE in the U.S. Army in World War II, and now a freshly minted U.S. citizen, my father returned to New York and to his work with Bergson, whose group was renamed the American League for a Free Palestine. The organization now focused on building political and financial support for the fight for independence from the British.

First and foremost, it sought to build American political support for the notion that it was finally time—in light of all that had just happened to the Jewish people—for independence for the State of Israel. It continued to run its full-page ads toward that end, to lobby in Washington and to build a base of support all around the country. Bergson was a public relations genius, credited with inventing the concept of advocacy advertising, starting with the group's full-page advertisements in the *New York Times* during the war to call attention to the plight of European Jewry.

It also initiated the marriage of Hollywood with political causes, the most visible and famous effort being the Broadway play *A Flag is Born*, written by Ben Hecht and starring Marlon Brando, Paul Muni and Celia

Adler. Tens of thousands of people in cities from New York to Baltimore, Chicago, Philadelphia and Boston saw the much-talked-about performances, and more than $400,000 was raised to "provide ships to get Hebrews to Palestine."

At the same time, the group was also raising money to buy arms and the boats to transport them to Israel where they would support the struggle for independence from the British by the Irgun, now led by Menahem Begin.

Perhaps their most high-profile achievement was the purchase and equipping of the *Altalena*. The boat, named for an early pseudonym of Ze'ev Jabotinsky, was a mothballed LST (Landing Ship, Tank) from World War II. My father raised the money to purchase it, led the effort to refit and arm it, and recruited the personnel who would make the transatlantic journey first to Europe and then on to Israel.

The ship, loaded with weapons purchased mostly from the French, set sail on June 11, 1948, from the south of France with my father and over nine hundred others on board, arriving in the waters just off Israel on June 19. The one-month-old government of Israel under David Ben-Gurion and the Irgun under Menahem Begin had been negotiating for months over how to deal with the Irgun's arms and men—with Ben-Gurion arguing that there must be only one unified fighting force under his command. In his view, all the arms on the *Altalena*—enough to significantly enhance the capacity of the Israeli Defense Forces—should be delivered to the IDF for use at its discretion in the War of Independence.

Begin argued that since his group had raised the money and purchased the arms itself, and was still fighting independently from the IDF in areas around Jerusalem but outside the boundaries of the new state, a percentage of the arms on board should be retained by the Irgun.

For his part, Ben-Gurion felt the principle at stake was crystal clear—there could only be one army under one command in the new country. The army of the brand new state was the outgrowth of the official defense force (or Haganah) of the Jewish community. He gave the order to Haganah forces commanded by a young Yitzhak Rabin to fire on and sink the boat.

Sixteen members of the Irgun died either on board the boat or in skirmishes on the shore. Dozens were wounded. My father avoided injury and arrest, but close friends died, and many of his oldest colleagues including Bergson, Merlin (who was also wounded) and Irgun leader Ya'akov Meridor were imprisoned in Israel's first jail. Three-quarters of the arms on board were lost, and the Irgun itself was crushed. My father's words sum it up:

> We had sailed, our hearts pounding with excitement, full of hopes that Jerusalem and the Jordan would soon be ours again, that we would have safe borders and a strong State for generations to come. We sailed bearing our future and our past with us all at once. . . . But when we reached our brothers, they destroyed the gifts we brought them and tried to destroy us as well; then slammed the door in our faces as we carried our wounded from hospital to hospital.[19]

It was a stark and powerful moment, not only for those involved, but for the thousands of Israelis who witnessed the ship burning off the coast of Tel Aviv, not far from where my grandparents had stood four decades earlier to choose their lot in the new city.

Ben-Gurion had drawn a clear line in the sand. The authority of the new state was not to be questioned, even by a loyal opposition—and the new state's leaders were willing to take the heat for that position.

For many like my father, that decision was simply inexcusable. He never accepted it as necessary or right for the cause of Jewish statehood. The day the *Altalena* was sunk was perhaps the most painful day of his life. He would relive it for decades afterward; I recall, in my childhood apartment in New York City, loud arguments in Hebrew over the fate of the *Altalena* that stretched long into the night. He never got over his personal anger at Ben-Gurion either, and, from that day on, he refused to live in Israel as long as Ben-Gurion remained in power.

Tough choices await the leaders on both sides of today's Israeli-Palestinian conflict should there be a peace agreement. Will the Israeli and/or Palestinian leaderships be willing to make comparably difficult decisions about enforcing discipline and the terms of the peace against dissident forces? The choices will not be easy, and the consequences—much like those surrounding the *Altalena*—will undoubtedly be debated for generations to come.

MY FATHER'S GENERATION achieved independence through war, but that was only the beginning, not the end, of the fighting. The wars of the future would not be to establish their state, but to secure its existence and survival. The fighters prevailed in each instance, but not without great suffering. Thousands died and tens of thousands were wounded. And the toll of the violence and conflict on the Israeli psyche has been perhaps as great as, if not greater than, the physical impact.

Many leaders of this generation aged with grace—producing statesmen like Menahem Begin, who returned the Sinai for peace with Egypt, and Shimon Peres, the Nobel Prize–winner, who envisioned a new Middle East in which old enemies cease their fighting and focus instead on integrating Israel into the neighborhood, bringing the benefits of peace to all.

Perhaps the greatest story of the generation was Yitzhak Rabin. Born in 1922, just a few years after my father, he commanded the unit on the Tel Aviv beach that June day in 1948 when Ben-Gurion ordered the attack on the *Altalena*. He was chief of staff of the Israeli Defense Forces in 1967, defense minister and prime minister twice.

His stirring words at the signing of the 1993 Oslo Accords challenged people on both sides of the Israeli-Palestinian conflict to face the historic necessity of ending it. His words remain the test for today's leaders:

We are destined to live together, on the same soil in the same land. We, the soldiers who have returned from battle stained with blood, we who have seen our relatives and friends killed before our eyes, we who have attended their funerals and cannot look into the eyes of their parents, we who have come from a land where parents bury their children, we who have fought against you, the Palestinians—we say to you today in a loud and clear voice: Enough of blood and tears. Enough.[20]

His singular recognition of the desperate need to resolve the Israeli-Palestinian conflict made the Oslo Accords possible and earned him a Nobel Peace Prize.

It also cost him his life. His dream of ending the conflict, of finally fixing Israel's borders, of securing its future, remains unfulfilled.

The early generations—the pioneers, builders and fighters—have all passed from the scene. Now it falls to my generation to complete their work.

We—their sons and daughters, grandchildren and great-grandchildren—must find a way to fulfill the dream that the Jewish people have chased for two thousand years. In the words of Israel's national anthem, we seek "to be a free people in our own land." That work is not complete so long as Israel remains a country without an internationally accepted border, still fighting to establish itself in peace and security with recognition of its permanent place in its neighborhood.

Whether we succeed depends on critical decisions in the next few years—some to be made in Israel, some right here in the American Jewish community.

3

BORN IN THE USA

I often wonder how shocked my grandparents would be that their grandchildren were born in New York City and not in the city or country that they helped build.

They did not live to see the center of my father's life shift gradually to the United States—to watch him fight in the U.S. Army in World War II, become an American citizen or marry his first wife (not my mother), who was a nice Jewish girl from New York. But when I remember that they were already reduced to bribing him with an orange grove to get him to come home in the 1930s, I realize they probably could have guessed that his adventurous spirit and fierce independence would ultimately lead him far from the Herzl Street of his birth.

Though my father struggled personally to get past the attack on the *Altalena,* he still nurtured a deep family connection to Israel, and, by the mid-1960s, we were traveling there almost every summer. Sometimes, we'd stay in Jerusalem and tour historical sites. Other times, we'd travel the length of the country, getting to know the land, our family and the history. Or we'd simply relax on the Mediterranean beach—the place in the world where my father was most at home.

In New York, we had very little family. By contrast, in Israel it seemed we were related to half the country. Everywhere we went—every town, every side road, every historical site, seemed to carry a story about how this or that part of my family helped build it, taught at the first school, built the first store and so on.

Politics—and in particular, the conflict with the Arab neighbors—was always front and center in our travels to Israel. I remember my cousins from Netanya making it a point to drive us on each visit from their home near the beach in Netanya to the old "Green Line" (the armistice line from 1948) near the Arab village of Tulkarim. I took the assignment very seriously as an eight- and nine-year-old to time how long the drive took. Of course, it was their way of showing us how quickly an Arab army could have cut Israel in half before 1967, implying, quite obviously, that we could never give back the land.

We spent, it seemed to me as a child, way too much time in cemeteries. In Jerusalem, we climbed the Mount of Olives. In Tel Aviv, we visited the old cemetery on Trumpeldor Street where my grandparents are buried. In Petah Tikva, we visited my other great-grandparents' resting place in the old section of the cemetery, where my wife's great-grandparents are buried as well, just one row away. They too were—it just so happens—among the very first pioneers of the settlement in the early 1880s.

I saw firsthand my father's deep attachment to the land and to the people. I absorbed that his connection wasn't simply to the last one hundred years but to thousands of years of Jewish history, to biblical times, to the Patriarchs and Matriarchs, to King David and to Herodian Jerusalem before the Romans destroyed the Temple. And I developed a similar affinity for the land and the history.

In the States, my parents hosted seemingly never-ending debates among graying ex–comrades-in-arms. They argued about history and politics and what could and should have been done differently either to save the Jews of Europe or to set the nation of Israel on a different course.

A constant parade of fascinating friends and colleagues was always on hand, and Israel was the number-one topic of conversation. The philosophical debates that began among the youth of Tel Aviv in the 1920s and '30s still fired the imaginations of these aging rebels well into the 1960s and '70s.

As with so many young Jewish Americans being exposed to Israel in that era, I was thoroughly steeped in—and loved—the mythology of the State of Israel, its miraculous founding and the astonishing accomplishments of its brief history. There was, however, one huge gap in my learning about the history and the culture of the region and the land. I never learned about the Palestinians. I knew them simply as the enemies of my people. Back then, we called them simply Arabs. My father and his friends were, to me, the true Palestinians.

I understood that the Arabs had tried—more than once—to destroy Israel and make the Jews leave. But never once did I hear their side of history. Not one book in our house told their story. Not one class in Hebrew School exposed us to their culture, their backgrounds and lives.

According to the history I learned, Palestine was essentially empty when the Jews arrived. My father was apt to cite Mark Twain's famous 1867 description of the land in *The Innocents Abroad:* "[a] desolate country whose soil is rich enough, but is given over wholly to weeds—a silent mournful expanse. . . . A desolation is here that not even imagination can grace with the pomp of life and action. . . . We never saw a human being on the whole route. . . . There was hardly a tree or a shrub anywhere. Even the olive and the cactus, those fast friends of the worthless soil, had almost deserted the country."

When I was seven, Golda Meir gave an interview in London to the *Sunday Times* that summed up what many Jewish Americans understood about the Israeli-Palestinian conflict at the time:

> There were no such thing as Palestinians. When was there an independent Palestinian people with a Palestinian state? It was either southern Syria before the First World War, and then it was a Palestine including Jordan. It was not as though there was a Palestinian people in Palestine considering itself as a Palestinian people and we came and threw them out and took their country away from them. They did not exist.[1]

The story line of the Israeli-Arab conflict as my generation learned it was simple and appealing—a tale of good and evil, a morality play pitting David against Goliath. On one side stood the country my family had helped bring back to life after thousands of years, the place where they made the desert bloom and saved the Jewish people from destruction. On the other were dozens of countries and hundreds of millions of people looking to wipe my people, my family and my history off the map.

My mother's family history added to the righteousness of the story. She had fled the Nazis in Austria with next to nothing at age sixteen. She had lost her grandmother and untold numbers of cousins, great-aunts and uncles in the camps. Hers had been a classically assimilated upperclass family in Vienna. My mother's father was an international bridge champion and successful attorney, his wife, a glamorous socialite whose photo on my mother's dresser showed her in fur and jewels.

All of that came crashing down in 1938. As my father was frantically trying in one part of Vienna to rescue Jews, my mother's family across town was scrambling to get out with the clothes on their backs. They were unable to convince her grandmother to leave—a far too common story among the generation that couldn't believe what was happening—and she spent her final days in the Nazi concentration camp at Theresienstadt.

Every part of my family's history drove home the lesson we relearned at each Passover seder—in every generation, enemies rise up to defeat the Jewish people. It has happened before. It will happen again.

It would be many, many years before I discovered that there is more than one narrative when it comes to the history of Israel and Palestine. In fact, it wasn't until I moved to Israel and started meeting those very Palestinians that I learned that, yes, the Palestinians are a people and, yes, they do believe that my people came and threw them out of their homes and took their country away from them.

Imagine my surprise when I found out that they had the keys to those homes to prove it.

UNSURPRISINGLY, AS MY father's son, I had a natural inclination toward politics from an early age. As a child, while my friends were outside playing sports or inside watching them, I was the only ten-year-old huddled over a board game called Election 1972. I'd play the game again and again, trying to figure out how George McGovern could get the 270 electoral votes necessary to beat Richard Nixon. Needless to say, I didn't win very often.

In 1976, I spent the summer at the Times Square office shared by the Moynihan for Senate and Carter for President campaigns. My baseball card collection may have been more valuable, but my collection of Carter for President buttons was my pride and joy. Green and white posters of Carter and Walter Mondale decorated my bedroom door.

Then Jimmy Carter made Israel give back the Sinai, and down came the Carter posters. My father's politics were liberal-left on all issues—easily traced, I suppose, to his days in the Socialist youth movement. But not when it came to Israel. Little did I know that this was a phenomenon I'd come to know all too well in the American Jewish community later in life.

My father was deeply opposed to the Camp David Accords—he believed that giving the Sinai back to Egypt, in fact giving any land back that had been taken in a defensive war, was a huge mistake. The strategic value of a physical buffer far outweighed, in his mind, the value of the paper on which a peace treaty with an Arab neighbor was written.

In 1980, he and some of his old Irgun buddies, along with some of their younger followers, put together a committee to defeat President Carter's re-election bid, running ads and organizing in the Jewish community against the president. While he couldn't bring himself to actually support Ronald Reagan for president, he knew he wanted to see Carter defeated.

I became enamored with the independent candidacy of John Anderson—allowing me to stay on my father's good side by not supporting Carter's re-election, yet not violating an unwritten family rule (and my own leanings) against actually voting for a Republican.

I spent the summer of 1980 working as Anderson's Manhattan coordinator, and to this day I am still proud that I was—that year—the youngest candidate for the Electoral College on the New York State ballot as a candidate to be an Anderson elector.

I arrived at Princeton that fall as a much more typical Jewish upper-middle-class kid than I would like to admit. Several of my classmates had parents who had escaped or survived the Holocaust. Others had grandparents whose flight from tsarist Russia had led them west to America rather than south to Palestine.

What we all had in common was that we were a personal link between the old world of our parents and grandparents and the new world in which our own children and grandchildren would grow up. We could still feel the force of prejudice, violence and hate our people had suffered, yet we were born in this country, far removed from those experiences. The only factors in our success would be our own ability, motivation and determination.

I remained interested in Israel and felt deeply my connection to the Jewish people. I wrote a few op-eds in the weekly student paper that touched on Israel. One I remember well defended Israel's behavior in

Lebanon in 1982, when its army chased Yasser Arafat and the PLO out of southern Lebanon and ultimately to Tunisia. The Israeli army faced accusations of having stood by passively as its Lebanese allies carried out atrocities in the Palestinian refugee camps, Sabra and Shatila. I wrote at the time that the real problem was that a biased media was unfairly focused on Israeli behavior while ignoring comparable Syrian actions in the same area.

Today, there are well-funded training programs to arm student activists with talking points and arguments like these. Back then, I just had my father.

But despite my interest in Israel, my passion lay elsewhere. I attended rallies against U.S. intervention in El Salvador and wrote regularly on the evils of nuclear weapons and the true costs of the Reagan military buildup. I attended services at the High Holy Days if I wasn't home, but I never once ventured into the Jewish dining hall or attended a Jewish student program.

My senior thesis brought together my passion for politics and my fascination with foreign policy; it concluded, based on twenty-eight years of polling data, that foreign policy actually has little impact on presidential elections. It's an argument I still find myself making over three decades later.

My father wrote and spoke prodigiously on all matters related to Israel in his final years. He was a regular commentator in the right-wing Jewish papers, and even had his own radio show in New York, called the "Voice of Herut"—named after the political party that most closely followed the philosophy of Ze'ev Jabotinsky.

He won the loyalty of a new generation of activists who respected the role that the Irgun played in establishing the toughness of the Jewish people and their willingness to fight. I hear from them today—some from the West Bank, some from Brooklyn—sharing angry, often venomous letters charging me with betraying my father's legacy.

I've reread my father's autobiography numerous times over the past three decades. I've taken from it a powerful sense of his commitment to the survival of the Jewish people, to their security and to the importance of a country that the Jewish people can call their own.

But it's also taught me about the danger of adhering to conventional wisdom and accepting the rulebook written by mainstream leaders and their institutions. My father fought practically the entire American Jewish establishment to get their attention over the looming danger of the Holocaust and to get them to act. In Palestine, too, he fought the leadership of the Jewish establishment because they were too willing to sacrifice the masses of Jews in Europe to preserve their vision of a properly developed Jewish utopia.

In each of these cases, history proved my father and his colleagues right, and the mainstream Jewish leadership wrong.

Today, I find myself on the center-left of the political spectrum, sounding the alarm about the looming existential threat to the democratic state of Israel as a Jewish homeland if the Israeli-Palestinian conflict is not resolved. My words and those of my colleagues in the pro-Israel, pro-peace movement are dismissed too casually, and we are attacked personally by a right-of-center establishment, both in the United States and in Israel.

The critics of my work today use terms frighteningly similar to those used to disparage my father before and during World War II—calling my colleagues and me fanatics, anti-Semitic, extremists and self-hating Jews. The rules as set out by today's mainstream leaders tell us to stay quiet, respect unity and avoid dissent. Just as my father wouldn't accept the rules as he found them in the 1930s and '40s, I think today's rulebook needs a fundamental rewrite.

I only hope that I will not spend the waning years of my life with as many regrets as my father had because he just couldn't get more people to listen.

My father passed away in 1984, the year I graduated from college. We never really had the chance to talk about Israel as adults or peers. I know we would never have agreed substantively or politically on the views I hold today. I do know, however, that he would be glad I care enough to be involved.

FOR MUCH OF MY first decade out of college, I gave little thought to Israel, the Israeli-Arab conflict or the role that Israel plays in American politics. I was busy trying to develop permanent housing for the homeless in New York City and figuring out how to organize ten thousand unruly liberal Democrats on Manhattan's Upper West Side into an effective political operation at my local Democratic club.

Though our club was probably 75 percent Jewish, never once in all my time as president or as an active leader in West Side politics did the issue of Israel come up as a factor in our politics. Far more important was the likely impact on the local subway station of Donald Trump's pending development of tens of thousands of housing units.

I spent 1992 working for Bill Clinton's presidential campaign and continued my focus on domestic policy, ultimately spending four years as part of the Clinton domestic policy team—including nearly two as his deputy domestic policy adviser.

While at the White House, my interactions with the Jewish community and the issue of Israel were sporadic. At times, I was the designated domestic policy briefer for Jewish community groups passing through Washington. I'd talk about health care, welfare reform, education or immigration. But Israel? I left that to my colleagues from the National Security Council, and I'd head back to my office when they started talking.

I did attend, and was moved by, the signing ceremonies on the road to peace that took place at the White House in 1993 and 1994 involving

Israel, the Palestinians and Jordan. I experienced them not as ideological events, but as mile markers on a historical road that seemed to me to be leading inevitably to the peaceful acceptance of Israel into the Middle East.

My family in Israel—whom I now connected with less frequently than in my childhood—seemed to be taking the developments in stride, falling in line behind the efforts of Yitzhak Rabin and Shimon Peres to once and for all end Israel's conflicts with its neighbors and establish its permanent place in the community of nations in the Middle East.

I was jolted—perhaps for the first time—out of my complacency by the assassination of Prime Minister Rabin in 1995. The prime minister of Israel killed at the hands of another Jew? It was one thing for the infighting among the Jewish people before the state was formed to have led to the sinking of the *Altalena*. It was another for it to lead to the assassination of a prime minister.

I began to read all the news I could get my hands on about the situation to try to understand. How could a deeply religious Jew, committed to his people and his country, have done this to one of the heroes of the state?

I grew frustrated by the limits of my ability to read Hebrew and to question what I really knew of the situation in Israel if such a moment could come to pass without my fully grasping the underlying dynamics.

I decided that I needed to spend some serious time in Israel, to learn the language, come to terms with my past and my father's politics and assess the potential for completing the late prime minister's work.

I had had enough of working on welfare reform and fighting the bureaucracy in Washington over regulations and budgets. I wanted to see and experience far more of the world and to reconnect with my roots. I was more and more fascinated by the question of what my life would have been like had my father stayed in Israel and raised his children there.

I left the United States on January 21, 1997—the day after Bill Clinton was inaugurated for a second term—and headed off with a backpack, a one-way ticket and a plan to see the world and learn Hebrew.

AFTER TRAVELING THROUGH the South Pacific and Southeast Asia for about three months at the beginning of 1997, I arrived in Israel intending to spend a few months reconnecting with my family and with the country—for the first time since my father died, a little over a decade earlier.

I enrolled in Ulpan Akiva in Netanya, an intensive language immersion program, generally intended for new immigrants to learn Hebrew. The school was unlike other language programs in that it brought together not only new immigrants—primarily from the Soviet Union—and tourists, but Palestinians from Gaza who were interested in learning Hebrew as well.

The inclusion of Palestinians in the program was part of a special effort by the school's founder to further the cause of peace and reconciliation between the Israeli and Palestinian peoples. I knew nothing at the time of so-called people-to-people exchange programs, but I did know that I was simply shocked to be sitting in *kita aleph*—basic first-grade Hebrew—learning my letters and basic grammar with Palestinians from Gaza.

Over the course of the next three months, I got to know my classmates well as we lived, learned, ate, played chess and toured the country together. I spent a lot of time talking to new immigrants from the Soviet Union who were struggling to find their way in a strange new land. Often, they were highly educated professionals with advanced degrees now being forced to start their lives all over, learn the alphabet, adapt to an insular society and overcome enormous gaps in language and in culture.

I also spent hours with my Palestinian classmates from Gaza—the first time in my life I'd met and talked in depth to Palestinians. After thirty-five years of knowing little more than the caricatures on which I had been raised, I was now getting to know pharmacists and schoolteachers, fathers and sons, real people with real stories—and I opened a window into a history of which I had been totally unaware.

As we toured museums in Israel as a group, celebrating the Israeli history of victory and conquest, they shared with me the Palestinian history of displacement and occupation. I learned again a basic rule of history—that one people's victory is likely to be another people's catastrophe.

I was astounded by the depth and layers of the situation in Israel, having arrived only a year and a half after the Rabin assassination. The country, so recently on the path to resolving its fifty-year conflict, was suddenly thrown wildly off balance.

Bombs and buses had been blowing up regularly since 1996, and the Israeli people had turned rightward, toward Benjamin Netanyahu and away from Shimon Peres and the likely completion of the work begun by his partner in peace, Rabin.

I found myself deeply attracted to the country and to the politics there. Everywhere I went, there was a lively and engaged argument over the future of the peace process, the proper course of action for the government, the legacy of Rabin, the intentions of Netanyahu.

Political life was far more vibrant in Israel than in the United States, and I began to consider whether or not to extend my stay in Israel and to explore what life would really be like in the country where I felt so alive and so at home. By the end of the summer, I was circulating my résumé, setting up informational interviews in Tel Aviv and Jerusalem, and generally exciting my cousins and shocking my mother with the thought that I would make Israel my permanent home.

Then, on July 30, I was in Jerusalem for a few days for some interviews. I loved walking through the city and was proud that I already knew how to get from the bus station to the Old City and down to the German Colony without a map. I stopped by Mahane Yehuda, the bustling nineteenth-century market, around 1:00 in the afternoon to pick up some food and fruit from the vendors.

I walked a couple of blocks away and sat down on a bench to eat my lunch, when suddenly a loud explosion filled the air, followed by an eerie silence. Nothing seemed to move around me for what seemed an eternity. There was no screaming or panic. It was as if the noise had never happened. Then, after no more than a minute, sirens began screaming and all hell broke loose.

The terror attack at the market—actually two separate bomb blasts, it turned out, not one—killed 16 people and wounded 178. The stalls where I had purchased my lunch were destroyed; most likely, the very vendors from whom I had just bought my lunch were dead.

Life is simply too random to contemplate the role of luck in making you five minutes late or early to such a fateful place and time. But I knew then and there that I was meant to come face to face with the violence, and that I would dedicate myself to ending it.

I spent over two years living in Jerusalem. Together with my friend Oriella Ben-Zvi, another American who had deep Israeli connections, I started a consulting business, working primarily with Israeli nonprofit organizations, helping them with their English language communications and with fund-raising in the United States.

Our clients included many of the mainstays of the peace and social justice movement in Israel, from larger organizations like Peace Now and the New Israel Fund, to smaller groups creating bilingual schools where Arab and Jewish children study together and Internet education programs teaching citizenship.

I got to know many wonderful Israelis—Jewish and Palestinian. I met hundreds of Jewish Israelis devoting their lives to building a national home for the Jewish people in accordance with the values that I was raised to believe are fundamental to Judaism.

I met Arabs living in East Jerusalem in a kind of limbo, without citizenship, yet technically permitted to vote in the municipal elections. I traveled to the West Bank and met Palestinians devoted to the cause of freedom and independence for their people.

I discovered more about myself, my family and my history than I had in the prior thirty-five years. I was exposed to every angle of debate and discussion about religion, politics, citizenship and conflict resolution.

But despite building an exciting small business, becoming relatively fluent in Hebrew, developing a circle of close and dear friends and connecting with my distant family—I ultimately realized that my life was simply too rooted in the United States. I felt that I would never be fully accepted professionally into Israel's political world as an English-speaking transplant. And on a personal level, I was feeling strangely old as a thirty-seven-year-old single person, and I was not finding a satisfying social life. I decided for all these personal and professional reasons that the time had come to return to the States.

So on December 31, 1999, I flew back to the United States and re-entered my American worlds—American politics and American Jewry. My perspective on Israel and the Middle East had been thoroughly altered. My understanding of the country, its history and its people was now much deeper than before. And I returned committed to helping the homeland of my people to find security, peace and justice by completing the work that the previous three generations of my family had begun.

II

THE RULEBOOK

4

SIXTY SECONDS
IN SANTA FE

I t was 10:30 at night, and I was grabbing a late drink at a bar in Santa Fe, New Mexico, where about two hundred supporters of Howard Dean's presidential campaign had gathered for their September 2003 Meet-Up (a fancy name for a meeting organized through the Internet). I was schmoozing with some of the national campaign staff and members of the national press corps. The first debate among the 2004 Democratic presidential candidates was to take place the next day in nearby Albuquerque.

The scene was typical of events on the road to the White House: music blasting, locals with no interest in the campaign mixing and mingling, and, in the background, the would-be leader of the free world delivering his stump speech through a third-rate sound system and then bracing himself for questions from the press.

As a semi-neurotic, controlling campaign aide, my radar was up. Why was the candidate taking questions for over an hour at 10:30 at night? Where was the press secretary to say thank you very much and good night? It's trouble waiting to happen when your candidate is fielding his fifteenth question the night before a big national debate. On a campaign, you want nothing but message discipline and focus. Tired candidates make mistakes, distracting from the story lines you hope to drive in the next news cycle.

I was only too right. As national policy director for Howard Dean's presidential campaign, I was developing a sixth sense for brewing trouble. I had joined the Dean campaign about six months earlier, when most of the country had never heard of Vermont's former governor. Since returning from Israel, I'd worked for two years on Mark Green's 2001 mayoral campaign in New York City and for another year at the New Israel Fund, a nonprofit promoting democracy and social justice in Israel. The Dean campaign was my first foray back into national politics since walking out of the White House on Inauguration Day 1997.

A doctor by training, Dean initially entered the race to put the issue of health care reform back on the national agenda, where it had been notably absent since First Lady Hillary Clinton's efforts had foundered a decade earlier.

His sudden rise from virtual obscurity to serious presidential candidate was fueled primarily by his willingness to publicly oppose the Iraq War—a position studiously avoided by the more-prominent Democrats against whom he was running, such as John Kerry, John Edwards and Richard Gephardt, not to mention Hillary Clinton, who was keeping her options open for the future.

Dean's claim to speak for the Democratic wing of the Democratic Party, and his view that the party could only win by standing up for its core principles, resonated with me. So, in a move that was becoming familiar in my career, I abandoned stable employment for the thrill of the campaign trail just when Dean was what's called an "asterisk" in the polls—someone not mentioned often enough by respondents to actually show up in reported results.

Six months after I made the leap, Dean was suddenly the hot commodity—and the candidate with the target on his back. The first campaign to harness the power of the Internet for presidential fund-raising (drawing on techniques pioneered by the advocacy group MoveOn.org), we had already changed the nature of political campaigns forever. Thanks to Dean for America, the whole world now knew you could raise more money at lower cost at the click of a button from large numbers of small contributors than traditional campaigns could raise from small numbers of large donors.

Dean was now part rock star, part cultural icon. Everywhere we went, the crowds were large and excited, and the press was eating it up. So, here we were in Santa Fe, with about a dozen members of the national press corps following the most exciting story of the election cycle.

An hour into the event, after the stump speech and a string of questions and answers, most of us at the bar were distracted by pre-debate chatter, keeping one ear on the impromptu press conference going on behind us. Suddenly, one of the reporters and I froze and looked at each other. Had Dean just said that the United States should "not take sides" in the Israeli-Palestinian conflict? That we should be "evenhanded" in our approach? The governor took one more question and wrapped up the evening. The moment seemed to pass, and I went back to my drink with relief.

American politics is governed by a rulebook that covers the tricks of the trade, including what you can and can't say as you run for office. Most candidates, staff and consultants memorize it from cover to cover the moment they start out in politics.

Its wisdom includes, for instance: Don't go to Iowa and attack government subsidies for ethanol as a waste of money. Don't pledge to end the embargo of Cuba on a campaign swing through southern Florida.

Don't order mayonnaise on a roast beef sandwich at Katz's Deli in New York City.

And don't talk about being "evenhanded" when it comes to Israel.

I hoped against hope that, given the lateness of the hour, most of the press who knew the Middle East well were at the bar with me rather than listening to Governor Dean. After all, back then—a mere seven or eight years ago—your comments weren't tweeted as soon as you made them, and the news cycle was actually more than twenty-four minutes long.

I woke up the next morning and immediately scoured the papers. Unfortunately, the Associated Press's chief political correspondent, Ron Fournier, had not missed the moment. There, in the third to last paragraph of a 774-word story that framed the day's debate as a major test for Dean, was the following:

> His position on the Israeli-Palestinian conflict might cause some problems in the Jewish community, a key Democratic constituency. Dean told the crowd there are an "enormous number" of Israeli settlements that must go.
>
> "It's not our place to take sides" in the conflict, he said.[1]

The paragraphs could easily have been dropped from the story—which had nothing to do with Israel—if only the editor had wanted seven hundred instead of eight hundred words. The statement would have been forgotten. No one else wrote about it.

But it wasn't forgotten. And the political football known as Israel was in play.

The story ran on Thursday, and by Monday Dean's rivals, Joe Lieberman and John Kerry, had seized on the remarks, looking both for political advantage in the Jewish community and to send a larger signal about Dean's readiness to be president.

Lieberman, who was having trouble getting any attention or momentum for his campaign on his own, accused Dean of calling for a "major break" from the longstanding American policy of explicitly siding with Israel. The *Washington Post,* in a page two article under the headline "Rivals Criticize Dean for Mideast Comment," quoted Lieberman saying, "If this is a well-thought-out position, it's a mistake, and a major break from a half a century of American foreign policy. If it's not, it's very important for Howard Dean, as a candidate for president, to think before he talks."[2]

John Kerry was quoted in the same article saying, "It is either because he lacks foreign policy experience or simply because he is wrong that Governor Dean has proposed a radical shift in United States policy towards the Middle East. If the president were to make a remark such as this it would throw an already volatile region into even more turmoil."

Dean couldn't understand the fuss. We talked about it briefly, and I organized a quick conference call for him with our foreign policy team to talk it through. He wasn't about to back down from what seemed to him a commonsense position. After all, the United States had been actively working to achieve peace under four presidential administrations of both parties. The U.S. role as a mediator had been central to the Sinai peace agreement with Egypt, and, under American auspices, Israeli-Palestinian peace efforts had nearly reached fruition in the waning days of the Clinton administration. I deeply supported Dean's inclination to stand by his remarks.

That Monday, he told *Washington Post* reporter Jim VandeHei, "Israel has always been a longtime ally with a special relationship with the United States, but if we are going to bargain by being in the middle of negotiations then we are going to have to take an evenhanded role." He felt his rivals were manufacturing a controversy, and he said he was "deeply disappointed" in Joe Lieberman for making this a divisive issue.[3]

A second Democratic debate took place in Baltimore on Tuesday, sponsored by the Congressional Black Caucus. The announced focus of the debate was issues of concern to the African American community, not a forum where one would ordinarily expect Israel to come up. But the

Israel football was in play now, and the moderator asked Dean whether he had meant to say that, "after all of these years of alliance and friendship between the United States and Israel, that the U.S. should maintain some sort of neutral stance."

Dean answered simply that the United States needs "to be a credible negotiator, a facilitator for peace in the Middle East, and that means we have to be trusted by both sides." Lieberman parried that Dean was essentially advocating breaking a critical American alliance, saying "he has said he wouldn't take sides, but then he has said Israel ought to get out of the West Bank and an enormous number of their settlements ought to be broken down. That's up to the parties in their negotiations, not for us to tell them."

Dean pushed back, "My position on Israel is exactly the same as Bill Clinton's. . . . I think America needs to be an honest broker. We desperately need peace in the Middle East. It doesn't help, Joe, to demagogue this issue."[4]

This kind of straight talk and honesty was why I went to work for the governor, but it certainly didn't constitute playing by the rules of American politics when it comes to Israel.

By the next day, thirty-four Democratic members of Congress, led by Nancy Pelosi, had already signed a letter saying, "American foreign policy has been—and must continue to be—based on unequivocal support for Israel's right to exist and to be free from terror. . . . It is unacceptable for the U.S. to be 'evenhanded' on these fundamental issues."[5]

On the same day, the head of the Anti-Defamation League, Abraham Foxman, dashed off a letter attacking Dean over the use of the word "evenhanded"—a critique that he would repeat in 2009 around the appointment of George Mitchell as special envoy for Middle East Peace. According to Foxman, "evenhanded" is "code" for tilting toward the Palestinians and away from Israel, and making a false equation between, say, Israeli intransigence on settlements and Palestinian terror.[6]

Later that day, Dean went on CNN with Wolf Blitzer to try to clear things up, but, rather than beginning to climb out of the hole, he dug deeper. Attempting to voice support for Israel's policy of targeted assassinations of Hamas militants, Dean said, "There is a war going on in the Middle East and members of Hamas are soldiers in that war, and, therefore, it seems to me, that they are going to be casualties if they are going to make war."[7]

That simply added fuel to the fire. Calling Hamas members "soldiers" rather than "terrorists"? Another violation of the rules.

Senator Kerry leaped on this one, charging, "In the wake of Howard Dean's statements last week on the Israeli-Palestinian conflict, many Democrats wanted to give him the benefit of the doubt and dismissed his comments as the flippant remarks of an inexperienced politician. But in going out of his way to term members of Hamas as 'soldiers,' Governor Dean insults the memory of every innocent man, woman and child killed by these suicidal murderers."[8]

The Jewish and Israeli press went into a feeding frenzy. By Friday, *Ha'aretz*—Israel's leading daily—was writing that the fracas had badly hurt Dean's chances to become president of the United States: "Sources in the Jewish community say that Dean has wrecked his chances of getting significant financial support from Jews. . . . Many believe Dean's statement will drive more Jews toward Lieberman and Kerry, enabling Kerry to take the lead again."[9]

The Dean campaign was now in full crisis-control mode. Steve Grossman, who had been national president of the American Israel Public Affairs Committee (AIPAC) for several years in the 1990s, was the chair of the Dean campaign. Together, he and I, as national policy director, brought our understanding of both the issue and the politics surrounding it to the table.

At my urging, after more than a week, we brought in Matt Dorf, a Washington-based consultant, to help with messaging and outreach to the

Jewish community, a resource that a traditional campaign would have had in place *before* hitting a full-blown crisis.

Steve was working the phones furiously. "Here's what I think happened," Grossman told *Salon*'s Michelle Goldberg. "Howard made some comments in someone's backyard in New Mexico that were shorthand, if you will, for some of his Middle East views. In the course of those remarks and some others in subsequent days, he used some language that gave people consternation, and it was immediately jumped on by Joe Lieberman and John Kerry that somehow Howard Dean was breaking faith with this 55-year tradition of the United States' special relationship with Israel, which is patently absurd."[10]

The reverberations continued to spread from national media circles to the broader Jewish community. By Saturday, Kerry was gleefully predicting that Dean was "imploding" over Israel.[11]

The Internet rumor mill in the Jewish community now lit up in shock and horror. In a tactic that has since been finely honed in the far-right reaches of the community, an anonymous email started making the rounds:

I KNEW I DIDN'T LIKE THIS GUY FOR A REASON.

HOWARD DEAN PROMISED THAT IF HE IS ELECTED PRESIDENT, THE UNITED STATES WILL NO LONGER SUPPORT ISRAEL THE WAY IT HAS IN THE PAST UNDER BOTH DEMOCRATIC AND REPUBLICAN PRESIDENTS. IN HIS OWN WORDS HE WILL INSIST THAT THE UNITED STATES BE "EVENHANDED." THIS IS A TERM REGULARLY EMPLOYED BY ARAFAT AND HIS COTERIE OF ADHERENTS THAT MEANS TO BE ANTI-ISRAEL!!

GOVERNOR DEAN MADE THESE COMMENTS ON CNN ON SEPTEMBER 10, 2003 ON THE WOLF BLITZER SHOW. HE HAS REPEATED THESE WORDS SINCE.

IN [*sic*] THESE WORDS WERE NOT ENOUGH, GOVERNOR DEAN ON THAT SAME SHOW CHARACTERIZED THE HAMAS TERRORISTS

AS "SOLDIERS." FOR THE FIRST TIME SINCE 9/11 WE HAVE SOME-
ONE RUNNING FOR THE OFFICE OF PRESIDENT OF THE UNITED
STATES CALLING TERRORISTS SOLDIERS.

I URGE YOU THAT IF YOU HAVE ANY LOVE FOR AMERICA AND
ISRAEL YOU SHOULD NOT AND CANNOT VOTE FOR HOWARD
DEAN FOR THE OFFICE OF PRESIDENT. THIS COMING ELECTION
MAY VERY WELL BE ONE OF THE MOST IMPORTANT IN DECADES.

PLEASE PASS THIS MESSAGE ON TO AS MANY OF YOUR FAMILY
AND FRIENDS AS YOU CAN.[12]

Dean never stopped doing penance for his offhand remarks in the
remaining months of the campaign. He spent hours in meetings, on conference calls and in briefings with Jewish community leaders trying to
atone. He did not have to take a trip to Israel to visit the Western Wall or
Yad Vashem as part of his penance (at least not until after the campaign),
though we did consider it for a time.

Despite being the campaign's national policy director—responsible
for overseeing a large staff and a team of experts developing positions on
a wide range of issues from the war in Iraq to health care reform and the
economy—I spent more time that fall working on Israel than on any other
issue facing the campaign. And I was furious. The notion that an American presidential candidate could be made to sweat and suffer for having
spoken out on the need for peace in the Middle East was to me simply
outrageous. I had returned from Israel fully convinced of the absolute necessity of achieving peace, and believing that the single greatest thing any
president could do for Israel would be to help it reach a deal with the Palestinians to end the conflict. At that point, the region was in the midst of
several years of intifada and violence that were killing hope for a peaceful
future among Israelis and Palestinians alike.

The Dean campaign did ultimately implode, though several months
after John Kerry's prediction and for reasons not directly related to Dean's

position on Israel. Kerry had warned that Governor Dean lacked the experience to make it through a national campaign. Maybe that was the case, if you take him to mean that anyone seriously contemplating a career in American politics—let alone a national candidacy—needs to know the rules of the game. And the chapter in the rulebook on Israel says never use the word "evenhanded." Instead, it commands, talk about your unwavering support for the State of Israel, your strong support for its security, and move on.

The lines you need to know are simple. Memorize them and you'll be fine. Questioned on Hamas? They're terrorists. Questioned about settlements? That's an issue for the parties to negotiate. Don't use the word "evenhanded." Abe Foxman will say it's code for being pro-Palestinian. Don't say resolving the Israeli-Palestinian conflict is critical to American strategic interests. Alan Dershowitz, looked to by so many Jewish Americans as the preeminent advocate in the United States for the state of Israel, will say it's code for blaming Israel for American casualties in its wars in the region.[13]

MY 2003 EXPERIENCE brought back bad memories from the 2001 New York City mayoral race. On returning to the States from Israel, I had decided to get back into New York City politics, where, prior to joining Bill Clinton in 1992, I had worked for eight years in local politics and for the city's government on homeless housing programs.

In 2000, several former colleagues and friends formed the inner circle around the city's public advocate, Mark Green, as he began his run for mayor. I'd worked a bit for Mark in his 1986 Senate campaign, and his good government, consumer-oriented approach to politics and policy attracted me. I came on board to oversee policy and manage the day-to-day operations of the campaign. My role expanded when a heart attack sidelined our campaign manager.

Israel entered the race as an issue in April 2001, when Mark released his taxes for the year 2000 and his charitable contributions included a $1,200 donation to Americans for Peace Now (APN), the U.S. support group for Israel's oldest and most established peace movement, Shalom Achshav (Peace Now).

The contribution caught the attention of New York Assemblyman Dov Hikind, an Orthodox Jew from Brooklyn representing Borough Park and other heavily Orthodox parts of the county. Even today, Hikind is as active promoting settlement of the West Bank as he is promoting the interests of his constituents in Brooklyn. Just recently, for instance, he led a mission of fifty Americans through the West Bank and East Jerusalem to encourage home purchases in the area and "to send a clear signal to Washington and President Obama that Jews will continue to live in Judea and Samaria and the ultimate commitment American Jews can make is to actually come and buy property in these areas as this will ensure these communities' security and growth."[14]

Hikind's wife, Shoshana, is the executive vice president of the Jerusalem Restoration Fund, a charity that purchases Arab property in East Jerusalem, to promote increased Jewish presence specifically in Arab neighborhoods, where Palestinians hope to one day have the capital of their new state. These ongoing efforts are likely to be one reason that efforts to achieve peace and a two-state solution go off the rails.

Needless to say, making Israel a political football is normal in New York City. This is, after all, the city where Rudy Giuliani burnished his tough-guy credentials by throwing Yasser Arafat out of a UN-sponsored party at Lincoln Center, and Ed Koch most likely cost himself a fourth term by saying Jews would be crazy to vote for Jesse Jackson partly due to Jackson's views on Israel.

When Hikind learned of Green's contribution to APN, he attacked Green's dedication to Israel, calling Peace Now the fringe of the Israeli Left and apologists for Yasser Arafat who condoned rock throwing at Israeli settlers.[15]

I was close to Peace Now, having consulted for them while living in Israel. I knew their work and their key activists firsthand. The group's politics were left-of-center, but they were absolutely part of the Israeli mainstream and could draw tens of thousands of people into the streets for rallies in the 1990s. In fact, at the time, the organization was certainly more mainstream than the settlers that Hikind supported in their efforts to push Palestinian families out of their homes in East Jerusalem.

I found it absolutely outrageous that a candidate to run the largest city in the United States should have to pass a loyalty test to Israel established by settler allies from the West Bank. But, as angry as I was, I agreed that it wasn't worth the energy to fight for Mark's right to support Israel's leading peace group when the only people paying attention were the handful of right-wing Jews whose support Mark might well have already lost over the issue. No one else in the city of New York noticed or cared.

So we searched around for a "kosher" charity to which Mark could contribute as our spokesman Joe DePlasco spent the better part of a week assuring the media that Mark had "spent his entire life supporting peace and safety for Israel." Mark ended up buying some bulletproof vests for Israeli ambulance drivers—a gesture Hikind's allies deemed sufficient penance for the "error" of his ways.

BY SUPPORTING Peace Now, Mark Green, a Jewish American, was showing his support for Israel in a manner that matched his American politics. And Howard Dean was articulating a mainstream position on American foreign policy, supported by countless experts and academics. Yet both candidates were treated as if they had blundered horribly—politically and substantively.

And these are but two minor examples of what happens every day, everywhere in the country, when American politicians interact with Israel's most vocal supporters, both in the Jewish community and beyond.

Strip away the spin and the politics, and what was so terrible about what Dean said or what Green did? Why the scrambling, apologies and fear? Why are politicians immediately on the defensive when they utter one word or make one contribution that those on the political Right of the Jewish community don't like? And where was the rest of the community? Where were all the American Jews I knew who agreed with me and with these candidates?

Five of Green's top advisers were liberal Jews who disagreed with Dov Hikind and his position on Israel. But when blackmailed by the right wing of the Jewish community and forced to back down from a "pro-peace" position, we could offer no protection for an American political candidate.

And as Governor Dean scrambled all fall to "make nice" to the official American Jewish establishment, to reassure them that he valued the special relationship between Israel and the United States, I kept thinking to myself, who gave these people the right to speak for me as a Jewish American? Who made Dov Hikind the arbiter of how a political candidate should talk about Israel in American politics?

How did it happen that sensible politicians like Nancy Pelosi and Steny Hoyer could act so irrationally when it comes to Israel? Why couldn't they say, when asked to write a letter condemning Dean (who went on to become chairman of the Democratic National Committee), that not only would they never sign such a letter, but that of course the United States should do whatever it can to broker a deal, create a Palestinian state on the West Bank and remove a major source of instability from an already volatile region?

How did it come to pass that the major national organizations of the American Jewish community—namely, AIPAC, the ADL, the American Jewish Committee and the Conference of Presidents of Major American Jewish Organizations—had come to present only right-of-center views on Israel to candidates for president and other federal offices? Who, I wanted to know, gave these groups and their leaders the exclusive right to set the rules on Israel in American politics?

What about my views, and the views of all my many friends and colleagues who had lived and worked in Israel, who passionately believe that it will serve Israel's and America's interests for the United States to be more evenhanded in its approach to the conflict? Why isn't anyone standing up for us? Why don't the rules reflect the truth—that a more balanced American approach will actually help Israel to save its future?

How these rules were written and codified is a fascinating tale of modern American politics.

The need to rewrite those rules has become the mission of my life.

5

THE LOUDEST
EIGHT PERCENT

Jim Gerstein started questioning the rulebook on Israel in American politics even before I did. While studying for his master's degree at Tel Aviv University, he was at the rally where Prime Minister Rabin was assassinated, and he saw Rabin walking down the stairs to leave the rally seconds before he was shot. Jim later spent much of the 1990s as executive director of the Center for Middle East Peace, a Washington-based think tank, and finally convinced the organization's primary funder, Slim Fast founder S. Daniel Abraham, to send him back to Tel Aviv to pursue his efforts to promote an end to the conflict.

As it happens, Jim has also worked for the Democratic National Committee and several Democratic campaigns, including President Clinton's re-election. Along with three legendary Washington strategists—Stan Greenberg, James Carville and Bob Shrum—Jim helped create Democracy Corps, a polling and strategy outfit providing data and analysis to

Democratic Party strategists. Today, Jim has his own public opinion research company, Gerstein Agne Strategic Communications, and advises the Democratic leadership in Congress.

Jim and I met when we were both living in Israel and he was advising Ehud Barak's campaign for prime minister in 1999. Jim had a lovely apartment in Tel Aviv overlooking the beach, where I distinctly remember watching President Clinton's effort to bring Israeli prime minister Ehud Barak and Palestinian leader Yasser Arafat together at Camp David fall apart in the summer of 2000. He married an Israeli woman and returned to D.C., where they now have two young sons.

After returning from Israel, we commiserated for hours about the state of the discourse on Israel in the American Jewish community. How was it, we kept asking, that with all the progressive and liberal Jews we knew, the voices heard in Washington on Israel were so far to the right of ours and of those of the community as a whole? Jim was one of the many people I consulted after the 2003–2004 Dean debacle, asking what it would take to create a new political voice for Americans with moderate views on Israel who felt the political dialogue on the issue had become drastically skewed.

We expanded these discussions to include numerous Jewish professionals with years of Washington experience in and out of politics and government, as well as some of the larger Jewish political donors we knew who had either lived or spent time in Israel or had Israeli family.[1] The funny thing was none of us could understand how the discussion of Israel in the United States—whether in politics or the Jewish community—could be so much more constrained than it is in Israel itself! There, lively political debates on Israel had dominated our family meals, the television talk shows and, of course, the floor of the Knesset, Israel's parliament. Passionate views ran the gamut from far left to far right.

We had plenty of personal theories about the shape of the problem we were grappling with and its root causes—mostly based on intuition and anecdotal experience. But Jim knew the data.

In the end, he identified the central phenomenon: While Jewish Americans do care about Israel and want assurances that the candidates they support do as well, like most Americans, they vote based on the issues that affect them on a daily basis—the economy, health care and, during the Bush years, the Iraq War. Israel is a "threshold issue" for Jewish voters. Once assured that the politicians they're considering do in fact support Israel, they'll cast their votes based on other, more immediately relevant issues.

Only a small percentage of Jewish Americans actually vote based primarily on whether or not a candidate adheres to their party line on Israel. For that minority, Israel is not simply a voting issue but the central cause of their political lives. And that minority definitely trends farther right than Jewish Americans as a whole when it comes to Israel. Polling done by J Street and others has consistently confirmed this phenomenon. When the American Jewish Committee asked in its 2008 Annual Survey of American Jews what issue matters most to Jews when they vote, only 3 percent answered "Israel."[2] The polls that Jim has done for J Street from 2008 to 2010 have also shown that only 7 to 10 percent of Jewish Americans pick Israel from a list of issues when asked to name the two most important factors in deciding their vote.[3]

Jim has taken to calling this minority "the loudest eight percent in the country" because their voices so dominate the public debate and the perception of where the community stands. This vocal group deserves credit because, without their passion and conviction, Israel might not have the critical backing and support of the United States that has helped ensure its survival. But the views of this minority are out of date and out of touch with the broader American Jewish public.

What really matters to the bulk of Jewish Americans today? Not surprisingly, it's whatever matters to Americans of all stripes at that moment. The economy headed the list in 2010; health care was front and center for a while; and the war in Iraq before that.

TABLE 5.1   SURVEY OF JEWISH VOTERS, ELECTION NIGHT, 2010

Which two of the following issues are most important for you in deciding your vote for Congress in November?

Issue	%
The economy	62
Health care	31
The deficit and government spending	18
Social Security and Medicare	16
Taxes	14
Terrorism and national security	13
Education	12
Israel	7
The environment	7
The wars in Iraq and Afghanistan	6
Illegal immigration	6
Energy	4
Iran	0
Separation of church and state	0

Source: "National Survey of American Jews," Gerstein Agne Strategic Communications, November 2, 2010, http://2010.jstreet.org.

Yet, despite the data, there is a perception in political circles that the "American Jewish community" is a single-issue voting bloc that cares first and foremost about U.S. policy toward the state of Israel and the broader Middle East. To win Jewish support—electoral and/or financial—you've got to be "pro-Israel," and it's assumed that there's only one way to do so—to tack as far right politically as possible.

As a result, candidates don't stand in front of Jewish audiences talking primarily about the economy and health care. They don't focus on jobs and global warming. They don't leave Israel to the eighth or ninth bullet point. They open their remarks by reciting their deep commitment to Israel, usually in very personal terms, and their understanding of the critical importance of the strategic relationship between the two countries. They'll talk about their most recent visit to Israel, and, yes, even the Jewish friends they had growing up and the role Israel played in their lives. They'll recite the threats Israel faces and the weapons systems they've supported. And, finally, they'll recount all that Israel has done for peace over the years in the face of intransigence, terror and violence.

What an amazing feat. Recall that just a couple of generations ago, Jewish Americans were afraid to take up the Zionist cause for fear that people would question their loyalties. Those who spoke too loudly about Jewish issues and problems were admonished by community leaders to tone it down a bit. The accomplishment isn't simply that Israel has been pushed to the front and center of the American political agenda. It's that both ends of the American political spectrum have been trained to speak with one voice on one of the most complex and dangerous issues in the world.

The real question is what *is* the actual range of views held by over five million Jewish Americans? It's always tricky to paint any large, diverse community with a single broad brush. But we can certainly start with the notion that Jews are liberal politically. They self-identify as liberal or progressive, and they vote Democratic. In fact, since the election of Warren Harding in 1920, Jews have voted Democratic in every presidential election, and, since Eisenhower, no Republican has gotten more than the 39 percent of the Jewish vote that Ronald Reagan won in 1980.

TABLE 5.2   AMERICAN JEWISH VOTE FOR PRESIDENT, 1972–2008

Year	Democratic Candidate	%	Republican Candidate	%
1972	McGovern	65	Nixon	35
1976	Carter	71	Ford	27
1980	Carter	45	Reagan	39
1984	Mondale	67	Reagan	31
1988	Dukakis	64	Bush	35
1992	Clinton	80	Bush	11
1996	Clinton	78	Dole	16
2000	Gore	79	Bush	19
2004	Kerry	74	Bush	25
2008	Obama	78	McCain	22

Source: L. Sandy Maisel and Ira Forman, eds., *Jews in American Politics* (Lanham, Md.: Rowman & Littlefield, 2001), 153, provides data through 2000. 2004 data are based on exit polls by CNN, 2008 data are from Edison Media Research/Mitofsky International.

In terms of party identification, Jewish Americans are one of the most reliable cornerstones of the Democratic Party. Gallup has regularly looked at religious identification in relation to party affiliation and concluded that "Jews are substantially more likely to identify themselves as Democrats than are members of any other major religious group in the country."[4] In 2004, Gallup reported that 50 percent of Jews say they are Democrats, 34 percent Independents and only 16 percent Republicans—and those percentages have remained constant since the early 1990s. Allocating Independents who lean toward a party, Gallup concluded that more than two in three Jews, 68 percent, either identify as Democrats or lean toward the Democratic Party. Gerstein's polls for J Street in 2008 and 2010 found, similarly, that 67 and 69 percent of Jews in those surveys identified strongly and weakly with the Democratic Party.

That, of course, doesn't stop Republicans from claiming in every election cycle that they are about to make major inroads into the Jewish community by spending large sums of money to convince Jewish Americans that Democratic candidates aren't strong enough on Israel. The story line is familiar. Several months before the elections, Republicans will claim that some perceived slight by a Democrat toward Israel means this will be the year that Jewish voters shift significantly toward Republicans. Then, when the results fail to bear it out, they retreat quietly until they repeat the same exercise in the next cycle.

In February 2004 Matt Brooks, executive director of the Republican Jewish Coalition, touted a new poll showing that 31 percent of American Jews would vote for President George W. Bush. "It [is] now undeniable that there is a major shift taking place among Jewish voters," Brooks claimed at the time.[5] But, in November 2004 Bush took just 25 percent of the Jewish vote according to exit polls, only six points better than his showing in 2000 when the Democratic ticket included Joe Lieberman, the first Jewish American from a major party to appear on the ballot for national office.

Republicans tried to make the case that George W. Bush was the "best friend" Israel had ever had in the White House. They argued that exerting zero pressure on Israel, stepping back from active leadership of the peace process and backing the Israeli security barrier no matter its route made Bush a "loyal friend" to Israel.[6] They regularly predicted that this would translate into tangible gains for their party in November. Representative Clay Shaw, a Republican from southern Florida, claimed in July 2006 to the *Washington Post* that "Jewish voters are becoming less partisan and more independent in their thinking, which I think gives an opportunity for inroads among Republicans."[7] They were in fact so independent that 87 percent of American Jews voted Democratic in the fall congressional elections according to CNN's exit polls,[8] and Shaw—representing a heavily Jewish district in Broward and Palm Beach counties—was swept from office after thirteen terms.

In 2008 the Republicans spent millions of dollars on ads trying to take advantage of the perceived weakness of the Democratic presidential candidate, Barack Obama, in the Jewish community. Early polls showed his support in the low 60s among Jewish Americans, and right-wing blogs began predicting that McCain might draw Reagan-like numbers, approaching 40 percent in the Jewish community. Joe Lieberman—the onetime national Democratic candidate—was among those McCain supporters predicting that McCain would receive more support from Jewish voters than any Republican candidate since the Great Depression.[9]

The Republican Jewish Coalition ran a series of borderline libelous and racist ads in Jewish papers trying to link Barack Obama to Iran's Mahmoud Ahmadinejad. Vicious smear emails—usually prominently featuring Obama's middle name, Hussein, and far worse than anything I had seen attacking Howard Dean in 2003 and 2004—made the rounds in the Jewish community, expressing doubts about his religion and country of birth and, of course, his support for Israel.

Their reward for all this effort? Barack Obama actually got 4 percent more of the Jewish vote for president than John Kerry got in 2004—and nearly as much as Al Gore received in 2000 with Joe Lieberman on the ticket.

In congressional elections, Jews consistently provide 60 percent or more of their support to Democratic candidates—62 percent in 2002, 76 percent in 2004, 87 percent in 2006—according to exit polls. In J Street's national survey on election night in 2010, 66 percent of Jewish voters reported voting Democratic, down significantly from the previous two cycles—in line with the national trend against the Democratic Party in 2010—but by no means out of line with traditional results. In strongly Republican years like 2002 and 2010, the Democratic Party's support drops to the low- to mid-60s. In strongly Democratic years like 2006 it can rise well into the 80s. And there is no evidence that these swings have any relationship to candidates' positions on Israel, events in Israel or the state of the U.S.-Israel relationship.

One of the story lines being pushed by conservative Jewish activists in the early years of the Obama presidency is that his activism in pursuit of a Middle East peace deal has somehow hurt his standing among the Jews. Sadly, this theory has gotten some traction among the media and opinion elites, because it is consistent with the well-worn chapter of the rulebook that America's leading political journalists and commentators have memorized.

In August 2010, under the headline "Oy Vey, Obama," Charles Blow, the visual op-ed columnist for the *New York Times*, presented data that in his words showed that President Obama hasn't been "good for the Jews" and that purportedly showed Jewish Americans disproportionately abandoning the president.[10] Citing a Pew Research Center Report, Blow trumpeted the finding that the number of Jews who identify as Republican or lean Republican increased by 50 percent between January 2009 and August 2010, from 20 to 33 percent. The piece was shockingly simplistic, perpetuating the myth that ethnic minorities like Jews make voting decisions based on the relationship of the United States to their home country, rather than on political issues affecting them where they now live.

Just days later, in a stroke of bad luck for Blow, the Gallup organization released data showing that Obama's approval rating among Jewish Americans had actually moved exactly in tandem with his rating among all Americans since the beginning of his presidency, dropping 16 points among Jews and 15 points in the public at large.[11] The Gallup data aggregated hundreds of daily tracking polls, which included over 6,700 Jews, providing a margin of error of 1.2 percent.

The story line of Jewish voters moving and shifting by large numbers based on the daily give-and-take between the president of the United States and Israel is naturally appealing to *New York Times* op-ed columnists, who get more page views for controversial headlines, and it's juicy fodder for political consultants too. Nevertheless, it remains one of the great myths of American politics, bearing little connection to data or reality.

What's more, Jewish Americans are not simply overwhelmingly Democratic; they are far more ideologically liberal than the American public as a whole and are one of the most reliably liberal constituencies in America. The American Jewish Committee, in its Annual Surveys of American Jewish Opinion, asks Jewish Americans to place themselves on a scale of ideological views from "extremely liberal" to "extremely conservative," and between 37 and 44 percent rated themselves liberal from 1997 to 2008, as opposed to the 18 to 27 percent who called themselves conservative. The remainder self-identify as moderate.[12]

In J Street's three polls, between 2008 and 2010, we gave people the choice of self-identifying as conservative, moderate, liberal or progressive. Between 21 and 24 percent have identified themselves as conservative, between 28 and 32 percent as moderate and between 44 and 50 percent as liberal and progressive.[13]

Meanwhile, a 2010 Gallup poll found that 43 percent of American Jews identified themselves as liberal, and just 20 percent called themselves conservatives. Comparatively, 30 percent of Muslims, 19 percent of Catholics and 16 percent of Protestants self-identified as liberal.[14]

There's a reason for this. It's an understanding built into the fabric of the Jewish community in the United States that helps to define the community's sense of place in the larger tapestry of America. American Jews grow up very conscious and proud of the accomplishments of their fellow "tribesmen" in this country. Nearly every Jewish child can name the star Jewish athletes or the Jewish celebrities of their generation in music, film and the arts.

Similarly, Jewish Americans grow up both conscious and proud of Jewish leadership of movements for justice and equality over the past century. As a very young child on Manhattan's Upper West Side, I grew up thinking that the civil rights movement was being led by young Jews from my neighborhood—like Andrew Goodman and Michael Schwerner[15]—who were going south to help people even more persecuted than Jews to get their rights. And, as my mother—who had been in this country all of seven years when I was born—was sure to emphasize, they were getting killed in a place far, far more dangerous for Jews than the Middle East: Mississippi.

Many of us grew up seeing photos in our rabbis' studies of Abraham Joshua Heschel marching in Alabama alongside the Rev. Martin Luther King. We heard stories of the role that Jews played in the labor union movement and in the great progressive movements that were spawned amid the masses of immigrants in the tenements of the Lower East Side and other cities at the beginning of the twentieth century. We understood that it was our role to help fight oppression and injustice, not simply because that was the right thing to do but because we Jews had known far too much of it ourselves.

The fight for justice was our fight wherever it was taking place, so it was not surprising to see the modern movements for equality being led by Jewish Americans—from Betty Friedan, Gloria Steinem and Bella Abzug in the women's movement, to Harvey Milk and Evan Wolfson in the gay rights crusade. Look at leading environmental groups or organizations dealing with human rights and poverty, and you'll find Jews disproportionately represented among the staff, leadership and funders, considering that we constitute only 2 percent of the entire American population.

All of this engagement stems from a deeply ingrained belief that charity (*tzedakah*), good works (*gmilut Chasidim*) and repairing the world (*tikkun olam*) are fundamental elements of Jewish identity. Young Jews today are continuing that tradition, finding deep connection to their Jewish identity through community service (in organizations like Avodah or American Jewish World Service) and in a range of new social justice projects and organizations, from the California-based Progressive Jewish Alliance to the leadership development programs of the Jewish Funds for Justice.

But what of the "loudest eight percent"? How does their political profile match up with that of the broader population of Jewish Americans? The polling shows that those Jewish Americans who mention Israel as one of their top two issues are less strongly Democratic, less liberal and progressive and more likely to have voted for John McCain over Barack Obama in 2008. They are also more likely to be religiously observant, male and opposed to active American leadership as a means to resolve the conflict. In other words, the face that American politicians see presenting Israel as a high political priority differs wildly from the face of the community as a whole.

Based on the hard data about the community's politics and its historical track record of support for and leadership of social justice causes, one might think that politicians would seek to appeal to Jewish audiences primarily on issues of economic and social justice. Yet the rulebook tells candidates and political operatives that Jewish Americans are best approached as single-issue voters who are relatively hawkish on Israel, the Middle East and foreign policy generally.

The "loudest eight percent" who've helped to write this chapter of the rulebook have done a spectacular job. Not only have they created the impression of a community with a single-minded focus on Israel, they have backed it up with just enough money and political muscle to skew the national conversation about foreign policy and the Middle East for more than a generation.

6

ENDING THE CONFLICT

Those who oppose efforts to end the Israeli-Palestinian conflict love to say that there's no point trying, because this is a fight that has been raging since time immemorial between mortal enemies destined to hate each other. In the words of Israel's foreign minister Avigdor Lieberman, "It is a clash of civilizations which you cannot solve with a territorial compromise."[1]

His view leads him to conclude that "signing a comprehensive agreement in which both sides agree to end the conflict and end all of their claims and recognize Israel as the nation-state of the Jewish people is a goal that is not achievable in the next year or in the next generation, so any historic compromises or painful concessions won't help."[2] Since there's no hope of solving this kind of conflict, this line of argument goes, why even bother trying?

In fact, the history of Jewish/non-Jewish relations in the land of Palestine, and throughout Arab and Muslim lands, was fairly positive. The first wave of new Jewish immigrants to Palestine—including my great-grandparents Shmuel and Chaya-Frieda Rosin and Ze'ev and Batya Yatkovsky—only began arriving a little over a hundred years ago, in the late nineteenth century. Before that, there had been a continuous Jewish presence in Jerusalem, in Jaffa and in other towns and villages across Palestine for centuries, and for most of that time, there was little hostility between Jewish and non-Jewish residents.

The roots of today's conflict lie not in ancient religious hatred but in the clash of national aspirations of two peoples unfortunate enough to stake a claim to the same small piece of land. Their subsequent struggle for land, resources and control echoes other global conflicts that have been successfully resolved.

Notions that Islam itself is hostile to Jews or Judaism are strongly rebutted by scholars like Princeton's Mark R. Cohen, who explains that:

> Anti-Semitism originated in Europe in the 12th century and came to the Middle East from the West in the 19th century with colonial settlers and Christian missionaries. It caught on first with Arab Christians and then spread to Muslims. With the rise of political Zionism at the end of the 19th century, it grew in intensity. The notorious European anti-Semitic book, *The Protocols of the Elders of Zion,* was translated into Arabic from French in the 1920s by a Christian Arab. Then the Nazis, who wanted to win over Arab countries as their allies, preached anti-Semitism to the Middle East through radio broadcasts in Arabic and Persian, quoting passages from the Quran that, taken out of context, looked anti-Semitic. This was later picked up by some Arab nationalists as a tool against the British, who were believed to be allied with the Jews. The formation of Israel in 1948 and the wars that have followed it have ratcheted up anti-Semitism in the Middle East even more.
>
> Today, the lines between anti-Semitism and anti-Zionism have become blurred. But from a historical standpoint, it is wrong to attribute anti-Semitism to Islam at its core. Once you say that anti-Semitism comes from the Quran, you are exonerated from doing anything about it—you don't have to make peace with the Muslims because they are inveterate anti-Semites.[3]

At the very birth of Islam, the Prophet Mohammed designated the Jews as a "people of the book" and promised that they would be protected, though consigned to a secondary status, in Muslim society. For centuries, Jewish philosophy, culture and society flourished under Muslim rule, and, right up through the nineteenth century, Jewish communities in the Muslim world were protected and lived peacefully with their neighbors.

Outright conflict between the Arab and Jewish communities in Palestine began as World War I ended, the Ottoman Empire crumbled and the British assumed the Mandate for Palestine. Early in the Mandate period, the British made contradictory promises to the rival nationalist movements vying for the land of Palestine. In the 1917 Balfour Declaration, Lord Balfour communicated on behalf of the British to Lord Rothschild that, "His Majesty's Government view [*sic*] with favour the establishment in Palestine of a national home for the Jewish people, and will use their best endeavours to facilitate the achievement of the object."[4]

However, after a change of prime minister in 1922, the British issued a "White Paper" in June 1922 stating that His Majesty's Government had not "at any time contemplated, as appears to be feared, the disappearance or the subordination of the Arab population, language or culture in Palestine. . . . The [Balfour] Declaration . . . does not contemplate that Palestine as a whole should be converted into a Jewish National Home, but that such a Home should be founded in Palestine."[5]

The root of the conflict at this point was clearly national and territorial—two people pursuing their national ambitions on the same land—without religious overtones. The resolution of this conflict was clear even then: the division of the land into two states, one for the Jewish people and one for the Palestinians.

The first time the British officially outlined a "two-state solution" following their assumption of the Mandate for Palestine was the Peel Commission, convened in 1936 in response to Arab-Jewish clashes that began that year and lasted until 1939. The commission's report recommended the creation of a state for the Jewish people in the north of Palestine and one for the Arabs in the south.

The Arab leadership, not willing to compromise at all, rejected the plan out of hand, while the Jewish leadership at the 1937 World Zionist Congress expressed a willingness to at least discuss it. The report was deemed impractical by the British a year later and ultimately shelved.

The idea of partitioning Palestine resurfaced following World War II and became the basis of UN Resolution 181, passed on November 29, 1947, ending the British Mandate over Palestine and partitioning the land into a Jewish and an Arab state. Once again, the concept was rejected by Arab leaders, though accepted by the Jewish Agency and confirmed by Prime Minister David Ben-Gurion's declaration of independence on May 15, 1948, the day the British Mandate expired.

When hostilities ended following the 1948 War of Independence, the front between Israeli and Arab forces became the so-called Green Line, the de facto boundary of the new Jewish homeland, defined not by the international community but by where each side was left after the fighting. The original partition established by the United Nations in 1947 accorded Israel 55 percent of Mandatory Palestine, with the Palestinian state to be on the remaining 45 percent. Yet now Israel controlled 78 percent of the land.

The Palestinian-Israeli conflict took a decidedly different turn in 1967 when Israel, faced with imminent attack by nearly all its neighbors, scored a surprising and overwhelming victory in the Six-Day War. In the brief conflict, Israel captured not just 100 percent of Mandatory Palestine from the Jordan to the Mediterranean but the Golan Heights and the Sinai too. Israel now had control for the first time over the entirety of the land both peoples desired.

In those early days after the stunning 1967 victory, many Israeli policy makers understood the significance of deciding whether or not to settle the newly acquired land. So did the nationalists who prized the land on the West Bank as part of the historic land of Israel—"greater Israel," as they termed it. For them, the territory of Judea and Samaria (their name

for the West Bank) was not the possible future homeland of another people but the cradle of Jewish history and civilization.

Other Israelis saw retention of the West Bank as the answer to the security dilemma posed by Israel's pre-1967 boundaries. Because the country was just nine miles wide at its narrowest point, they always feared that
armies attacking from the east could easily split the country in two, and in
doing so isolate Jerusalem. One advocate for retaining the West Bank was
Shimon Peres. "Unlike Dayan, he did not speak of the Bible, but stuck to
security arrangements. He proposed a settlement east of Tel Aviv to widen
Israel's narrow waist—and more settlements east of that, creating a strip
slicing across the West Bank, 'for defensive purposes.'"[6]

The consequences of these initial decisions have loomed over Israel
for more than four decades. Scholars now have access to records of Israeli
cabinet deliberations of the time and the papers of the leaders who pre-
sided over the country, and they clearly show that some of these early leaders did understand the depth of the problems the occupation would cause.
As Gershom Gorenberg reports:

At the first cabinet debate on the future of the occupied territories, shortly
after the war, Defense Minister Moshe Dayan proposed giving the West
Bank limited autonomy under Israeli rule. Justice Minister Yaakov Shim-
shon Shapira attacked that idea. "In a time of decolonization in the whole
world," he said, "can we consider an area in which mainly Arabs live, and we
control defense and foreign policy? . . . Who's going to accept that?" Shapira
also warned against annexing the land outright. That, he said, would turn
Israel into a bi-national state, in which Jews would eventually become the
minority. Unless Israel gave up nearly all of the West Bank, Shapira said,
"We're done with the Zionist enterprise."[7]

Others warned of the consequences of prolonged occupation of the territory as well. Cabinet minister and ex-general Yigal Allon went on record in

1968 saying that a Palestinian enclave under Israeli rule "would be identified as . . . some kind of South African Bantustan." Finance Minister Pinhas Sapir warned that rule over Arabs without granting them equal rights would put Israel in a class with "countries whose names I don't even want to say in the same breath."[8]

However, these were isolated and minority voices, and the Israeli government—under first the left-of-center Labor Party and then the right-of-center Likud—began a policy of settling Israeli Jews on the occupied West Bank and across the Green Line. Today, over 500,000 people—nearly one-tenth of all Jewish Israelis—live over the Green Line, 200,000 in East Jerusalem and more than 300,000 in the West Bank.

Israelis developed settlements all across the West Bank—particularly in the Jordan Valley along the eastern edge of the territory and in a ring around Jerusalem. Today, the population of Jews over the Green Line is concentrated in a series of settlement "blocs" around Jerusalem, where roughly 70 percent of Jews living on the West Bank reside.

Israeli and world leaders knew they needed to address the future of the territories, even in the years immediately after the Six-Day War. They put it on the table in negotiations over the Sinai at Camp David in 1977, and a commitment to address the issue was critical to enabling Egyptian president Anwar Sadat to participate in and conclude the Sinai peace treaty.

In the intervening years, the broad parameters of a reasonable deal that could end the conflict have been well known to the parties, to the international actors seeking to help end the conflict and to scholars of the region's history and politics. As early as 1988, the Palestinian Liberation Organization (PLO) expressed its recognition of this reality, making what its leaders call its "historic compromise" in its declaration of independence, accepting that a Palestinian state would be on only 22 percent of the land of Mandatory Palestine, instead of the 45 percent proposed by the United Nations in 1947.

Since the 1990s, negotiators have embraced the same basic outline—from Oslo to Camp David, through Annapolis and the new efforts of the Obama administration. The resolution was outlined by President Bill Clinton in 2000 and became known as the "Clinton Parameters." These same parameters were incorporated into model peace agreements over the last decade like the 2003 Geneva Accord and the 2002 Ayalon-Nusseibeh Initiative. Perhaps one day someone will come up with an entirely new framework to end the conflict, but until then, the outline remains as follows:

- The land between the Jordan and the Mediterranean should be divided into two states—Israel and Palestine—each the national homeland of its people.
- The border between the two countries should be based on the Green Line that existed in 1967, dividing Israel from territory controlled by Jordan on the West Bank and by Egypt in Gaza. This amounts to 22 percent of Mandatory Palestine for the Palestinians and 78 percent for Israel.
- The new border should take into account the largest settlement blocs that Israel has established over the Green Line since 1967, by including within Israel about 2 to 4 percent of the territory of the West Bank, including new Jewish neighborhoods established within the municipal boundaries of Jerusalem over the Green Line. Approximately 65 to 80 percent of Israelis living in the West Bank and 200,000 Israelis living in East Jerusalem could be accommodated within Israel's border in such an arrangement.
- In return, Israel would swap on a one-for-one basis land that is inside Israel's pre-1967 territory that would become part of the Palestinian state so that the territory of the new state of Palestine amounts to 100 percent of the territory captured by Israel in 1967.
- The city of Jerusalem would be shared—with the Jewish neighborhoods under Israeli jurisdiction and the Arab neighborhoods under Palestinian jurisdiction. Each country would establish its capital in Jerusalem.

- The so-called historic or holy basin of Jerusalem, including some of the most sensitive religious and historic sites in the one-square-kilometer area in and around the Old City, would be subject to a special administrative regime, perhaps under some form of international administration, including representation of both Israelis and Palestinians.

- Palestinian refugees would not return to the State of Israel. Their claims would be recognized, their grievance acknowledged, and they would be financially compensated and offered resettlement in the new State of Palestine or in third countries. A small number of refugees might be allowed to participate in a family-reunification program that would bring them back to Israel proper.

- The new State of Palestine would be demilitarized, and rigorous security arrangements would be negotiated between the parties, including a third-party presence (possibly NATO) on the borders between the states and on the borders of the new Palestinian state to the east to prevent smuggling of arms and rockets into the West Bank and to oversee and verify the agreed security protocol.

The leaders of both peoples understand the general contours of the likely deal, and polling on both sides indicates that, even after a generation of unfulfilled promises and overblown expectations, a strong majority prefers the two-state solution over available alternatives. A joint Israeli-Palestinian poll released in March 2010 by the Harry S. Truman Research Institute for the Advancement of Peace at Hebrew University and the Palestinian Center for Policy and Survey Research showed that 71 percent of Israelis and 57 percent of Palestinians support the two-state solution, as opposed to a single binational state.[9]

The Dahaf Institute conducted a poll in January of 2010 of just Israelis and tested support for a two-state solution[10] that incorporates the principles of such model peace agreements negotiated by civil society leaders as the Geneva Accord and the Ayalon-Nusseibeh Initiative. The poll found

67 percent of Israelis (and 63 percent of Israeli Jews) in favor of such an agreement. Interestingly, it also examined the attitudes of members of Knesset on the exact same questions and found the public was more willing to accept such a deal than were members of the Israeli parliament.[11]

Numerous other polls in recent years have shown support in the neighborhood of 60 to 75 percent among both Israelis and Palestinians.[12] The Dahaf poll in particular dug more deeply into the reasons why people were opposed to the two-state solution, finding that 37 percent of Israelis who opposed the agreement did not believe that the Palestinians would live up to their commitments, while only 24 percent were simply ideologically opposed to the creation of a Palestinian state under any conditions.

Despite widespread public support for a two-state solution and a broad understanding of its outlines, three factors make resolving the conflict increasingly difficult and urgent. First is the ever-improving technology and ever-more-lethal weaponry available to those looking to undermine peace. For the past two decades and through two intifadas, the greatest security threat to Israel was terrorism—often in the form of suicide bombers capable of claiming dozens of lives at a time. The threat, at its peak, kept the population of entire cities on edge for months or even years on end. It was finally overcome through a security barrier on the West Bank, assistance from American-trained Palestinian security forces and an apparent recognition by those resisting the occupation of the futility of the tactic itself.

Today, the weapons and technology used in the armed struggle against the State of Israel have advanced considerably, including tens of thousands of rockets in southern Lebanon and Gaza. Hezbollah in Lebanon has rearmed following the 2006 war in southern Lebanon, and Hamas in Gaza has rearmed following Israel's most recent invasion of Gaza in 2008–2009, called Operation Cast Lead, which was aimed at stopping the rockets. Both Hezbollah and Hamas in fact are probably stronger militarily now than before the last rounds of fighting. Their rocket stocks are larger, and the range of those rockets longer.

Rather than simply threatening the border towns of the north or the south, these non-state armies can likely threaten all of Israel's major population centers and reach the entire length of the country with their weapons. The threat is real that one day these forces will gain access to, and learn how to deliver, nonconventional weapons.

With each passing round of conflict, the toll that can be inflicted by armed Palestinian and Arab resistance groups increases, and Israel, in turn, increases the level of military force it brings to bear to defeat it. This spiral of violence is leading inexorably toward a clash with unprecedented consequences if a peaceful resolution is not soon reached.

In his final testimony before the Knesset, General Amos Yadlin, the outgoing chief of Military Intelligence, warned that Israel's next war will be fought on several fronts and will "cause far heavier damage and casualties than other recent conflicts."[13]

The second factor making the conflict more dangerous is its shift from a national dispute over territory to one that is increasingly religious and ideological in nature. More and more hard-liners on both sides are saying that they seek not simply to fulfill their right as a people to a home of their own, but that their cause is divine—rooted either in fundamentalist Judaism or fundamentalist Islam.

The more religious overtones the conflict takes on—the more it is framed as a struggle between the divine right of the Jewish people to all of the land that God bequeathed them and the Muslim imperative to "conquer the infidels"—the harder it will be to solve. And as the religious hard-liners in Hamas and the religious hard-liners in Israel gain more and more power, the odds of finding a territorial compromise or a win-win resolution diminish—and the conflict becomes a zero-sum situation.

The third factor that makes the lack of a two-state resolution a more serious threat to Israel over time is demography. There are over 11.4 million people living today between the Jordan River and the Mediterranean Sea. Of those, about 5.7 million are Jews living either in Israel proper, or in

East Jerusalem, the West Bank and the Golan Heights. Another 5.2 million are Arabs: over 1.2 million citizens of Israel, a quarter million residents of East Jerusalem, 1.5 million Gazans and another nearly 2.2 million Palestinians on the West Bank. The remainder are foreign workers and non-Jews in Jewish households in Israel.[14]

In other words, roughly half of the people living in the area under Israel's political control are not Jewish. Given demographic trends, at some point soon the number of non-Jews in the area will exceed the number of Jews, who as a minority will then be exercising political control over a majority that is denied equal political rights on the basis of their ethnic background.

Given these threats—the improved technology, the deepening extremist ideology and the inexorable march of demography—Israel finds itself at a critical fork in the road, facing a choice of existential proportion: Either end the Israeli-Palestinian conflict now through a two-state solution or cling to an untenable status quo that leads to the decline of its Jewish character, its democratic values and its international standing.

The creation of a political home for the Palestinian people at some point in the coming years is inevitable. The question is whether the Israeli political system can muster the will to swallow the compromises necessary to achieve this outcome peacefully and diplomatically now, or whether it will take years or decades, not to mention thousands more lives lost.

The lack of strong and politically courageous leadership on either side is one of the great tragedies of the conflict. One common observation is that one side has the capacity to take the steps necessary to end the conflict, but not the will. The other has the will, but not the capacity. On both sides, the political class faces major hurdles to offering the necessary leadership on the issue. Israeli coalition politics leave prime ministers dependent on smaller parties at the extremes of Israel's political spectrum. And the Palestinian political leadership lacks the credibility and political legitimacy to deliver on the promises they are making.

Leading Israelis and Palestinians have been negotiating with each other for the better part of two decades through both formal and informal channels. They understand each other's red lines, they know the parameters of the conflict's resolution and the sacrifices they must ultimately make.

Yet, here we are, after nearly twenty years of a "peace process," farther than ever, it seems, from a deal. Left to their own devices, the Israelis and Palestinians are unlikely to muster the political will to hash out the details of an agreement. One can speculate as to the reasons—lack of actual interest, shortage of political capacity or imbalance of power—but there is no doubting the result.

That's why the assistance of third parties, in particular that of the United States, is indispensable. But third parties must do more than convene and host talks, or simply play the role of shuttle negotiator, sustaining the process for its own sake, keeping diplomats employed, journalists engaged and the public distracted. What's needed is active and sustained leadership that focuses not on keeping talks going but on bringing them to a successful conclusion.

President George W. Bush recognized the importance of Israeli-Palestinian peace, though his administration chose to play a relatively passive role until convening the 2007 Annapolis peace conference. He committed the United States publicly to supporting the creation of a Palestinian state as early as 2002. He used the term "occupation," spoke of America's readiness to help the parties achieve "two states living side by side, in peace and security" and talked of how liberty on the West Bank and Gaza "will inspire millions of men and women around the globe who are equally weary of poverty and oppression."[15]

The role of a third party both as a mediator and as guarantor has become indispensable. And only the United States has sufficient trust from, and leverage over, both sides to do it successfully. Luckily, it also has a strong self-interest in ending the conflict.

7

THE CROSSROADS
OF POLITICS AND
POLICY ON ISRAEL

M any conversations in Washington about achieving peace in the Middle East follow a predictable pattern. First comes easy agreement that the shape of the resolution to the Israeli-Palestinian conflict will likely follow the outlines of the two-state solution set forth in President Clinton's parameters.

Second, there's consensus that resolving the conflict is a fundamental national interest of the United States, a conclusion that's not the least bit controversial among policy makers given the massive upheavals in the region, two American wars and the growing challenges posed by Iran and other sources of extremist terrorism throughout the Middle East.

Third, there's acknowledgment that, left to their own devices, the Israelis and Palestinians will remain locked in a divisive status quo that at some point will spark another regional conflagration or worse. That the United States—for its own sake and for that of the parties involved—should play a far more active role in resolving the conflict, specifically by helping to close gaps between the parties, ultimately putting its own ideas on the table and using its influence to close the deal.

Finally, there's agreement on the urgency of the situation, an understanding that if we don't solve this conflict now—diplomatically—the consequences will be felt on the ground and around the world in the not too distant future.

This seems almost too easy: consensus among policy makers in Washington—even across party lines and in and out of government. How often does that happen? It's amazing but true. With the exception of a small number of analysts housed at traditionally neoconservative or pro-Israel lobbies and think tanks, there's surprisingly little debate in Washington about the direction American policy should follow in the Middle East. Reading a joint op-ed by former national security advisers Brent Scowcroft, who worked for President George H. W. Bush, and Zbigniew Brzezinski, who worked for Jimmy Carter, you might even think wistfully that the tradition of partisan differences stopping at the water's edge could still be alive.[1] Maybe a determined president could actually find a way, with bipartisan support, to act forcefully, pull the parties together, advance America's interests and bring peace and stability to a volatile region.[2]

Not so fast.

The conversations always have one last step. The decision makers at the table—whether members of Congress, diplomats, congressional or State Department staff—will look around, check the door to be sure it's closed and give you a look that says, essentially, "You don't really expect me to repeat all this publicly, do you?" Whether at private meetings, dinner parties or policy conferences, conversations on Israel and the Middle East nearly all end with hands thrown in the air and the conclusion that it's really too bad that nothing is ever going to change on this issue.

The 800-pound gorilla lurking around these conversations is the impact of domestic politics, specifically those of the American Jewish community as represented by traditional pro-Israel lobbying groups, on America's Middle East policy. "You can't really expect me to say the things I believe publicly," the politicians and policy makers are saying, "because it will cost me Jewish support." In a very few instances, "support" means Jewish votes. In most cases, it means money, specifically campaign contributions.

This political dynamic goes a long way toward explaining how the United States—the world's sole superpower and the most generous patron of both parties to the Israeli-Palestinian conflict—is unable to find a way to end the conflict when both the need and the solution are so evident.

In keeping with their customary high levels of political engagement, activism and generosity, Jewish Americans do provide a disproportionately large percentage of funding for American political candidates and committees. Exact data are not available on the ethnic or religious background of political donors, but political professionals are well aware that Jewish Americans contribute substantially more as a group than their roughly 2 percent of the American population.

In his landmark 1996 book on the role of Jewish Americans in politics, *Jewish Power*, J. J. Goldberg cites "conversations with numerous Jewish and non-Jewish Democratic party figures" in suggesting that roughly 50 percent of the money raised at that time by Democrats in national races came from Jewish sources.[3] He puts the number for Republicans at less than 20 percent. The perception—inaccurate as it may be—is that access to those resources demands being "pro-Israel" as defined by those who have established themselves as "the" voice of the Jewish community on Israel for the past several decades. Fifteen years later, my own informal conversations with party insiders suggest that the figures may be slightly lower, but Jewish support for Democratic candidates remains substantial nonetheless.

Washington insiders seem surprisingly unaware, however, how little of this financial support from Jewish Americans has anything to do with Israel. They don't seem to grasp that Jewish Americans aren't single-issue voters on Israel or that the majority of Jewish Americans actually hold moderate to liberal views on Israel. In J Street's November 2010 poll, for instance, we found 78 percent support among Jewish American voters for a two-state solution to the Palestinian-Israeli conflict, which would result in Arab countries establishing full diplomatic ties with Israel in return for creating a Palestinian state in the West Bank, Gaza and East Jerusalem. This is consistent with prior surveys showing broad support among Jews for a diplomatic resolution to the conflict along these lines.[4]

The 2010 J Street poll also found that, by a margin of 82 to 18, Jewish Americans understand that a two-state solution is necessary to strengthen Israel's security and ensure its Jewish, democratic character.[5] Further, 69 percent of Jewish Americans believe that Israel should suspend, either partially or totally, construction of Jewish settlements on the West Bank. This, too, reflects a consistent view among Jewish Americans that the settlements are counterproductive to efforts to resolve the conflict peacefully.

Finally, Jewish Americans support by a margin of 65 to 35 percent an active American role in resolving the Arab-Israeli conflict, even if that means exerting pressure on both sides to make the compromises necessary to achieve peace. What's critical to ensuring Jewish support for such efforts, we found, is simply that they be pursued in a balanced manner, with recognition of the responsibility of all sides to take action and make sacrifices.[6]

It is clear to me, after several years of presenting these polls to decision makers in Washington, that the political establishment just does not hear this moderate voice. Instead, what they hear constantly is vocal support for Israel, whether current Israeli actions are right or wrong; implacable opposition to any American pressure on Israel; and real doubts about the feasibility of a two-state solution. This voice tells them that the only way to truly support Israel is by not questioning any legislation, resolutions or letters related to the conflict that express unwavering commitment to one side in the conflict (Israel) and frustration and doubt about the other (Palestinians or Arabs).

The Jewish community that Washington knows is the one that has established warm relationships with both the right wing of the Republican Party and the Christian Zionists in the broader evangelical community. Year after year, politicians witness national groups like the American Israel Public Affairs Committee (AIPAC) honoring and promoting Newt Gingrich, Tom DeLay and Rick Santorum, local Jewish Federations celebrating Israel with Pastor John Hagee, and the Conference of Presidents of Major American Jewish Organizations inviting figures like Sarah Palin to their rallies, with far less representation of Democrats of comparable stature.

So it's no shock that a community so fundamentally liberal and overwhelmingly moderate in its views on the Middle East is perceived as monolithically hawkish and right-of-center when it comes to Israel. That's what the people see. The challenge to the rest of us could not be clearer.

In stating this challenge, I do not wish to minimize in any way what AIPAC, among other groups, has accomplished over the past several decades. It has solidified the U.S.-Israel alliance, locked in broad bipartisan support for a generous military aid package and helped to ensure that Israel has a qualitative military edge over its neighboring enemies. The accomplishments of those supporting Israel in Washington certainly helped ensure Israel's security and survival in its early years. They also form a near-perfect case study on the effective accumulation and deployment of political power in Washington.

In fact, AIPAC is unfairly and at times simplistically attacked when discussing the exercise of political power by the Jewish community in Washington. It's not uncommon, for instance, to hear people imply that members of Congress fear that, if they take a particular position on Israel, "AIPAC is going to beat them." This is a massive oversimplification of the facts, but it's always easier to have one all-powerful bogeyman than to actually explain the complex political structures and processes surrounding the issue.

AIPAC and its associated charitable arm, the American Israel Education Foundation, do raise massive sums of money to fund their operation, over $80 million combined in 2009; nearly $100 million in 2008. In operation for well over fifty years now and with staff and chapters all over the country, it is a finely tuned political and lobbying machine, with a vast reach. *Fortune* magazine and the *National Journal* have both ranked AIPAC as the second or third most powerful interest group in Washington behind the AARP.[7]

AIPAC, however, is only one of a number of forces. National powerhouses such as the American Jewish Committee and the Anti-Defamation League, each with annual budgets of over $50 million in 2006–2008, weigh in regularly and meaningfully in the national debate, generally reiterating the same Israel-right-or-wrong positions. And the Conference of Presidents of Major Jewish Organizations, an umbrella group for over fifty Jewish organizations, has acted as the primary conduit through which presidential administrations get the views of American Jews for several decades. The conference may not have a large budget of its own, but its leaders can easily raise hundreds of thousands of dollars to sponsor, for instance, ads saying that the status of Jerusalem shouldn't be the subject of negotiations.[8] Jewish Federations and the Community Relations Councils that are their public affairs arms engage significant numbers of Jews around the country, and most have Israel advocacy committees that organize regular meetings with members of Congress or take political leaders on trips to Israel with local supporters. Sometimes the leaders of these committees are active in AIPAC; sometimes they are independent. But they're all working from similar talking points.

There's also a host of smaller organizations—polling outfits, media watchdogs, think tanks and the like. Most have a strong security orientation and a conservative political outlook. They include such organizations as The Israel Project, the Committee for Accuracy in Middle East Reporting in America (CAMERA), the Middle East Media Research Institute (MEMRI), Stand With Us, the Jewish Institute for National Security Affairs (JINSA), the Foundation for the Defense of Democracies and the Zionist Organization of America, to name a few.

None of these many organizations are actually in the business of electoral politics. In fact, AIPAC, despite its name ending in the letters PAC, is not itself a political action committee, which would have to be registered with the Federal Election Commission for the purposes of endorsing candidates for office and raising money for them. Given the organization's reputation and the fear of crossing it that pervades Washington, one might assume that the organization specifically endorses candidates and raises money for them. Most people are surprised to discover it's not true. AIPAC decided decades ago that its leaders around the country should engage politically either as individuals or through other local committees.

At one time, there were fifty to sixty PACs supporting federal candidates around the country that specifically identified themselves as pro-Israel. Today, there are approximately thirty, a reduction partly tied to the shrinking number of single-minded Israel voters. Some are explicitly tied to national AIPAC leaders, while others look to it informally for guidance as to which candidates are acceptably "pro-Israel." Some, like NORPAC in northern New Jersey or the Washington PAC of former AIPAC director Morrie Amitay have developed independent identities and agendas. Together, in the 2004–2008 election cycles, these pro-Israel PACs contributed roughly $3 million to federal candidates per cycle.[9]

In the 2010 election cycle, the primary vehicle for attacks on candidates perceived as being insufficiently pro-Israel was a newly formed body called the Emergency Campaign for Israel (ECI). ECI was formed by Bill Kristol, Gary Bauer and Rachel Abrams. Kristol is the editor of the *Weekly*

Standard, one of the leading right-of-center journals, and the son of Irving Kristol, perhaps the godfather of modern neoconservatism. Neoconservatives support an assertive foreign policy and military strategy that favors the use of American power, unilaterally and even preemptively, both to protect American interests and to impose American values abroad. The neocons, as they are called, descend ideologically from Cold War liberals, who worried greatly about the antiwar and pacifist tendencies of "the Left" beginning with the Vietnam War in the 1960s.

The neocons differ from traditional conservatives, who favor limited engagement abroad and smaller government domestically. Many of the leading neoconservatives are Jewish, and one significant factor that drives their worldview and foreign policy agenda is strong, unquestioning support for Israel. They believe that Israel, as an ideological ally of the United States in a nondemocratic part of the world, represents a critical outpost in the battle to promote and export democratic values. Their contention that strength and military power are more useful tools than diplomacy and conciliation meshes well with the right-of-center views now dominant in Israel, and there is strong cross-fertilization between Israel-focused and neoconservative think tanks in the United States.

The views of neoconservatives could not differ more from those of the overwhelming majority of Jewish Americans. For instance, while the neocons were providing the intellectual justification for the war in Iraq and the Bush doctrine of preemptive war, 70 percent of Jewish Americans were opposing the war in Iraq and viewing not only President Bush but Vice President Dick Cheney extraordinarily negatively.

Another partner in the creation of the Emergency Committee for Israel was Gary Bauer, whose résumé includes working for Ronald Reagan on domestic policy, serving as president of the Family Research Council for eleven years and even running for the Republican presidential nomination in 2000. He also serves on the executive committee of John Hagee's Christians United for Israel. Bauer is president of the nonprofit American

Values, which, according to its website, "is deeply committed to defending life, traditional marriage and equipping our children with the values necessary to stand against liberal education and cultural forces."

The third founder, Rachel Abrams, is the wife of Bush Middle East adviser Elliot Abrams and the daughter of legendary neoconservatives Norman Podhoretz and Midge Decter. ECI itself does not appear to be associated directly with AIPAC. Rather, it looks more like a partisan Republican political operation, staffed by two young Republican and neoconservative political operatives—Michael Goldfarb and Noah Pollak. Goldfarb was John McCain's spokesman on Jewish issues in the 2008 presidential campaign and worked closely with Kristol at the *Weekly Standard*. Pollak, the group's executive director, has written for *Commentary* (whose founding editorial board included Kristol's father Irving and which was edited for thirty-five years by Podhoretz) and worked for the Shalem Center in Jerusalem, the think tank that was home to Israel's current ambassador to the United States, Michael Oren, prior to his appointment.

ECI ran television ads attacking a number of Democratic members of Congress for signing a letter to the president in early 2010 urging that the closure of Gaza be eased. They painted those members as friendly to Hamas and anti-Israel.[10] Their attacks meshed with those of the explicitly partisan Republican Jewish Coalition (RJC), which ran more than $1 million in television ads to paint Representative Joe Sestak, a retired three-star admiral, as weak on terror for supporting civil trials for terrorism suspects.[11] The RJC has run harsh attacks ads in several recent political cycles, all aimed at peeling Jews away from their traditional Democratic affiliations—efforts that, as mentioned earlier, have never succeeded.

I do not accept that these groups, each with its own agenda and leadership, constitute a vast "Israel Lobby," a coordinated effort to skew American policy, control the media or shut down political debate, as the most vociferous conspiracy theorists assert. For example, Philip Giraldi, a former CIA officer who is the executive director of the Council for the National Interest, says:

> Pro-Israeli interests control much of the media, and, more important, dominate the opinion and editorial pages, making the only narrative that most Americans hear about the Middle East highly favorable to Israel and highly critical of all Israel's enemies. As a result, Israel is able to control U.S. foreign policy as it relates to the Middle East and much of the Muslim world.[12]

In fact, I believe that efforts to overstate Jewish power in this way are playing into nasty historical stereotypes that have fueled prejudice against the Jewish people over the centuries.

I do believe, however, that the professional efforts by the Jewish community to support Israel have succeeded in conveying an image of power perhaps beyond what those who started the work in good faith ever intended. Making use of the leverage and access that come with even modest political contributions, recognizing the lack of knowledge that most people going into national politics have about Israel and the Middle East and taking advantage of politicians' natural inclination to please their constituents, the community has masterfully written the chapter on Israel in the rulebook of American politics.

It all starts when a politician first sets foot on the road to national office. Representatives of the Jewish community—whether from their district or national fund-raisers—set up a meeting at which they ask the hopeful candidate if he or she supports Israel. The "yes" they receive is supplied in good faith, no doubt, as is, I'm sure, the offer from those representatives to help the candidate figure out what it actually means to "support Israel."

Often, the representatives come prepared with position papers and talking points on Israel for the candidate's use. These position papers may go straight up on campaign websites, and the talking points become the basis for standard responses the candidate will memorize and fall back on for the rest of his or her political career. After all, they know how important it is to their political future that they learn the proper way to be "pro-Israel"—meaning no criticism of Israeli policy, no vocal opposition to settlements and no talk of active American leadership to achieve a two-state deal. Undoubtedly, not long after these initial interactions, one or more of these newfound friends offers to hold a fund-raiser as a way of demonstrating their support and thanks.

After a candidate wins, even if it's not a national office, he or she will get invited to take a trip to the Middle East, courtesy of AIPAC or another arm of the Jewish community. When it comes to Congress, the process has become very disciplined and organized. Every August after a congressional election, the educational arm of AIPAC sponsors a trip to the region for the freshmen of that Congress. The leadership in Congress strongly urges the members to go, and high-ranking Republican and Democratic members usually lead the trips.

In August 2009, House Majority Leader Steny Hoyer led twenty-nine Democratic members of Congress on a mission to Israel, and House Minority Leader Eric Cantor took twenty-five Republicans, meaning that over 10 percent of the U.S. Congress spent a portion of their first August break in Israel. For some members, these AIPAC missions are their first trip to Israel and the region. They'll get background briefings and they'll learn of the security threats facing Israel and the depth of its ties to the United States.

During their time in office, they'll get regular visits not only from representatives of AIPAC but from their local Jewish communities, giving them refreshers on what it means to be "pro-Israel." The campaign contributions will continue to flow from these same friends and leaders, as will the phone calls when there's an issue of consequence to be voted on or a letter to be signed.

Newly elected officials are trained as well, often by colleagues and the political operatives who staff and advise them, to live with an element of fear of what might happen if they start to toe a different line when it comes to Israel. They worry about the possibility of an electoral challenge. They worry that some of their funding will dry up. They worry about the angry calls from a handful of energized activists—often long-time supporters—and about the meetings they'll have to take to answer tough questions from a few dozen motivated constituents or donors.

There'll be talk of what happened to Senator Charles Percy of Illinois in 1984 or what happened to Cynthia McKinney and Earl Hilliard in 2002—all defeated in races when out-of-state donors contributed hundreds of thousands of dollars to challengers because they believed those candidates were in some way anti-Israel. The examples of challenges directly related to Israel are few and far between, but they're sufficient to send the message to newly elected members. (It's important to note as well just how little money is involved in these challenges in the context of a political system that now raises money by the billions.)

Representative Donna Edwards, a Democratic congresswoman from Maryland, was a recent target of this pressure after she and twenty-one other colleagues voted "present" on House Resolution 34 in January 2009. The resolution held Hamas responsible for the escalation of violence in Gaza and southern Israel and made no mention of Israel's policies or issues related to humanitarian conditions in Gaza either before or as a result of the military operation. The resolution passed the House by a vote of 390 to 5. The head of the Washington, D.C., area Jewish Community Relations Council was quoted in an article about rumblings of a primary challenge to Edwards over her vote and position on Israel generally, saying, "The relationship between the Jewish community and Donna Edwards got off to a rocky start. . . . I would be lying if I told you there wasn't concern."[13] Two local rabbis concurred. The threat was not particularly veiled.

Edwards had knocked off a veteran member of Congress, Al Wynn, in the 2008 Democratic primary. Wynn had been a staunch ally of traditional pro-Israel supporters and organizations, but Edwards struck a decidedly different tone in her pro-Israel positions. While supporting aid to Israel and regularly restating her commitment to "a peaceful and secure democratic state of Israel," she also recognized the legitimate rights of the Palestinian people to a state—like Presidents George W. Bush and Barack Obama.[14] She visited Gaza and refused to sign or support the stream of Israel-related letters and resolutions that crossed her desk in her first few years in office. Rumblings about challenges continued throughout the 2010 primary season, but never took shape. Edwards was duly put on notice, but went on to win re-election overwhelmingly in 2010, with a larger number of votes than any other candidate in Maryland for the House of Representatives. She has found considerable support in her district for her reasonable positions, and the handful of voices making noise in the media continue to grumble but pose no real threat to her continued service.

BEWARE THE BACKLASH

The traditional pro-Israel community employs a powerful combination of political assistance for those who follow the line and a healthy dose of fear for those who don't. Students of politics looking to learn how to fight effectively in the national arena would do well to study the techniques they use for accumulating and exercising political power. However, there's a question in my mind regarding where these efforts cross the line from an admirable exercise of political power to overplaying one's hand.

I would argue that we're there already, and that the long-run interests of the Jewish community and of Israel are not well served by the level of resentment building up over how the game is being played. I regularly hear from members of Congress and their staffs about the dread they and some of their colleagues feel as they head to the floor of the House or Senate to cast votes on Israel-related resolutions. They often get no more than a few hours to review resolutions, which rarely go through the traditional committee hearings or get extended debate on the floor. They know that what they're being asked to support is one-sided or over-the-top, but few members of Congress are willing to say no. It's just not worth the political price.

More than a few members of Congress and their staffs resent the treatment they receive from pro-Israel lobbyists—both staff and volunteer—but few are willing to talk openly about it. One exception to that rule is Congresswoman Betty McCollum of Minnesota who lost her temper with AIPAC after one of its local leaders disagreed with her on a 2006 bill that would have significantly restricted American assistance to the Palestinian Authority (a measure that was questioned even by the chief of staff of the Israel Defense Forces[15]) and told her office that her "support for terrorists will not be tolerated." Rarely do members of Congress take such an argument public out of fear of the repercussions, but McCollum published her letter to AIPAC demanding an apology in the New York Review of Books.[16]

While few of McCollum's colleagues are so bold, observers of Capitol Hill will share, off the record, their sense that the resentment over the tone and tactics of pro-Israel lobbying is building up like steam in a boiling pot. At some point, the steam will need to be released. The Jewish community should be concerned about what the blowback against the community in Washington and around the country could look like. It is time for an open conversation within the Jewish community about the atmosphere that has been created in its name and whether it serves the long-term interests of either Israel or the Jewish community.

THE MAJORITY of national political leaders know from personal experience that, beneath the surface, there is a diversity of political views and voices in the Jewish community. They have worked with Jewish Americans on a wide range of efforts aimed at making both the United States and the world more equitable and more just. They see the community's leadership in efforts to end the genocide in Darfur. They see Jewish lobbyists working to achieve immigration reform. Members of Congress know that their colleagues Bob Filner and John Lewis, one Jewish and one black, were Freedom Riders together in the 1960s. Where, they wonder, are these moderate, rational voices when it comes to talking about Israel? They know they must exist, but their impact in the political process is limited at best.

By the spring of 2004, I was convinced that the rulebook of American politics needed a thorough rewrite. The limits on American policy makers imposed by domestic political considerations were not only skewing the conversation for candidates like Howard Dean and Mark Green. They were skewing the substantive discussion in Washington, D.C., about actual American policy.

After all, shouldn't there be at least as much space for discussion here as there is in Israel itself? If Israel's politicians can talk openly and honestly about the difficult sacrifices Israel needs to make to achieve long-term peace and security, and the serious consequences of failure, why can't America's?

It was crystal clear to me that a more open dialogue on American policy would only happen if American leaders were given the space to stake out their positions without fear of the "loudest eight percent." And I was certain that, given that space, they would adopt sensible policies toward the Middle East, grounded in friendship to Israel, and make it a priority to end the Arab-Israeli conflict with a two-state resolution. Time was running out on the two-state solution and, without U.S. action now to achieve it, the consequences for the region, the United States and our allies could be severe.

Those who might naturally stake out such pro-Israel, pro-peace positions need to know that if they do, there will be meaningful political support for them. They need to see evidence that for every prominent donor they think they may lose, another will take its place. They need to know that someone's got their back.

The key to changing these rules is to rally moderate Jewish Americans who care deeply about Israel to express themselves politically. We have to deliver campaign funds. We have to rally Jewish community leaders—rabbis and other pillars of the community—to stand by politicians who take these positions. We have to deliver hundreds of people to community meetings to cheer and applaud rational positions on Israel, just as those on the right do for their own.

In 2004, there simply wasn't such a mechanism. The majority of the Jewish community had been far too silent for far too long—their political voice claimed by those to their right, purporting to speak for all of us.

In Washington, D.C., the streets run in a grid pattern from A Street to W Street in alphabetical order. There is, however, no J Street. It's the missing street in Washington's grid. Similarly, there was a gap in Washington in the way the Jewish community was being represented. The voice of what I call the "passionate moderates" in our community was being lost.

That's why we started J Street. We sought to fill this gap by providing a political voice for friends of Israel who care deeply about its long-term survival and security and who are willing, when appropriate, to break with Israeli government policy. Who are ready to say that the United States may need to press not only the Palestinians and the Arabs to make peace, but the Israelis, too.

These discussions, with a small group of colleagues and friends including my good friend and former Israeli peace negotiator Daniel Levy, veteran Washington insider Mort Halperin, Jim Gerstein and others, would go on for over three years. They centered on creating a new voice on Israel, coming from the center-left mainstream of the Jewish community, that would advocate a two-state solution, lobby policy makers and raise and distribute political money—and in the process rewrite the rules of American Jewish politics.

We approached this in several different ways. First, we tried convening a large number of wealthy Jewish American philanthropists who had stood up for traditionally liberal Jewish politics but had not necessarily found their political home in the existing lobbies or political vehicles.

On October 25, 2006, we called a meeting, inviting such notable philanthropists and political funders as George Soros, Peter Lewis, Charles
and Edgar Bronfman and others. We planned to present a program for
creating a comprehensive progressive voice for peace and security in the
Middle East that would build on existing efforts and add a political arm to
work already being conducted by other groups.

We tried to keep the meeting confidential, as those invited were not
yet committed to the project. Unfortunately, in the days leading up to
the meeting, the story broke in the press, and the role of George Soros
in particular was highlighted. Soros had had some run-ins with the Jewish communal leadership and had been critical, at times vocally, of Israeli government policies and of the way AIPAC in particular operated in
Washington, D.C. Among other things, he had been blasted in 2003 for
connecting a rise in European anti-Semitism with the policies of President George W. Bush and Prime Minister Ariel Sharon, saying "There is a
resurgence of anti-Semitism in Europe. The policies of the Bush administration and the Sharon administration contribute to that. . . . It's not
specifically anti-Semitism, but it does manifest itself in anti-Semitism as
well. I'm critical of those policies."[17]

The publicity around the 2006 meeting led a few participants to pull
out before it even took place. Soros himself opened the meeting by reading a prepared statement explaining why he felt he could not take part
in launching the effort—a conclusion he repeated the following year in
an essay in the *New York Review of Books:* "Anybody who dares to dissent
may be subjected to a campaign of personal vilification. I speak from
personal experience. Ever since I participated in a meeting discussing
the need for voicing alternative views, a torrent of slanders has been released. . . . I am not sufficiently engaged in Jewish affairs to be a part of
the reform of AIPAC."[18]

The project had numerous fits and starts. We scaled back our vision
from an effort that would start with a minimum $10 million budget to

one that might begin with a merger of existing organizations, such as the Israel Policy Forum, Americans for Peace Now and Brit Tzedek v'Shalom (the Alliance for Justice and Peace).

Finally, in the fall of 2007, realizing that major philanthropists weren't going to kick in large-scale funding up front and that merger talks among existing groups were no longer progressing, we faced the decision of whether to simply forge ahead or fold up the whole idea, sacrificing three years of planning.

We decided in November to move forward, and I began working full-time on the effort with one assistant. We had two significant pledges of financial support—one from Israeli-American businessman Davidi Gilo, who would become chairman of the board, and the other from philanthropist and political activist Deborah Sagner and her father, Alan. I worked out of my basement, raising more money and pulling together a roster of supporters.

On April 15, 2008, we formally launched J Street—with four full-time staff members and a budget of about $1.5 million. We set up a legally independent political action committee, called JStreetPAC, and in six months made it the largest pro-Israel PAC in the country, distributing more money to federal candidates than any of the other pro-Israel PACs in that cycle.

Over the next three years, J Street grew steadily. Today, it has an operating budget of nearly $7 million with fifty staff in eight cities and 170,000 supporters, including many who had at one time been active in Brit Tzedek v'Shalom, with whom we integrated. In the 2010 election cycle, JStreetPAC distributed over $1.5 million to federal candidates, nearly two and a half times what it had distributed in 2008, and more than any pro-Israel PAC in history.

We ultimately did gain the financial support of George Soros, who began contributing to the effort in the late fall of 2008. Our decision to keep Soros's support confidential, as we were legally entitled to do, ended up generating controversy when, in the fall of 2010, the Internal Revenue Service illegally posted our confidential list of donors for our first fiscal year on the Internet. Soros's prediction was on the mark: The revelation of his support generated a storm of controversy. So did the decision not to make his support public when it began.

I am proud to have George Soros's support. I believe his philanthropy and political activism represent the best of Jewish values in action, and I regret that I succumbed to the very political pressure J Street is trying to defeat in arguing that we should keep his support quiet.

Happily, none of the controversy—from funding issues to our overall mission to shake up the status quo—has stopped the effort from taking off successfully. Over forty local J Street groups have been formed. A new arm of the group is organizing on more than fifty college campuses. Over six hundred rabbis have joined our Rabbinic Cabinet. J Street's first national conference in the fall of 2009 attracted not only controversy—Michael Goldfarb and other right-wing activists tried to frighten members of Congress out of serving on our Host Committee—but over 1,500 people, 200 media outlets and, in the end, about 150 members of Congress. The second drew over 2,000 people. Groups with similar identities and agendas have popped up in continental Europe and England.

The vacuum is being filled. As I said on our first conference's opening night, the "majority" of Israel's supporters, the moderates, were silent no more. The Obama administration, coming into office just months after J Street launched, recognized this emerging power center and sent National Security Advisor Jim Jones to address our conference and invited me to a meeting of American Jewish leaders with President Obama in the summer of 2009.

J Street's early record of accomplishment is but a first step on the road to changing the dynamics of American politics when it comes to Israel and the Middle East. Some of the organizations speaking for the Jewish community have been around for decades, others for over a century. It's simply not possible for a new organization to come onto the scene and drastically shift these well-established dynamics overnight.

But for the first time, American policy makers and politicians are hearing a new political voice in the mix. They're hearing that, for Israel's sake, for the sake of U.S. interests and for the good of the American Jewish community, the conflict between the Israelis and the Palestinians needs to end. And American policy makers and politicians who choose to take up that cause now know that there is a base of political support for them. Many of them have had only one question when they meet with us: "What took you so long?"

The goal of J Street is to be a new voice for Israel, not to be "the" voice of the American Jewish community. We have no pretense to represent the entirety of the community. We know that we disagree substantively and politically with many in the community who are more skeptical of chances of reaching a peace deal, of the capacity and willingness of the Palestinians and of the long-term viability of such an arrangement.

And that's their prerogative. We simply want the message that reaches Washington to reflect the true diversity of opinions in the American Jewish community. We want a voice in the American political debate that reflects the progressive and liberal tendencies of that community and that is consonant with the values on which we were raised.

We want nothing less than to rewrite the rules of American politics. Our job won't be complete, however, unless we change the rules of the American Jewish community as well.

8

GENERATION OY!

The Jewish emigrants who headed to Palestine from Russia in the late nineteenth and early twentieth centuries were far outnumbered by the hundreds of thousands who sought a fresh start in the New World. Over the past hundred years, these two communities of Jews—in Israel and in the United States—have charted wildly different courses.

In the States, Jews were one minority in a sea of immigrants from various nationalities and backgrounds. Their history of survival as strangers in new lands fit neatly with America's melting-pot culture, and they fared well, integrating quickly.

The dynamic in Palestine was very different. There, the new arrivals aimed not to integrate into the existing society so much as to transform it, with the ultimate goal of re-establishing a national homeland of their own.

Today, the Jewish communities in the United States and in Israel are the world's two largest, by one estimate accounting for over 81 percent of all the world's 13.4 million Jews. Putting a precise number on the Jewish population in the United States is not simply difficult, it's political, since the number is heavily affected by determining how exactly to define who counts as a Jew. One estimate by a leading Israeli demographer is that there are roughly 5.2 million Jews living in the United States, only slightly less than Israel's 5.7 million.[1] Another says there are nearly 6.5 million Jewish Americans.[2]

The level of direct connection between Jews in America and Jews in Israel is hard to measure precisely, but still surprisingly low. Recent polls like J Street's and one out of Brandeis University found that only 33 and 36 percent of American Jews have traveled to Israel,[3] while a 1983 study by Steven M. Cohen found the number only slightly higher at that time (40 percent).[4] Overall engagement with Israel seems to be trending downward over time. For instance, the 1983 Cohen survey found that 75 percent of respondents "often [talked] about Israel with friends and relatives,"[5] while J Street's 2010 study found that only 37 percent discuss Israel every week or even once or twice a month.[6]

The relationship between Jewish Americans and Israel helps shape American politics and foreign policy, as discussed earlier. It also helps to define the nature and character of Jewish communal life here in the States. To understand this evolving relationship, we must look at important fissures in the American Jewish community, some related to religious practice and political outlook, and some—perhaps the most critical—generational.

BORN IN 1962, I find myself squarely on the dividing line between two very different American Jewish generations—one with a deep personal connection to the tragedy of World War II and the immigrant experience that brought their families to the United States, and another for whom those experiences are, at best, distant memories.

Those older than me—especially those born before World War II in the United States or abroad—understood first-hand the costs of war, the threats to the Jewish people, and the reality of the extermination of a people. My mother's and father's lives and worldviews were defined largely by World War II. Images of Hitler addressing the German masses, of SS troops goose-stepping in military parades or of starving Jews dying in concentration camps were not pages in history books or grainy footage in old newsreels. They were reality.

Jewish Americans born after me have—thankfully—little to no first-hand experience with prejudice and fear on the basis of their religion. The stories of suffering—of pogroms and blood libel, of *Kristallnacht* (Night of Broken Glass) and trains to Auschwitz—are not their own memories or even the living memories of friends, neighbors and parents. They are at best the hazy recollections of grandparents, dusty diaries or fading photographs in the attic. Second- or third-hand accounts of the suffering and tragedy that have befallen the Jewish people may still hold personal meaning, but the impact of these events is inevitably blunted by the passage of time.

Similarly, I find myself at a crossroads when it comes to the relationship between American Jews and the State of Israel. I turned five the day after Israeli soldiers miraculously emerged victorious in the Six-Day War. My earliest recollections include the overwhelming fear, the week of my fifth birthday, that Israel would be destroyed by invading armies, and the subsequent joy at its improbable victory and the sight of Jews at the Western Wall in Jerusalem.

My habit of saving the front page of the *New York Times* to mark important memories began with the banner headline announcing Israel's victory. My childhood bookshelf was filled with biographies of the Israeli heroes of that era and stories of their miraculous achievements. The music and words of "Jerusalem of Gold" stirred pride in my heart. I looked forward to marching in the Israel Day Parade with our synagogue. An Israeli flag flew proudly in my room.

On birthdays and holidays, I got certificates informing me that trees were planted in Israel *with my name on them*. And I'll admit to being hugely disappointed when I finally understood that it wasn't possible to visit *my* trees when we took our family trips to Israel. I don't think I'm the only one who expected to find little plaques marking each tree planted in my name. In fact, I expected an entire grove.

I also remember well the dread we felt in synagogue on Yom Kippur in 1973 as the congregation prayed for the survival of the State of Israel. I can still summon the anguish and tension nearly forty years later.

The kidnapping and subsequent slaughter of the Israeli Olympic team in Munich in 1972 was a searing experience for a ten-year-old. The stirring rescue of Israeli hostages at Entebbe in 1976, by contrast, was a moment of enormous pride in Israeli daring and ingenuity.

My father's background and the unusual level of connection to Israel in my childhood undoubtedly heightened my awareness of all these experiences, but I think that my deep sense of pride in Israel was common among the children of my generation.

Jews my age and older may experience terrorism differently as well. Images of bombed-out buses or shattered pizza parlors conjure memories of prior waves of anti-Jewish violence, the kind that drove our parents and grandparents out of Europe and helped justify the creation of the State of Israel. Confronted with such violence in our own homeland, what choice is there but to stand and fight? After all, there's nowhere else to go.

This particular mix of emotions—deep pride in the achievements and victories of Israel on the one hand, and existential fear on the other—is, in my experience, far less common among those born two decades after me. The children of the 1980s and later, in college today or recently graduated, have known a far different world and have a far different relationship to Israel than their parents do.

Israel, to today's younger generation, is less a miracle than a fact. With one of the world's most powerful armies and a presumed nuclear arsenal, Israel's survival is, it would seem, a given. The notion of Israel as David and of the Palestinian people as part of an Arab Goliath sounds backward to them. In fact, for some in this generation, the defining images of Israel are of intifada and occupation. They see less an Israeli fight for survival and more a Palestinian fight for freedom, in which the underdogs are no longer the Jews.

They struggle with the communal narrative grounded in an image of Israel on the defensive against large and powerful armies arrayed to destroy it. Their hearts may go out to Israelis who have been the victims of terror, and they may respect the dangers faced by those on the front lines, threatened by rockets. But they still see Israel as the party with the power, battling not so much a mortal enemy but a people seeking their own liberation. And, based on what they've seen in their short lives, that fight for liberation and justice resonates.

Jewish children in the United States today are unlikely to forge an emotional connection with the Israeli settlers reclaiming the land of their forefathers across the Green Line. They are much more apt to relate personally to the young Christian woman from Gaza denied permission to re-enter the West Bank in order to complete her university degree in Bethlehem weeks before graduation. And they're shocked when they hear that rabbis rule that it is a sin to rent a home to an Arab, and that a majority of Jewish Israelis support this discrimination, not the Arabs who are its victim.[7]

The sociologists Steven M. Cohen and Ari Y. Kelman's 2007 study "Beyond Distancing: Young Adult American Jews and Their Alienation from Israel" makes the case that there is a wide generational gap between non-Orthodox Jews who are sixty-five and older and those under thirty-five in their level of attachment to and attitudes toward Israel. Their data address a range of indicators from following news coverage about Israel to feeling emotional attachment to it and caring about its fate and survival. If the generational gap was present on one or a few indicators, they suggest, it could be dismissed as an outlier, "but the gaps between younger and older Jews for all measures suggest that a broad-based distancing from Israel is well under way and has been under way for decades."[8]

With each age cohort (65 and over, 50–64, 35–49, and under 35) progressively less attached to Israel than the one before it, they conclude "that we are in the midst of a long-term and ongoing decline in Israel attachment." They observe "a massive shift in attitudes toward Israel" underway, in which an older generation that was more deeply connected to Israel is being replaced by a younger one that is less Israel-engaged.[9]

Cohen and Kelman are careful to say that this trend among the non-Orthodox doesn't mean that the importance of Israel among the younger generation has disappeared altogether. Most young Jews under thirty-five still express attachment to Israel, even if it is weaker than that of their parents. And, of course, including the rapidly growing younger Orthodox population would impact those numbers. Overall, only 9 percent of American Jews identify as Orthodox, but they are a higher percentage of younger Jewish Americans, owing to their custom of having large families. Twenty-two percent of the remaining Jewish Americans identify as Conservative, 28 percent as Reform and 41 percent with another form of Jewish practice or simply "just Jewish."[10]

Intermarriage directly affects levels of connection to Israel and is far more common today than a generation or two ago. A report based on the National Jewish Population Study conducted in the early 1970s found that only 9.2 percent of all Jews at that time were intermarried. The same report revealed, however, the beginning of the massive shift ahead in the next generation, with a stunning 32 percent of Jews marrying outside their faith between 1966 and 1972.[11] A 1991 study reporting that the rate of intermarriage in the whole community had risen to 52 percent sparked such controversy that it was later revised down to 43 percent. By 2006, it was estimated to be 47 percent.[12]

While the far higher level of intermarriage among the younger generation of non-Orthodox Jews helps to explain the weakening attachment to Israel across the generations, their ideology does not. Using party identification and political ideology, Cohen and Kelman break the population into "left leaning" (Democratic *and* liberal), "right leaning" (Republican *or* conservative) and "other." Thirty-seven percent of Cohen's non-Orthodox sample fell into the left-leaning category, 21 percent into the right, and 42 percent into the middle. Interestingly, they find no meaningful distinction in attachment to Israel among these three groups. Progressive Jews are as tied to Israel as are their right-leaning peers.[13]

Jewish liberals, young and old, should find it reassuring and empowering to have data proving that they care as much about Israel as do their conservative neighbors. Too often, liberal Jews find their views dismissed on the grounds that they are somehow less supportive of or connected to Israel than community members from the right of center. Furthermore, the data should serve as an impetus to Jewish institutions such as federations, community relations councils and synagogues to provide Israel-related programming that includes left-of-center political perspectives. If liberals care just as much about Israel as do conservative community members, their concern for and perspective on the future of Israel deserve equal respect and airtime.

One upshot of these demographic shifts is that American Jews are not as likely as they used to be to channel their charitable giving through Jewish organizations and charities, and nearly every established Jewish institution is struggling to deal with this challenge. Only 45 percent of Jewish Americans reported that they donated to such organizations in 2010,[14] compared, for instance, to 1983 when 64 percent said they "usually give to UJA/Federation" (the main established charitable arm of the Jewish community).[15] Making pro-Israel liberals more comfortable in traditional communal settings might be a start toward reversing the nearly 50 percent decline in donations that has the community's established leadership so concerned.[16]

There may not be a relationship between ideology and connection to Israel, but there most certainly is a relationship between one's politics and how one reacts to events there. A team of Brandeis scholars looked specifically at Jewish responses to Israel's actions in the summer of 2010, when a Turkish flotilla attempted to break the Israeli naval blockade of Gaza.[17] The study presented participants with two statements—one concurring with Israel's narrative of events, and the other with Turkey's.

Agreement with the Israeli statement was directly correlated with middle age, political conservatism and religious observance. The differences in reactions by age, in particular, were startling. Only 18 percent of those 60 and over agreed strongly or somewhat with the Turkish statement, or judged themselves halfway between the Turkish and Israeli statements, as opposed to 49 percent of those 18 to 29.

Younger Jews today are no less connected as individuals to their Judaism than their parents are.[18] They are, however, finding new and creative outlets for engagement with their faith outside traditional synagogues, and they identify more with their faith and heritage at a personal level than they do with the institutions of the Jewish community. For instance, there is a real commitment to community service among younger Jews, and they are often excited to do it through a Jewish lens. But fewer of them are pursuing communal activism, as their parents or grandparents did, through traditional organizations like Hadassah or B'nai B'rith. Meanwhile, programs like Avodah, which sponsors community service programs in the United States for young people, or the American Jewish World Service, which provides similar experiences overseas, are enjoying tremendous growth.

Recent efforts to document the extent of this burgeoning world suggest that several hundred thousand Jews are participating in new activities, organizations and initiatives outside the mainstream affecting the practice of the Jewish religion, education, community service, the media and more.[19] They include independent minyans (lay-led worship communities) all over the country, social justice organizations like Progressive Jewish Alliance and Jewish Funds for Justice, educational initiatives like Limmud and new media outlets like J-Dub. The leaders of these initiatives—many under forty—have not pursued communal engagement by climbing the leadership ladder at federations or AIPAC or by joining the Conference of Presidents of Major Jewish Organizations. They have sought connection to and expression of their Jewish identity in innovative, non-traditional forums.

In mid-2009, J Street convened thirty-five leaders of these groups, all under forty, to talk about how they relate to Israel through their work and to see whether we could help them connect to Israel in a way consistent with their agenda. We wanted to know whether a progressive approach to Israel could be an asset to their work and what J Street as a progressive, pro-Israel group could do to help bridge the gap between Israel and young liberal Jewish American activists.

Frankly, we expected to find a naturally receptive audience among these young Jewish leaders. Instead, we were taken aback by how many of the participants rejected the premise that Israel is an issue that they should be expected to deal with or that should figure in their efforts to put Jewish values to work. One of the surprises for me since starting J Street has been that the next generation of leaders in the Jewish community seems to see Israel largely as a headache or impediment, rather than a potential asset to their work.

This strikes me as a shame and, worse, a missed opportunity. Israel is the one country where the Jewish people are putting their values into practice as national policy, with the Jewish people fully responsible for the outcomes. It should be as natural and exciting for young American Jewish activists to help Israel be the finest example of our people's values that it can be as it was for their parents and grandparents to help build and secure the country in the first place. Their disengagement from Israel is not simply a challenge to Jewish continuity in the United States. It is a loss for the State of Israel, which could benefit greatly from the idealism and energy these young people bring to the table.

In Israel, there is also a vibrant network of young activists working to make Israel a more democratic, just and peaceful society. Scores of small non-governmental organizations and networks of activists are working passionately on such causes as protecting the rights of foreign workers, promoting equal rights for all Israelis regardless of race, religion or sexual orientation, and supporting nonviolent resistance to the occupation of the West Bank. The young activists engaged in these efforts in both societies have far more in common with each other than either group has with the established leaders of their respective communities.

These two sets of cousins should get to know each other. Young American Jews should be exposed, for instance, to the passionate activism of young Israelis who have finished their military service and are now speaking out against the occupation. Instead, those Israeli speakers are often blocked from traditional American campus organizations and are certainly not on the itinerary for most Birthright trips that bring young Jewish Americans to Israel for the first time.

Similarly, there would be real value in connecting young Israeli activists with Americans engaged in community service, *tikkun olam* and other values-based activism. These American activists could inspire their Israeli counterparts at a time when they feel increasingly alone and on the defensive, surrounded by the growing power of right-wing politicians like Avigdor Lieberman and the ultra-Orthodox.

THERE HAS BEEN so much communal handwringing over this waning connection between young American Jews and Israel or the traditional Jewish community that I've come to call the whole dynamic "generation oy." The community's establishment has mobilized significant resources to better understand the problem and to plan a response. Pollsters have been commissioned to run focus groups and field surveys. Communal leaders and philanthropists hold conferences. Academics publish papers. Will the young people of today be there for the Israel of tomorrow? Will the next generation and their children and grandchildren remember where they came from? Will they still have a connection to their faith, tradition and people?

In one such study published in 2003, called "Israel in the Age of Emi-nem," pollster Frank Luntz introduced the issue to traditional Jewish lead-ers and philanthropists as follows:

> Most traditional communications and marketing strategies are not reaching
> the vast majority of young Jews. We are writing for ourselves, and talk to
> ourselves and because of this we may even be alienating the young Jewish
> audiences.
>
> The young Jews we listened to relate strongly to their identity but not in
> the same way as their parents and grandparents. For this audience, culture
> has replaced tradition and spirituality has replaced religion. Their associa-
> tion with Israel is frighteningly weak. . . . The impact of this is immediately
> evident in their use of the word "they" rather than "us" when they talk about
> Israel. The Jewish state is tangible and emotional for most Jewish organiza-
> tions but is an abstraction for many younger Jews.[20]

Major philanthropists have spent hundreds of millions of dollars over the past decade trying to address the problems Luntz outlines in his re-port. Communal funders and organizations have looked at the problem as one of communications and programming. As Jeffrey Solomon, the president of the Andrea and Charles Bronfman Philanthropies, wrote in the introduction to the Luntz report: "We are not connecting effectively with young Jews. Indeed, the messages, messengers, and mechanisms we are using for advocacy and fund-raising campaigns may even be turning them off."[21]

The response of the communal establishment to these trends has been sadly off the mark. Viewing the problem as one of communications, they blame themselves for not doing a good enough job conveying what a won-derful place Israel is or making the case adequately for why Israel is right when it comes to the Israeli-Palestinian conflict. So philanthropists pro-vide free trips to Israel that show young Jewish Americans a good time, filled with tours, parties and concerts—none of the troubling reality of the ongoing conflict. A little hummus, a good-looking, sun-tanned Israeli tour guide, a quick dose of history and culture—and, *voilà,* an instant connection with Israel is established that will last a lifetime.

I support the vision underlying the Birthright program, namely, to provide free trips to Israel for young Jewish Americans. I do believe every young Jewish American should go to Israel and connect with their people, their culture and their history. But they should see Israel in full and be encouraged to engage with the complexity of the conflict and the history of the region—rather than have trip itineraries that purposefully strive to avoid dealing with the conflict.

Because so many Birthright and other Israel experiences organized for young people fail to address these issues, they're not preparing their participants adequately for the discussion of Israel that's taking place on their campuses today. More and more students are looking for a way to express concern and anger over the plight of the Palestinian people. They are joining a movement that seeks to exert pressure on Israel to change its policies—through boycotts of Israeli goods, divestment from companies doing business in Israel, or other sanctions—called the "BDS movement" for the boycott, divestment and sanctions that it promotes. Progressive Jewish students are often at the forefront of these movements as they have traditionally been for so many other causes in the past half century.

To address this phenomenon and the difficult position in which many Jewish students find themselves, traditional Jewish communal organizations are putting together new pro-Israel counterweights. They sponsor speakers who present Israel's point of view, generally with an Israel-right-or-wrong narrative. They set up projects to monitor professors of modern history or political science for signs of anti-Semitism. They place Israel advocates on campus with talking points, prepared for a battle in black and white, even though young people today are anxious to see the shades of gray.

None of it's working, and here's why. Not because we haven't trained young American Jews adequately to be Israel advocates on campus, or armed them with the tools to counter professors whose presentation of history or current events casts Israel in a less than perfect light.

The problem is that the policies of the State of Israel and the behavior of parts of the Jewish community in Israel are simply tremendously disturbing to large numbers of students and even to their professors. A response grounded in denial that there is anything wrong with the ongoing occupation of the West Bank simply deepens the anger rather than alleviating it.

Friends of the State of Israel consistently suggest that Israel has a "PR problem"—that it hasn't done an adequate job of explaining itself, or of making its case in the court of public opinion. When news media run stories critical of Israel, the ensuing discussion in the community isn't about whether Israel should look more closely at what it is doing or consider adjusting its behavior. It's about the underlying anti-Israel bias in the media.

And the campus activists leading boycott or divestment campaigns aren't there because the Hillels on campus or the synagogues in their hometowns have failed to instill the proper messages and values. They're there precisely because their parents and their community *have* succeeded. They are wonderful young Jews, moved by their values, conscious of justice and wanting all people treated fairly and equally.

The proper response to the organizations that are successfully rallying young people around positions that the community doesn't like is not to label them anti-Israel or to throw them out of the communal tent— as, for instance, the Anti-Defamation League does by including Jewish Voice for Peace, a pro-BDS organization, in the list of Top Ten Anti-Israel Groups for 2010.[22] The best response to criticism of Israeli policy, when it's grounded in concerns over justice and human rights, is not a vigorous reiteration of Israel's right to exist. This does nothing but imply that the State of Israel and justice for all are mutually exclusive.

The American Jewish establishment needs to acknowledge that many young liberal Jews are turned off by its inability to admit that Israel's actions, policy and behavior are at times wrong, or to permit a nuanced discussion that addresses sensitive issues in a respectful manner. The history of this issue is complex. There is plenty of blame to go around. But in the end, the only way Israel will be secure, not to mention Jewish and democratic, is if it balances the Palestinian desire for freedom and independence with its own right to security and survival.

NO ONE HAS THROWN down the gauntlet to the Jewish community's leadership as clearly as Peter Beinart in his summer 2010 article in the *New York Review of Books* entitled, "The Failure of the American Jewish Establishment." In it, Beinart places the blame for the falling levels of connection to Israel among younger, more secular Jewish Americans not on underlying anti-Semitism or an anti-Israel atmosphere on campus, but on the policies and practices of the American Jewish establishment itself.

Beinart himself was once warmly welcomed in the heart of the establishment, as a popular speaker on the AIPAC circuit and, for seven years, as editor of the *New Republic*. Since 1974, when the magazine was purchased by Marty Peretz, it has been a leading voice for Jewish thinking that marries liberal politics domestically with a security focus abroad, grounded in hard-line, Israel-right-or-wrong views on the Middle East.[23]

Beinart was part of a cadre of writers and thinkers—many Jewish— who provided the intellectual capital that, in the early part of the Bush administration, helped promote the U.S. march to war in Iraq (though he also published a formal apology for doing so in the magazine in 2004). He was a prominent critic of Democrats who were not committed strongly enough to the war on terror and the battle against "totalitarian Islam."[24] He argued that the Democratic Party had a "national security problem" and that the Democrats lost in 2002 and 2004 because Americans did not trust them to keep the country safe.

As Howard Dean's national policy director, I argued the opposite case during the 2004 presidential primaries. While the *New Republic* was editorializing in support of the war and urging Democrats to be more hawkish, those of us on the Dean campaign were arguing that Democrats should act less like Republicans and more like a vocal and principled opposition—to the war in Iraq as well as the overall thrust of Bush's foreign and domestic policies.

That's why it caused such an uproar when a writer of Beinart's pedigree penned the seminal brief indicting the American Jewish establishment, not just for rigid adherence to a hawkish orthodoxy on Israel but for driving young, liberal American Jews away from Israel and from their community. In his words, "For several decades, the Jewish establishment has asked American Jews to check their liberalism at Zionism's door, and now, to their horror, they are finding that many young Jews have checked their Zionism instead."[25] How did they fail? By not providing a way for young liberal Jews to mesh the values on which they were raised with the devotion to the State of Israel so dear to their parents and grandparents.

Beinart reviewed the challenges and threats to Israel's democracy and to the very principles on which the nation-state of the Jewish people was founded, from increasing levels of prejudice and racism, to decreasing support for democratic rights and growing intolerance for dissent. He pointed out that, at the very moment Israel confronts the most serious challenges in its brief history, the American Jewish establishment is shutting down an open and vibrant conversation about the issues that threaten its future.

Beinart concludes that the current Israel conversation in the Jewish community is putting both the future of liberal Zionism and support for the State of Israel among young Jewish Americans at risk.

I would go further. I would argue that the state of the Israel conversation is putting the heart and soul of the entire American Jewish community at risk. Jewish Americans take deep pride in the role they have played in helping the United States strive for its ideal of justice and equality for all. We regularly speak out with moral clarity on challenging issues, not only at home but around the world.

Our community will suffer greatly if we refuse an open and honest discussion of how those same values manifest in the national home of our people. And it's not just younger, liberal Jews, but Jewish Americans of all ages, who are being turned off from organized Jewish life.

The American Jewish community today increasingly clusters around two poles. One is more Orthodox in its practice of Judaism, less intermarried, and defines itself as Jewish more as a religious than an ethnic identity. This group is also more politically conservative and more attached to and active in matters related to Israel. At the other pole are those Jewish Americans who are far less observant, more likely to be intermarried and less directly connected to the practice of Judaism or to traditional institutions of the Jewish community. This latter group is more liberal in its politics and, while emotionally attached, far less likely to have a direct connection to or relationship with Israel.

We've seen already that the "loudest eight percent" of the Jewish community on Israel is drawn from those clustered around the first pole. Their impact on American policy and politics has been enormous. Their impact on the community itself is just as significant.

The answer to all the handwringing over how to engage younger, non-Orthodox Jews clustered around the other pole seems to me painfully obvious. We need to change the rules of engagement to give Jewish Americans a voice for their values on Israel, whatever they may be.

Criticism of Israel needs to be met not with condemnation and censure but with rational dialogue. And the community's leadership should speak up loudly not just to defend Israel when it is in danger and under attack, but when Israel's behavior and actions run counter to both its own self-interests and our American values.

Of course, the conversation between the generations should be a two-way street. Those young Jews who cannot understand how or why Israel acts as it does today will benefit enormously from listening to their elders who can ground today's events in historical context and explain how their security concerns stem from generations of persecution and hatred. Similarly, those who see every Israeli action as justified by the necessities of survival can benefit from a call to conscience, reminding them that the values we've been taught on all other issues also apply to Israel itself.

Such a conversation will require rewriting the rules for a new century. The process may be painful, but it's existentially important to the American Jewish community, and critical to maintaining the bond between the world's two largest Jewish communities.

Until the American Jewish establishment welcomes debate and dissent, no amount of "improved messaging," advocacy training or even free trips will overcome the disconnect that many Jewish Americans of all ages feel between the values with which they were raised and the national homeland of their people. Without fundamental change, the long-standing Jewish institutions of the United States will see their support base shrink until there's only one pole standing.

9

FIVE MILLION JEWS, ONE OPINION?

A classic joke tells of a Jewish man who's been in a shipwreck at sea. He washes ashore on a desert island where he lives alone for many years, surviving off the land and waiting to be rescued.

One day a boat comes to the island and its crew discovers the man. The sailors go ashore, and the man proudly shows them how he's been living all this time. The rescue party is deeply impressed by the life he's built, but they have to ask him one nagging question: "You're living on this island all alone, why would you build two synagogues?"

"Well, that's obvious," replies the man. "One is the synagogue where I go to pray. The other is the one I would never go to if you paid me."

Jews love to joke about being people with strong opinions. They revel in argumentation, proud that the roots of Jewish learning lie in debate and disagreement. You know the saying: two Jews, three opinions. Even when it's just brunch at my house, it takes fifteen minutes to agree on what flavor bagels to buy.

Perhaps that's why it's so hard to see why anyone would expect all American Jews to have only one opinion, and to speak with one voice, when it comes to Israel. Debate and discussion over Israel has been going on since early in the last century, when some Jewish Americans opposed Zionism from the get-go, while its supporters argued over how best to achieve its goals. And lively arguments certainly go on every day in Israel from the family dining table to the halls of the Knesset.

However, since Harry Truman's recognition of Israel in 1948, Jewish community leaders in the United States have consciously sought to present a unified voice on issues relating to Israel. For some, any lack of unity around a "shared Jewish political agenda" portends a "serious crisis." In this view, "as a minority community, Jews cannot afford the luxury of being seen as a house divided. Ethnic communities operate within a particular framework of influence and credibility. When their power is understood to be compromised or weakened by internal discord, their capacity to be politically effective is proportionally reduced."[1] This argument is regularly used to justify the exclusive right of certain groups (notably AIPAC and the Conference of Presidents, the umbrella body of established American Jewish organizations) to speak for the community on Israel and to determine the content of the views presented.

Perhaps there was a time when Israel needed just such a unity of voice. In its early decades, it faced an ongoing series of life-or-death struggles, and aid and assurances from Washington were one of the country's few strategic assets. That's not the case anymore, yet some use this line of thinking to label any dissent as a threat, not just to Israel but to the Jewish community here.

I've never been sure exactly what threat dissent poses. Of course, there is anti-Semitism here in the United States and even more in Europe and around the world. Neo-Nazi movements fester at the fringes of society, anti-Jewish vandalism persists and nasty shadows of old stereotypes creep into daily life too frequently. But Jews live in the United States today as securely and comfortably as they ever have in history. So why the underlying pressure on dissenters to keep their views to themselves and not to air their differences in public?

From where I sit, it's unhealthy, un-Jewish, and in the long run extraordinarily counterproductive, not only to our community but to Israel itself.

As I travel the country, I regularly meet with rabbis and Jewish community leaders to talk about J Street's work and about the Israel conversation in their congregations and communities. Over and over, I hear, particularly from the spiritual leaders of Reform and Conservative synagogues, "we would love to introduce a richer, more robust dialogue on Israel, but there's a small group of hard-core Israel activists in my synagogue, and they just won't let me bring in views with which they disagree."

This dynamic usually plays out behind closed doors with little publicity or fanfare. However, in November 2010, Temple Beth Avodah, a Reform synagogue in Newton, Massachusetts, abruptly canceled an event at which I had been invited to speak. The *Boston Globe* reported that "Rabbi Keith Stern, who has led Temple Beth Avodah for thirteen years, said a 'small, influential group' within the congregation voiced strong opposition to hosting the event. Synagogue leaders decided to cancel after 'an agonizing process,' he said, because they felt the controversy would 'threaten the fabric of the congregation.'"[2]

Just the previous week, the Columbia Hillel (the official home for Jewish students on campus) had pressured J Street's student group at the university, called Just Peace, to withdraw its sponsorship of an event featuring John Ging, the director of operations for the United Nations refugee programs in Gaza. Worried that Ging might paint a negative picture of Israel or its policies, Hillel officials deemed it inappropriate for Just Peace to sponsor the presentation without another speaker to, apparently, put Ging's remarks into the "proper" context. Of course, no one recalls similar demands to balance out the many right-of-center speakers invited by other groups under the Hillel umbrella.

Back in February 2010, J Street launched the grassroots organizing arm of our movement in twenty-two communities that held simultaneous events across the country. I was to give remarks in Philadelphia that would be simulcast to other venues nationally. Our local Philadelphia leaders immediately thought to hold their event at the University of Pennsylvania Hillel, given that it's centrally located, well known and a venue relevant to our work. So they rented a room, signed a contract and started planning the event.

Some national and local Jewish activists were outraged over this decision. They wrote emails, held emergency meetings—tried everything in their power to get the event pulled from Hillel. "It is a shame that there will be any connection between Hillel and J Street," Lori Lowenthal Marcus, a member of the board of Hillel of Greater Philadelphia told right-wing blogs. "J Street does not deserve to be considered a mainstream pro-Israel organization, as it has demonstrated repeatedly that it is 'pro-Ishmael' and not 'pro-Israel.'"[3] Right-wing blogger Pam Geller wrote:

> The wolf in Jewish clothing, J Street, the anti-Jewish-Soro$ 'Jewish' group working furiously for the elimination of the Jewish state, scored a victory with a craven lapdog Jewish organization. The limp-wristed, soft and pathetically stupid Hillel, that sad excuse that passes as the passive "Jewish" presence on college campuses, has agreed to let J Street desecrate their space with the launch of the J street kapo network.[4]

The event ultimately went forward—but not before the debate reached Hillel's national office in Washington. In Boston, too, I eventually ended up speaking—down the block from the synagogue at a public school. And John Ging did speak at Columbia, but without the involvement of any campus Jewish organization.

The message from the right wing to synagogues, Hillels and other communal venues was clear: Don't expect a moment's peace if you bring dissenting views into your community. And mainstream organizations like AIPAC and the American Jewish Committee only reinforce the message by refusing to participate in panel discussions about Israel if they don't like the views of the other groups invited.

The chilling effect is intentional—and it works. All across the country, rabbis, Hillel directors and other organizational leaders are forced to consider whether they can or want to deal with the headaches, slander and vitriol from conservative voices in their community before they think of giving a platform to views outside the party line. Rabbis won't speak freely because they fear offending significant donors in their congregations, and institutions stop bringing in controversial speakers for fear that their funding will be cut. As at the Columbia Hillel, they'll say they can't present our views without "balancing them," yet they'll have right-wing speakers appear without rebuttal all the time.

Despite all this, J Street is making some headway. In a handful of communities, our local activists have been invited to participate on the local Community Relations Council. Over six hundred rabbis have joined our Rabbinic Cabinet, and many institutions do welcome our voice within their walls. But this is still, sadly, more the exception than the rule, and as a result, those who never hear their views affirmed decide either to stay quiet or just stay away.

The dynamic extends even into the Jewish home. People simply won't raise the issue of Israel with their family or friends if they hold centrist or left-of-center views because they fear a severe reaction. Non-Jews don't dare to raise the issue with their Jewish friends, even if they agree on just about everything else. The overall atmosphere in the United States when it comes to discussing Israel is becoming one of intimidation and fear—not exactly conducive to rational discussion either in the halls of government or in the Jewish community.

THE CAMPAIGN TO SILENCE DISSENT

How has it happened that an otherwise rational community has created a situation where one can't question or criticize Israeli policy or actions without being branded an outcast? The extraordinarily effective campaign against dissent has operated on several levels: intimidating personal attacks on individuals; threats to funding; and a modern-day McCarthyism that charges "guilt by association" for connecting with people who become communal persona non grata for simply expressing their opinions when it comes to Israel.

I know from my own experience how painful and difficult the attacks on those who dissent can be. Far too often, those who disagree with dissenters in the Jewish community label us "Israel haters" and "self-hating Jews" or intimate that somehow we would have assisted the Nazis in World War II. Of course, the attacks achieve their purpose on some level, because some who would dissent are scared into silence.

Such vitriol should simply be out of bounds in the Jewish community. Having lost family in the Shoah, having nearly been killed in a suicide attack and having descended from a family whose blood, sweat and tears have soaked the land of Israel for over a century, I do what I do precisely because I care so deeply about the Jewish people, Israel and their future. Our community should not be accepting—and I do not accept—name-calling, lies and smears as a legitimate substitute for rational discussion about the difficult issues we confront.

To sample the vitriol, simply read the comments at the end of any story about Israel on the Web, or scan the letters to the editor of the Jewish community papers. Here's just one example from a letter to the editor that the *Massachusetts Jewish Journal* actually allowed to print in November 2010:

Jew-hater George Soros, who funds J-Street, seeks Israel's annihilation. Soros' ally, President Obama, relentlessly drumbeats that Israel is a liability in support of whom Americans are dying needlessly. According to J-Street Director Jeremy Ben-Ami, the role of J-Street is to be President Obama's "blocking back" with the Jewish community. As during the Holocaust, J-Street is [sic] to convince Jews to dig their own mass graves.[5]

What kind of signal does it send to those at the fringes of the debate when such language is fully acceptable under the banner of leading media outlets and advocacy organizations? Writing for the *Washington Post*'s blog, Jennifer Rubin constantly labels J Street "Israel-bashing" and makes regular allusions to the notion that J Street is anti-Semitic.[6] And what does it say when a prominent public face of the American Jewish community, former AIPAC spokesman Josh Block, says of working with J Street that "when you lie down with dogs, you get fleas. You can kill the fleas, but the treatment is unpleasant and it's not cost free"?[7]

The challenge for the organized Jewish community is not simply to launch, as it has, a high-profile initiative to urge civility in the communal dialogue around difficult issues, but to call to task those who take the argument beyond the acceptable boundaries of civil discourse.[8]

The impact of attacks like these can be devastating on a personal and emotional level. Abby Backer, the leader of J Street's Columbia University chapter, recounted in the *Jewish Week* her experience at a synagogue in Stamford, Connecticut, where she went to hear me debate Alan Dershowitz. Following the contentious debate, Backer was approached by a woman who identified her as a J Street supporter. Backer writes: "'I should spit on you!' she yelled at me in front of a group of shocked onlookers. 'Excuse me?' I replied. Glaring, she taunted: 'Are you a Palestinian? You must be a Palestinian.'"[9]

Actually, Backer is the daughter of a rabbi and deeply connected to the Jewish community. That night, however, given the tenor of the debate and the reaction of some in the crowd, she felt that "I was a stranger, an outcast, and that my presence in this conversation [was] not only undesirable but threatening."

Luckily, Backer is strong willed and concludes, "We can only change the conversation if students like me demand to be included, and ensure that no amount of scorn will silence us." Unfortunately, for too many younger liberal Jews, such confrontations would be more than enough to ensure their permanent withdrawal not simply from the conversation but from the community.

FUNDING

Another tool in the right-wing playbook is to throw around financial clout. Hardliners tell the institutions they support who they can and cannot have as speakers and the types of programs that are acceptable. Until now, this has happened on an ad hoc basis, with one or two calls from funders enough to make an institution shut down a controversial program. Recently, though, institutions have simply started to put into writing what is and is not acceptable, both for purposes of funding and for simple expression.

One of the highly publicized episodes in recent years involved the San Francisco Jewish Film Festival. Started in 1980, the festival is the oldest and largest of its kind in the world—a real trend-setter, recognizing the potential of film to connect back to the community people who are unaffiliated with or even disaffected from traditional Jewish institutions. It has attracted large audiences and enormous support, becoming a model for the over one hundred film festivals around the world centered on or incorporating Jewish themes.

The films it has shown over the years have been deliberately chosen to stretch the boundaries of thought and discussion both about and within the Jewish community. The festival describes itself this way: "SFJFF offered a departure from commercial presentations of Holocaust themes, which tended to emphasize Jews' victim status, while providing alternatives to the often uncritical view of life and politics in Israel available in the established American Jewish community."[10]

In 2009, the Festival's program included a showing of the controversial film *Rachel*—a documentary about Rachel Corrie, a young Evergreen State College student from Washington who was killed in Gaza in 2003 while protesting in front of an Israeli bulldozer. Corrie's mother was invited to speak at the festival, and the film was screened before a raucous crowd. Festival director Peter Stein introduced the film with the question, "Is it appropriate for a Jewish Film Festival to screen a movie critical of the Israeli government?" He added that, "We're trying to be a model for civic discourse . . . but what makes for acceptable discourse will not be solved with one movie or one speaker."[11]

One part of the Jewish community had a clear answer for Stein as to whether showing the film was appropriate: "No." As Michael Harris, one of the founders of the San Francisco Voice for Israel, a branch of the national group Stand With Us, said at the festival, the program—film and speaker—is "inappropriate for a Jewish film festival." And the reception accorded Harris at the festival for his ten minutes of remarks was equally hostile and unwelcoming, with shouts of "liar" and boos and catcalls, loud enough at times to prevent Harris from speaking.

The firestorm around the film focused as much on the lineup of speakers—particularly on Corrie's mother, Cindy—as on the film itself. Following her daughter's death, Cindy Corrie became an outspoken opponent of Israel's policies and a well-known anti-occupation activist. It's not surprising that her inclusion in the program would upset some people. But whether the proper reaction was to try to prevent her from speaking or to prevent the film from being shown is another question entirely. Five festival board members resigned over the incident, and several conservative funders withdrew support from the festival.

Most significantly, the local Jewish Federation was pressured by a few major donors to re-evaluate not just its support for the festival but how it funds all Israel-related programming. In February 2010, the Federation announced new parameters for groups that it works with or funds. Specifically, the new guidelines state that the Federation will not fund groups that "advocate for, or endorse, undermining the legitimacy of the state of Israel . . . including through participation in the Boycott, Divestment and Sanctions (BDS) movement."

The BDS movement is a loose but growing aggregation of activists who seek to raise pressure, primarily economic, against Israel to end the occupation. Those rallying around BDS tactics hold a variety of specific views and positions. Some involved in the BDS movement are vehemently anti-Israel and deny its right to exist. Some of the rhetoric used by BDS activists is taken by the Jewish community as anti-Semitic. But many of the activists are simply protesting Israeli policies related to the Palestinians, and would certainly support Israel's right to exist in peace and security alongside a Palestinian state. The Israeli government and many of the Israel-right-or-wrong activists in the United States, however, refuse to make any distinctions among these different positions.

The San Francisco Federation guidelines don't just draw a line against funding BDS activists and activities. They strongly suggest a form of prior restraint, implying that Jewish community programs and speakers on the Middle East must be cleared in advance with community leaders. In addition, the guidelines prevent the Federation from supporting programming that is co-sponsored or co-presented by organizations that participate in the BDS movement, establishing a kind of guilt by association. *Forward* columnist Jay Michaelson described this phenomenon in June 2010 after he helped put together a program on the tensions over Israel advocacy in the LGBT community, called Queer Perspectives on Zionism: "In helping to assemble a diverse panel, I ran into problems. I spoke with tenured professors afraid to express their critical-of-Israel views in public. . . . I had several people refuse to be on the panel because they feared for their jobs."[12]

San Francisco was the first Federation in the country to formally adopt content-based guidelines for programming and funding related to Israel. Other communities and other organizations are considering similar approaches, further polarizing American Jews and undermining open debate. In protest, a group of seventy prominent Bay Area Jewish Studies professors, rabbis and community activists signed onto an ad in the national Jewish newspaper, the *Forward*, headlined, "Warning: We members of the San Francisco Bay Area Jewish community are sorry to inform you that our usually liberal community has set a dangerous precedent that may affect the range of American Jewish voices on issues concerning the Israeli-Palestinian conflict."[13]

The Federation guidelines start the Jewish community down a very slippery slope. Granted, funders have a right to determine the organizations and projects their money supports. But should support from, and membership in, the official "Jewish community" depend not only on one's own views but on the views of those with whom one partners and works? What these guidelines are saying, in effect, is that some views and activities are outside communal bounds and if you hold those views, you're not welcome.

This raises troubling questions. Is an organization working on public interfaith dialogue to be prevented from receiving support from the Jewish community because it works with a Muslim group that has qualms about Israel's treatment of Palestinians? Should we really be pressuring rabbis to stop engaging in established Jewish-Muslim dialogue programs that bring together moderates from both communities? The Foundation for Ethnic Understanding and the Islamic Society of North America have for several years overseen a program of "twinning" synagogues and mosques in local communities to further understanding and interfaith dialogue. In November 2010, the same Boston-based group (the ironically named Americans for Peace and Tolerance) that pressured Temple Beth Avodah to disinvite me from speaking pressed two rabbis in Buffalo to drop out of the twinning project by raising fears about the moderation of the local Muslims involved.[14] How can groups in conflict make progress at explaining themselves to each other if they are prevented from talking? And what should the larger community do when a small group of hard-core activists can stifle the national debate through sheer fear?

Campaigns to impact the agendas of nonprofit organizations around Israel are not limited to the Jewish world. Human Rights Watch (HRW) is one of the world's leading organizations devoted to investigating, exposing and reforming human rights abuses around the world. An overwhelming number of its funders, board members and staff are Jewish, undoubtedly—perhaps even unwittingly—drawn to the group's work by the values and traditions on which they were raised.

Yet, what happens when the organization turns its spotlight on Israel? A public and well-documented fight breaks out over whether or not its exposés constitute bias or anti-Semitism. The most recent example happened in the wake of HRW's investigation into the early 2009 Gaza War. Robert Bernstein, a well-known New York–based Jewish philanthropist and businessman, was one of the founders of Human Rights Watch in the 1970s. He has also been the most public voice challenging the organization over its approach to Israel.

In October 2009, Bernstein took to the op-ed page of the *New York Times* to question the organization he had helped to found over its approach to the Middle East: "The region is populated by authoritarian regimes with appalling human rights records. Yet in recent years Human Rights Watch has written far more condemnations of Israel for violations of international law than of any other country in the region."[15] Human Rights Watch, in response, says that reports on Israel account for only 15 percent of its output on the Middle East, which in turn is only one of sixteen research programs at the organization, accounting for no more than 5 percent of its budget.[16]

The attacks on Human Rights Watch have been withering and broadbased. The attackers have included Israeli government officials such as Natan Sharansky, whose plight as a Soviet dissident ironically was part of the inspiration for the founding of HRW's predecessor Helsinki Watch.

Sharansky now finds himself in the unusual position of leading the attack against the organization that fought for his freedom, saying it "has become a tool in the hands of dictatorial regimes to fight against democracies."[17] HRW has been beaten up by traditional American pro-Israel groups like AIPAC,[18] which called it anti-Israel, and the ADL, which called it "immoral"[19]; the *New Republic* ran a lengthy April 2010 exposé cataloguing decades of charges against the organization, accusing it of bias against Israel and of giving "disproportionate attention to Israeli misdeeds."[20]

The breadth and ferocity of the attacks would be enough to scare off all but the most strong-willed and well-funded of nonprofits. A charge of bias against Israel or a hint of anti-Semitism can spread like wildfire in the Jewish community through online networks. The goal of the campaign against Human Rights Watch was not so much to stop that group, which is large and respected, but to send a message to smaller nonprofits to steer clear of the Israel issue. Why offer themselves up for such treatment when it could interfere with all the other good work they're doing? Progressive Jewish groups are paying attention. They put their Jewish values to work here in the United States, or in Darfur, or where earthquakes and floods strike. But they steer clear of the one place in the world where the Jewish people are actually in charge and can be held accountable for their actions.

Executives at progressive Jewish organizations tell me quite bluntly off the record that they avoid the Israel issue out of fear that a major funder or two might pull their support if the organization says something that could be interpreted as critical of Israel. So they stay silent, even though most of them know exactly what they should—and would like to—say when it comes to Israel.

But there is another way. A whole range of Jewish philanthropists hold progressive values and jump at the opportunity to support groups who speak out for those values. Look, for instance, at the $100 million grant that Human Rights Watch received from George Soros. Look at the consistent budgets that the group has been able to raise from a heavily Jewish funding base, supporting a program in the $40 million range for the past several years.

Rather than live in fear of the consequences, progressive Jews need to lead the way. We need to stand up together and speak out confidently with a vision of how best to secure Israel's future, and how to protect its democratic and Jewish character. Engage in the debate and embrace the controversy that follows. Describe how the Jewish values you're fighting for elsewhere need to be applied in the one place where Jews have the power to put their principles into action.

THE ENEMY OF MY ENEMY

Personal attacks and threats to funding aren't the only tactics used to enforce the acceptable parameters of the Israel conversation. Organizations and individuals are also attacked for having "unacceptable" friends and supporters—a form of guilt by association that feels at times like a flashback to 1950s McCarthyism.

"Let me go down your membership list and I'll tell you who is 'unacceptable' in your organization." That's essentially what Alan Dershowitz said to me in the fall 2010 debate in Stamford, Connecticut, that brought Abby Backer to tears.

To be clear, he didn't have any specific names in mind. He was simply sure that J Street was full of dangerous subversives, and he felt comfortable smearing the entire organization as giving cover to "anti-Israel" forces. Jonathan Sarna, a noted and respected scholar of Jewish history at Brandeis, when asked about J Street, questioned whether the effort is "a Trojan horse for anti-Israel activists."[21] When I personally asked Sarna later if he could name one "anti-Israel" activist associated with J Street, the only name he could give me was George Soros—who has criticized Israeli policy but explicitly supported the country's right to exist and to defend itself.[22]

The pro-Israel community has unfortunately developed a list of people who are "good" and "bad" when it comes to Israel, however vague those
definitions may be. Usually, those on the "bad" list are people who criticize
some Israeli government policies or behavior as counterproductive, citing
either the suffering or the rights of the Palestinian people, or how the ongoing conflict negatively impacts the interests of the United States.

Those who consider themselves guardians of the pro-Israel brand also
hold it against you if any of the people on the "bad" list say something
positive about your work. So, for instance, *The Atlantic's* Jeffrey Goldberg
attacked me and J Street because Stephen Walt said in a September 2009
Washington Post op-ed on the floundering peace process, "The good news
is that there is a new pro-Israel organization, J Street, which is committed
to the two-state solution and firmly behind Obama."[23] Of that line, Goldberg wrote, "J Street would be better off with Osama Bin Laden's endorsement than it would with Stephen Walt's."[24]

Stephen Walt and John Mearsheimer's 2007 book, *The Israel Lobby*,
made the case that a powerful confluence of forces, centered around
AIPAC, has driven American foreign policy off course—tilting our country too closely toward Israel and taking our foreign policy in directions
that don't serve core American interests over the long run. The book—
which grew out of a shorter academic paper the prior year—caused a huge
stir in the Jewish community and in Washington and came to frame many
discussions about U.S. policy and politics around Israel in the past five
years. The two scholars quickly assumed an especially exalted place in the
pantheon of supposedly "anti-Israel" scholars and activists.

Interestingly, one of their observations in the book was that the American Jewish community needed to establish other voices that more accu-
rately capture the diversity of views on Israel within the community. So
when J Street came along, Walt in particular had some nice things to say
about our effort. That, of course, was far too much for some in the established pro-Israel community. If Walt and Mearsheimer have something

nice to say about you, then you must be dangerously anti-Israel yourself—and you become accountable not just for what you stand for, but for what they stand for as well.

In an August 2009 interview, Jeffrey Goldberg of *The Atlantic* asked me a series of questions about my views and J Street's positioning—kind of an interrogation to determine if I passed pro-Israel muster according to Goldberg's moderate brand of Israel boosterism. He started the interview as follows: "Let's go right to the Stephen Walt question. Why do you think Walt (the co-author of the book *The Israel Lobby*) likes J Street?"[25]

I answered, "I don't know and I don't care." Goldberg had previously called on me to "renounce" Walt's favorable comments about J Street, and I had refused. I added now, "One of the reasons that I won't answer your call to quote-unquote renounce him is that it really smacks of witch-hunts and thought police."

I then went on to say that though I won't engage in these kinds of tactics, I will say that I personally don't agree with some of what they have written in their book—specifically I don't buy that the organized Israel lobby (AIPAC in particular) really exercises control over the direction of American foreign policy. I think it is *one* influence, not the only or even necessarily the most important force. It's extraordinarily effective (as I discussed in chapter 7). But it's certainly not the be-all and end-all when it comes to American foreign policy.

I went on to say that implying, as some do, that Jews control foreign policy or that Jews are covertly running the country to benefit their own agenda, crosses the line from scholarly analysis to something closer to such anti-Semitic polemics of the early twentieth century as the "Protocols of the Elders of Zion." Suddenly, those attacking me from the right for being associated with Walt and Mearsheimer were joined by those on the left who saw me as "throwing Walt under the bus."[26]

The very idea that there is a list of people with whom one is not allowed to associate if one actually is pro-Israel defines the guilt-by-association attack politics perfected by Joe McCarthy in the 1950s. The list is long. Its highlights include Walt and Mearsheimer, George Soros, Richard Goldstone, who led the UN Human Rights Council investigation into the Gaza war, John Ging, Jimmy Carter and on and on. Pretty much anyone who has ever even mildly criticized Israeli policy is off-limits, un-kosher.

This is one of the most shameful aspects of the rulebook that governs the conversation on Israel. It reflects badly on the community and turns what should be a rational and substantive policy discussion into a verbal food fight.

Instead of simply labeling people anti-Israel, the guardians of the pro-Israel gospel ought to be able to address the substantive questions raised. It is not an adequate defense either of Israeli behavior or of Israeli policies to simply attack the funders of those asking the questions. Israel and the Jewish people face a critical challenge: Namely, can the Israel we love and care about survive as both a Jewish and a democratic nation without ending the occupation and establishing a Palestinian state living alongside it in peace and security? Name-calling and personal attacks on those raising the question don't make it go away. And they don't relieve our communal obligation to answer it.

THE TAUNTS, the funding threats and the guilt by association all add up to an undemocratic and un-Jewish pattern of limiting dissent. Those on one end of the political spectrum in the Jewish community have created an atmosphere in which communal centers, synagogues, Hillels and other organizations hesitate to invite a broad spectrum of views to be heard in their halls. Worst of all, the bullying has worked. The self-appointed "pro-Israel" forces have skewed the conversation so severely that only one point of view is regularly heard and everyone else finds themselves blacklisted almost before they open their mouths.

This dynamic has been going on for years, if not decades—day in and day out, in community after community, facility after facility, program after program. And too many have decided that it's far easier to avoid the topic of Israel altogether or to go along with the approach represented by the loudest voices, thereby avoiding the headaches, the angry phone calls and the scathing letters to the editor.

It's no surprise that, in such an atmosphere, many people simply throw up their hands and walk away from the conversation and even the community. Young people on college campuses avoid Hillel and other established Jewish groups, preferring not to have to deal with the right-wing views that they are spoon-fed. Adults steer clear of the local synagogue or Federation so they don't have to hear another vitriolic and un-illuminating argument about Israel.

Communal leaders wring their hands over increasing numbers of unaffiliated Jews, shrinking donations and young people less connected than ever to their community and to Israel. Yet, they continue to drive away a huge group of people by limiting debate and enabling a suffocating atmosphere.

Far too many of the community's leaders flatly deny this dynamic. When challenged, they'll point to my own busy speaking schedule as proof that there is no problem. Well, I invite those same leaders to join me when I speak to observe the dynamics. Usually, I speak for about fifteen or twenty minutes to an audience that is very polite. I'm often warned in hushed tones ahead of time about the presence of vocal opponents in the room. I'm regaled with stories of severe tensions, emergency meetings and angry letters preceding my arrival. Often extra security has been hired, the police put on notice. There's even the occasional bomb threat.

When I do finally speak, I'm rarely if ever interrupted. I see lots of heads nodding in response to my key points—even a few knowing smiles—and I'm given a polite, sometimes even warm, round of applause when I'm done. Then come the questions. Undoubtedly, if there's an open microphone, the first half dozen people who race to speak or who seek to vigorously catch my attention with their hands waving are critics from the right.

Their questions are almost always the same—as if they're reading from a prepared script. "Haven't the Israelis tried everything for peace—Barak offered everything to Arafat and he said no. What more is Israel to do?" or "Doesn't it weaken Israel to have an alternative voice on Israel?" or "How can you talk about peace when Hamas is trying to destroy Israel?"

More often, they'll avoid the substance of the issue entirely and launch into harangues about who funds our work, the supposed anti-Israel nature of our staff, board and advisers and the like.

Their voices might shake with emotion, even anger. The questioners are often older than me, usually in their sixties and seventies. There will be a direct or indirect challenge at some point about why I don't live in Israel if I'm going to criticize it. What right do I have to question Israeli policy when I'm not paying Israeli taxes and my children aren't serving in the army?

I'll respond and, again, I'll see many heads nod, as well as a number of satisfied smiles—but rarely does a hand go up from those whose body language indicates agreement. Perhaps, after a half dozen questions along these lines, one or two timid voices will emerge to say that they appreciate my remarks and J Street's efforts. Occasionally they will pose a slightly more moderate and nuanced question.

After the session, a good chunk of the audience will come to thank me emotionally for what I've had to say, for giving voice to their views, for having the courage to speak up. They're much more supportive than you would have guessed as a fly on the wall at the lecture.

The rulebook of the Jewish community has left these people on the outside looking in. They have been driven from the room over the years by invective and intimidation.

It is time to let them back in. It is time for them to know that they are not alone. It is time to rewrite the rulebook governing the Israel conversation in the American Jewish community.

10
REWRITING THE RULES

How should a small but diverse community such as Jewish Americans manage its internal conversation on a difficult question like Israel? How should the community present its views on these sensitive matters to the broader community of which it is a part? How much freedom should be granted to younger people in the community to critique the way business has been conducted by prior generations? These are among the difficult questions facing the American Jewish community as it grapples with its relationship with Israel.

The growing gap between America's liberal and secular Jews on the one hand and those who are more observant and politically conservative on the other only enhances the challenge of constructing a single political and communal home for all Jewish Americans. In fact, it may be that no single voice can or should speak on behalf of all Jewish Americans on any issue, let alone on Israel, where passions and feelings run so deep. Can people as disparate as the ultra-Orthodox of Borough Park in Brooklyn, the retirees of Miami Beach and the college students at Ann Arbor really be represented as holding a single monolithic view of anything, let alone what it means to be "pro-Israel"?

The flip side of this question, which has also been neglected, is what happens as Israel continues to become more religious and conservative, more isolated internationally and less democratic domestically? Over the past couple of decades, the number of ultra-Orthodox in Israel has continued to rise, as has their political power as the swing vote in putting together a governing coalition. Though still representing a small percentage of the Israeli population, parties like Shas that represent the ultra-Orthodox have used their political power to exert control over life in Israel and to deny the Jewish legitimacy of those who deviate from their brand of Orthodoxy. They control who can get married and divorced. They have final say over who counts as a Jew.

At the same time, the wave of Russian immigration in the 1990s has brought to power politicians like Avigdor Lieberman, Israel's foreign minister, who are far less committed to basic democratic rights and freedoms and push proposals such as loyalty oaths or the transfer of non-Jewish citizens out of Israel.

What happens to the relationship between American Jews and Israel as the face of Israel shifts from that of Yitzhak Rabin and Shimon Peres to that of the national religious settlers and the ultra-Orthodox rabbis?

One thing is certain: The task of maintaining that relationship will become virtually impossible if Israel fails to resolve its conflict with the Palestinian people in a manner that preserves both Israel's Jewish values and its democratic character. Those in the Diaspora who related so well to the country's idealistic Labor Zionist founders will find it increasingly difficult to provide unquestioning support, even as others to their political right argue that Israel has never needed it more, given the deepening threats and tensions in the region. The desire for unity will run headlong into the instinct of American Jews to speak out when self-interest or fundamental values are at stake.

The established leaders and institutions of the American Jewish community need to take a close look at these trends and address some tough questions:

- Will we draw a workable distinction between legitimate criticism of Israeli policy and delegitimization of Israel itself?
- Will we step back from efforts to limit participation in the organized life of the community based on the content of beliefs and speech?
- Will we control the manner in which the discussion takes place inside our community, effectively restraining ad hominem attacks and slander against those who dissent or criticize Israeli policy?
- Will we stand up for the rights and religious freedom of another embattled religious minority, Muslim Americans, as we have expected others to stand up for us?
- Will we step back from a deepening political alliance with right-wing evangelical Christians on the subject of Israel that belies our deep disagreements on a range of moral and political issues?
- Are we going to give young people—in particular on college campuses—the space to freely and openly discuss the situation in Israel, or will we insist on an ideological litmus test before allowing the use of communal space and funds?

These are not questions the American Jewish establishment can dodge by shifting the focus to shared external enemies—whether Arab nations out to destroy Israel, Iran's nuclear program or global efforts to de-legitimize Israel. This may be a time-tested and successful tactic for the short term, but it is not a formula for a community's long-run strength and success.

Rather, the enduring health and strength of the American Jewish community requires answering the questions above with a resounding "yes." The best answer to growing criticism of Israel here and around the world is not to circle the wagons, but to engage the questions and the critics and ground our responses in the principles and values that have guided us as a people for thousands of years.

The following are suggestions for refreshing the rulebook. Failure to adapt the rules to new realities will, I fear, contribute to the long-term disintegration of the community and dramatically shrink, rather than expand, the American Jewish communal tent.

1. SUPPORTING AND LOVING ISRAEL SHOULD BE MORE THAN A SIMPLE YES-OR-NO PROPOSITION. IT SHOULD BE A MEANINGFUL RELATIONSHIP FILLED WITH HUGGING AND WRESTLING, QUESTIONING AND ARGUING.

It may have been possible for the generations that experienced the tragedy of World War II and the thrill of Israel's founding—and even for their children—to provide Israel with unqualified support in a simpler time. It is asking too much of recent generations, who have no personal experience of those events, particularly since the situation has become infinitely more complex. In the best Jewish tradition, today's youth have been taught, and encouraged to embrace, the value of critical thinking on all other issues. They will undoubtedly seek to apply those tools to Israel as well.

My own synagogue in northwest Washington, D.C., sports a simple sign on its façade saying, "Temple Sinai Supports Israel." Signs like that have sprouted in front of synagogues all across the United States over the past few years—in many cases as a result of organized communal responses to the wars in Lebanon and Gaza. They give Jews in the Diaspora a way to express connection to Israel as the country comes under greater international pressure and appears increasingly isolated. The

signs come in different flavors. Some say, "We Support Peace and Democracy for Israel" or "Support Israel, Support Democracy." Much of
the time, though, like the one at my synagogue, they're simple, unconditional expressions of support—communal bumper stickers standing
behind the home team.

My wife, Alisa, and I first noticed the sign one day in the summer of
2010, soon after we became members. We learned that the sign had been
the subject of spirited discussion within our new community for a couple
of years and that it had immediately become a major topic of conversation with our new senior rabbi, who had started at the synagogue that
summer as well. Some congregants questioned the need for it, and others,
its wording. Apparently these signs have sparked similar conversations, if
not agita, in other synagogues from coast to coast, tapping into the well of
emotions that surround the Israel issue.

So I wasn't surprised when our new rabbi devoted his first major sermon at Yom Kippur to the sign and to his commitment to making Israel a
central part of the life of our synagogue and community.[1] He talked about
three meanings of the sign. First, he said, it signifies our rejection of efforts to question the legitimacy of the Jewish people making their national
home in the land of Israel. Our foundational belief as a people is that God
entered into a covenant with Abraham thousands of years ago, promising
the land to him and his descendants. Through slavery in Egypt, exile in
Babylonia and nearly two thousand years of yearning after the destruction of the Second Temple, the Jewish people have prayed passionately to
return to their Promised Land.

Second, he said, we as a community should endorse a vision of supporting Israel that is grounded in support for human rights, democracy
and justice—because those values are fundamental to the Jewish people
and woven into the Declaration of Independence for the State of Israel
by its founders. Now that's a vision of Israel that I can rally behind. I'm
thrilled to have a little content injected both into the meaning of the verb

"support" and the concept of "Israel." But none of that is actually expressed in the sign, which explains why many synagogues endure hours of debate over the wording of their signs. The simple assertion of support—without qualifiers—implies a relationship that lacks content, depth and texture. If anything, it expresses love and backing without question—another iteration of Israel-right-or-wrong.

Third, the rabbi said, the sign indicates that, in our community, Israel will be constantly present—in our educational programming for our children, in the sermons of the clergy, and in communal activities like lectures and discussions. People in the community should be free, he says rightly, to disagree with the policies and direction of the State of Israel, but there would be no debate over whether Israel itself should be a part of our communal life. Again, for me, a wonderful sentiment. I want nothing more than for my family and my community to be engaged with and vibrantly connected to Israel.

My notion, too, of "supporting" Israel includes the vibrant debate that of necessity flows as Jewish Americans "hug" Israel as a family member and wrestle with difficult issues the country faces and with their own evolving relationship with the homeland of our people. The notion that struggling and wrestling with difficult issues is fundamental to the Jewish people dates back to the patriarch Jacob. According to the Bible, Jacob earned the name "Israel" after wrestling with an angel (the word literally means "the one who wrestled with God"). The name came to stand for the entire Jewish people who were encouraged, as the latest Reform Jewish prayer book puts it, "to question and delve into the nature of a faithful life."[2] I question whether simply "supporting" Israel adequately captures the complexity of the relationship between the Jewish people and their national home.

Saying that we should give content to the sort of Israel we support demands that we define the content. And, if part of the content is that Israel should embody the values and principles that are central to our people, then it's reasonable to ask whether and how Jews who don't live there are going to hold Israel accountable for measuring up to those standards.

For instance, we could say that the Israel we support is one that values human rights, one that promotes equality for all regardless of religion or ethnic background, and one that practices a vibrant form of democracy. That, in fact, is a vision of liberal Zionism that I can believe in and that I think would be attractive to many American Jews.

But how does the modern-day reality in Israel measure up to that standard? Is it, in fact, consistent with "supporting Israel" to raise the troubling treatment of 1.5 million residents of Gaza? To ask what the impact is on Jewish values and identity when, over the course of several years, those residents are denied free access to food, medical supplies and building materials; when young students are prevented from leaving to study on the West Bank or abroad; or when businesses are prevented from exporting their goods?

Is it acceptable to talk about the occupation of the territory beyond the Green Line and the gradual taking over of land and property that belongs to another people? Is it still considered "supportive of Israel" to criticize the treatment of the country's Arab minority and to question whether the democratic promises in its Declaration of Independence have been kept?

And is the inverse true? Is a sermon that defines support for Israel as incorporating fundamental values and principles of Judaism complete if it never mentions any of the troubling ways in which Israel is failing to live up to the values of our people? Is a generalized commitment to justice and human rights sufficient if there is no effort to ensure that they are being put into practice in Israel and the occupied territories?

The first change to the rulebook, then, should be a redefinition of what it means to be pro-Israel, so that support for Israel is no longer a one-dimensional bumper sticker, and nuance and criticism are welcome. As long as "support for Israel" in the established community looks more like a loyalty oath than a multifaceted relationship, we can't be surprised when Jewish Americans turn elsewhere either to establish their identity or to provide a home for their activism.

2. BEING PRO-ISRAEL SHOULD NOT REQUIRE ACCEPTING EVERYTHING ISRAEL'S GOVERNMENT SAYS ON ITS FACE OR PLEDGING UNQUESTIONING LOYALTY TO THE POLICIES OF THE GOVERNMENT OF ISRAEL.

Dissent and criticism should be as vibrant and welcome in the American Jewish community as they are in Israel. One popular way to question whether Jewish Americans should criticize Israel publicly is to say, "What right do you have to question Israel when you don't live there? It's not your kids who are serving in the army or getting blown up at bus stops on the way to school."

Even ignoring the fact that many American Jews, including me, do have family in Israel, we also have three clear bases for taking positions on Israeli policy. The first is that much of the communal debate revolves around the role of American policy in the Middle East. As Americans, we have every right to stake out strong positions on our own country's policy, particularly when resolving the Israeli-Palestinian conflict is so widely regarded as a fundamental national interest of the United States.[3]

Second, Israel is the national home of our people—all our people, not just those who live there. Even Prime Minister Benjamin Netanyahu told American Jewish leaders at the 2010 General Assembly of the Jewish Federations of North America that "Israel must always be a place that each and every one of you can call home."[4] We are only going to be comfortable doing that if we also have a right to speak out to help "our home" get on, and stay on, a path that leads to security and peace for years to come.

Third and most important is the impact the conversation is having on the health and vitality of the Jewish community right here in the United States. Criticism and dissent will need to be welcomed if Israel is to remain a source of intellectual, spiritual and moral engagement in American Jewish life, particularly for the younger generation.

Rather than establishing guidelines and parameters that seek to define the voices and views that should be kept *out* of the discussion, the community should really be focusing on creating an atmosphere that brings people *in* for open debate and civil conversation. Funding and energy should be going not into efforts to root out critics of Israel, but toward engaging critics in productive conversation and debate within the community.

Interestingly, the whole argument against criticizing Israeli policy if you don't live there seems to disappear when you look at issues such as who the State of Israel recognizes as a Jew. During the summer of 2010, a committee of Israel's parliament passed a bill granting exclusive control to the Orthodox rabbinate over conversion to the Jewish faith. The proposed law called into question the legitimacy of conversions through the Reform and Conservative movements and created distinctions between the rights of Jews by birth and those of converts to Judaism. For instance, the Law of Return granting Israeli citizenship to all Jews might not apply to those who have converted to Judaism under the supervision of non-Orthodox rabbis.

The American Jewish establishment exploded in opposition, with leaders of the community flying to Israel to register their objections in person with the prime minister. Consideration of the bill was ultimately delayed, thanks largely to the serious opposition of American organizations and leaders. So it seems that criticism of Israeli policy on some issues is acceptable to the Jewish establishment in the States—particularly those that threaten their own rights and standing. Yet issues like the ongoing occupation of the West Bank and the isolation and treatment of the civilian population of Gaza remain firmly off the table.

The hottest buzzword in pro-Israel advocacy today is "delegitimization"— a catchphrase brought to the forefront in a 2009 report by the Reut Institute, an Israeli think tank. Reut's report defined de-legitimization as criticism that "exhibits blatant double standards, singles out Israel, denies its right to exist as the embodiment of the self-determination right of the Jewish people, or demonizes the state."[5]

The Israeli government and the Jewish community have declared dele-gitimization the biggest new threat against Israel, and they're rallying the troops. The Jewish Federations of North America together with the Jewish Council on Public Affairs announced in the fall of 2010 a new three-year, $6 million initiative to combat delegitimization of Israel. Organizers of the campaign say that "recent years have witnessed an escalating campaign to demonize Israel in the court of public opinion and to weaken and isolate the country through steps such as boycotts, divestment and sanctions. The ultimate goal is to deny Israel its very right to exist as the nation-state of the Jewish people."[6]

Unquestionably, the lack of diplomatic progress has led to a growing movement around the world, including in the United States, to pressure Israel to end the occupation through boycotts of Israeli products, institutional divestment from Israeli companies and governmental sanctions on Israel. Taken together, this is the Boycott, Divestment and Sanctions (BDS) movement we touched on earlier. The movement has many forms and faces, with no one organization or person speaking for it as a whole. Many websites devoted to BDS and organizations that adopt these tactics do, however, fail to explicitly recognize Israel's right to exist, to acknowledge its legitimate security concerns, and to support "two states for two people" as the appropriate solution for Palestinians seeking their freedom and rights.[7]

Many engaged in the BDS movement also call for the right of Palestinian refugees to return to their homes in Israel. The "right of return" to Israel of those whose families were displaced from their homes in 1948 is possibly the most complex issue to be resolved if there is to be peace between Israelis and Palestinians. There is no question, however, that any deal acceptable to Israel will not include that right. Equally clear is that Israel will have to recognize and acknowledge in some way the claims of Palestinian refugees in any peace deal. Hence, those who support the right of return for refugees essentially put themselves on record opposing the State of Israel as the national home of the Jewish people.

Not all those engaged in the use of boycotts to express opposition to the occupation, however, are "anti-Israel." There are Israelis and Zionists who support forms of nonviolent protest of the occupation of the West Bank, such as labeling products made in settlements so consumers can avoid purchasing them or urging artists not to perform over the Green Line. As diplomats and politicians in Israel and elsewhere fail to bring about a just and peaceful resolution of the conflict, even some strong supporters of Israel have concluded that the only route to ending the conflict is to raise the costs to Israel of continuing the occupation. As the peace process breaks down and the prospects for diplomatic success dim, popular support for BDS is sure to grow.

Faced with increasing boycotts and more efforts to get companies and institutions to divest from Israel, the path of least resistance for the organized Jewish community will be to oppose all forms of civil protest as "delegitimization" and to attack all those who engage in such tactics as Israel haters.

As it puts together its new efforts to counter delegitimization, the organized Jewish community needs to clearly recognize, as Reut's own director, Gidi Grinstein, does, the need to distinguish between legitimate criticism of Israeli policy and delegitimization of Israel itself. Those who criticize from a place of love and concern, and believe in the right of the Jewish people to a national homeland of their own, are far different from those who oppose the very notion that there should be a Jewish homeland in the first place.

It would also be a huge mistake if the anti-delegitimization campaign failed to address what the State of Israel itself can do to stop these efforts by changing its own behavior. The quickest and most effective way for Israel to take the steam out of the growing BDS movement would be to end the occupation. Then it would be unmistakably clear who are simply critics of Israeli policy and who are intransigent enemies of the state itself—since any efforts to boycott after the occupation ends could only be motivated by the existence of Israel itself. As the noted Israeli journalist Akiva Eldar writes, "Indeed, it is necessary not to dismiss the increasing delegitimization of Israel in foreign countries. But instead of whining and blaming the messengers, the captains of the ship of state would do well to change its direction."[8]

The American Jewish community would serve Israel best at this moment not by circling the wagons in unquestioning support but with a friendly reminder to Israel that its long-term survival and security depends on reaching a viable peace with its enemies. Only if Israel changes its behavior and policy can it avoid the full weight of international criticism and isolation that it is currently on its way.

3. THE AMERICAN JEWISH COMMUNITY SHOULD ALLY WITH THOSE WHOSE VALUES WE SHARE AND BE WARY OF SELLING OUT OUR VALUES IN AN EFFORT TO GROW THE BASE OF AMERICANS SUPPORTING ISRAEL.

Over the past two decades, perhaps the most important political alliance the American Jewish establishment has struck on behalf of Israel is with those Evangelical Christians known as Christian Zionists. And no single person has been more central to that friendship than Pastor John Hagee of San Antonio, Texas. Yet this alliance between the Jewish establishment and right-wing Christian Zionists turns off large numbers of mainstream Jewish Americans. They see their community sacrificing some of its core values and principles to ally with a group with whom we have little in common, simply to build a broader base of unquestioning support for Israel.

Pastor Hagee, founder of the John Hagee Ministries and Christians United for Israel (CUFI), invented the concept of Nights to Honor Israel, partnerships between local Jewish Federations and his organizations. Since 1981, the Nights to Honor Israel have been extremely lucrative, raising more than $73 million for Jewish and Israeli causes, in particular for local Jewish Federations, such as Houston's, which has served as the conduit for much of Hagee's giving. At the 2010 Houston event alone, Pastor Hagee donated $8.25 million to various Jewish charities in the United States and in Israel, including $250,000 to the Houston Federation.[9]

Hagee is a major supporter of institutions across the Green Line on the West Bank, as well as of groups that promote expanding Israeli settlements and a broader right-wing ideological agenda. The sports complex in Ariel, one of the largest cities on the West Bank and also one of the toughest challenges to drawing a border, is called the John Hagee Sports Center. The Convention Center in Efrat, another settlement on the West Bank, is called the John and Diana Hagee Lovingkindness Convention Center. Organizations receiving Hagee funding include Friends of Gush Katif, Christian Friends of Israeli Communities and the Gush Etzion Regional Council—all devoted to settlement expansion over the Green Line. Unlike most American charities and foundations giving money away, Hagee's are registered as religious institutions, so there is no full public record of their giving and no way to know how many millions flow from Hagee's groups to deepen Israel's occupation of the West Bank.

This is the same John Hagee whose endorsement John McCain was forced to turn down in 2008 after a Hagee sermon came to light in which he portrayed Adolf Hitler as being sent by God to force "Jews to come back to the land of Israel."[10] Hagee has also made a litany of controversial statements on topics ranging from Catholics (for which he has publicly apologized), Islam, and gays and lesbians, going so far as to say that Hurricane Katrina was "an act of God for a society that has become Sodom and Gomorrah." On other occasions, he has questioned whether the hurricane was God's retribution for the evacuation of Gaza: "I want to ask Washington a question. Is there a connection between the 9,000 Jewish refugees being forcibly removed from their homes in the Gaza strip, now living in tents, and the thousands of Americans who have been expelled from their homes by this tremendous work of nature. Is there a connection there?"[11]

Hagee has been featured at major national Jewish organizational events; he was even the keynote speaker at AIPAC's 2007 national conference. Senator Joe Lieberman has likened him to Moses.[12] He's been greeted by the prime minister of Israel, Benjamin Netanyahu, who said, "I salute you, the people of Israel salute you, the Jewish people salute you."[13] His organization brings over five thousand people at a time to lobby on Capitol Hill, where they greatly contribute to cementing the Israel-right-or-wrong grip on Congress and influence American policy toward the Middle East.

The cozy relationship between established leaders and organizations of the American Jewish community and the far right of the Christian evangelical community is far larger than simply one man and his organization. Another leader of the Christian Right who plays a very active role on Israel is Gary Bauer, noted earlier for his role in founding the Emergency Committee for Israel in the 2010 election with Bill Kristol and Rachel Abrams. Bauer's views on Israel are well known from his run for the presidency and his work with CUFI. In 2000, he said of the Clinton administration's effort (before Camp David):

> This administration has been tougher on Israel than it has been on China. It's outrageous that our ally Israel has been getting the back of the hand from this administration. You've got this tiny little democratic country in the middle of the Middle East surrounded by adversaries with much more land. And what are we doing, and the rest of the world, expecting that little Israel has to sacrifice more land for peace and security? I will stand with Israel as President and I will not waste billions of dollars of the taxpayers'

money to try to make up for mistakes that this administration is making in the Middle East.[14]

Bauer has not endorsed a two-state solution. He has raised a series of questions and objections to the proposal and says he is reserving support "until I'm sure that the ultimate result would not be the destruction of Israel as an independent, Jewish state."[15]

Mike Huckabee is an Evangelical Christian who could well garner much of that community's support if he runs for president again in 2012. He was feted in 2009 at one of the most controversial sites in East Jerusalem, Shepherd's Hotel, where Jewish settlers are looking to establish a foothold in a solidly Arab neighborhood with money provided by right-wing American bingo millionaire Irving Moskowitz. Demolition to make way for new Jewish housing began there in early 2011. While at the site, Huckabee told reporters: "The question is should the Palestinians have a place to call their own? Yes, I have no problem with that. Should it be in the middle of the Jewish homeland? That's what I think has to be honestly assessed as virtually unrealistic."[16]

What's troubling here is not so much the substance of Hagee, Bauer or Huckabee's positions on the issues as the comfortable alliance that has emerged between leading representatives of the Jewish community and their counterparts on the Christian right. "Strange bedfellow" alliances, as they're called—working relationships on a particular policy issue between groups that have little else in common—are widespread and essential to successful advocacy in Washington. For instance, environmental groups have worked hard to engage Evangelical Christians in efforts to combat global warming, and liberal children's advocates have employed more conservative law enforcement officials as key validators of the importance of investing in early childhood education.

I can see the strategic and tactical benefits that the Jewish community—as a small minority in America—might seek in developing strong relations with the far larger community of Christian Evangelicals. Large sums of charitable funds flow from Christian communities to Israel, large numbers of tourists visit and large numbers of Christians become lobbyists for Israel in communities that don't have large Jewish populations.

However, this alliance comes at an enormous strategic cost as the liberal American Jewish community grips the most culturally conservative of American political forces in an enormous bear hug. On almost every issue, including a woman's right to choose, separation of church and state, social justice and the rights of gays and lesbians, these are two communities whose core values and principles could not be farther apart. So why would Jews, whose core identity often lies in striving to put our values into practice in our lives and our communities, want to spend a night at our local Federation honoring Israel with John Hagee? How do Jews feel when seeing him likened to Moses by Joe Lieberman or getting a standing ovation at AIPAC? How do we feel about lining up our political interests with Gary Bauer and watching the political candidates we actually support get attacked by a Bauer-Kristol alliance as "anti-Israel"?

Am I saying that pro-Israel advocates should never look to advance their agenda—from defending aid to Israel to maximizing Christian tourism to the Holy Land—by working with Christian allies? Am I am saying that, at the local level, there should be no room for cooperation regarding Israel with groups and individuals with whom we may disagree on other issues? Absolutely not.

I am saying, however, that there is something more than a little inappropriate and that turns off less-engaged community members, when they see the fuss made over people like Hagee or Bauer with whom they have so little in common, elevating these far-right icons to centerpieces of our communal life.

Of course, this isn't the only reason younger, non-Orthodox progressive Jews aren't banging down the doors of traditional Jewish communal organizations. But perhaps if we found ways to honor and work with leaders of other faiths with whom we are closer on other issues—say working toward immigration reform, improving schools, closing social and economic gaps—we might find that attendance at and contributions to traditional institutions would be going up, not down. If nothing else, perhaps we'd save some of the money we're spending on studies to figure out why younger Jews are "distancing" themselves from the traditional Jewish community.

4. NOT EVERY "PRO" REQUIRES AN "ANTI"

The Israel conversation should not be conducted in simplistic black and white terms or viewed through an us-versus-them lens. We should not demand that being *pro*-Israel require being *anti*-something or someone else, whether it's Palestinians, Arabs, Muslims or Islam itself. We should not ask people, organizations, or even countries to pick sides—either with us or against us.

American Jewish organizations too often commission polls that ask respondents to choose between supporting Israel and supporting the Palestinians. They then tout results such as "Bipartisan Poll Shows Voters Want America to Stand with Israel" or "By a 3 to 1 ratio, the American people express more sympathy towards Israel than the Palestinians"[17] and highlight trends that show "supporters" of Israel outnumbering "supporters" of the Palestinians by ten to one.[18] Why is it that in such polls there is no option to support both sides? Is there really no win-win scenario?

It is time to redefine what it means to be pro-Israel, to break out of the us-versus-them paradigm and to view support for the creation of a Palestinian state as a legitimately pro-Israel position, since without a Palestinian state living alongside Israel in peace and security, Israel cannot remain both Jewish and democratic.

The application of a zero-sum lens to the conflict clouds not just perspectives on the conflict over there, but also reactions to events right here at home in the United States and attitudes toward the American Muslim community. In 2010, attitudes toward Muslims—and toward Islam itself—became focal points for discussion all over the country after a long-standing plan to build an Islamic community center in downtown Manhattan near the site of the 9/11 attacks suddenly became national news. Much debate ensued about the location of Muslim places of worship, highlighting the prejudice and racism Muslims confront as they seek to find a place for themselves in the United States, despite having been part of American society for decades.

Such attitudes toward immigrant groups are, of course, nothing new in American history. Nearly every religious and national minority has confronted prejudice as it has integrated into American society—whether it's the Irish and Italian Catholics who were targeted by the Know-Nothing movement of the mid-nineteenth century, or the Jews who faced relentless anti-Semitism in the first half of the twentieth century—to say nothing of the racism and prejudice ingrained into the country's relationship with black people right from the beginning.

Given the Jewish people's history both in this country and in others, one might hope that Jewish Americans would be especially sensitive about the prejudice and racism being displayed today toward Muslim Americans. One might hope that Jews would be among the first to stand up for the right of Muslim Americans to follow the path of so many immigrant groups before them as they integrate into American society.

One can't help but wonder, then, what role the us-versus-them mentality around the Israeli-Palestinian conflict played in the reaction of some among the Jewish communal leadership to plans for an Islamic community center called Park 51 in Lower Manhattan. One of the most significant moments in the public debate came when Abe Foxman, national director of the Anti-Defamation League (the leading American Jewish voice against anti-Semitism, bigotry and racism), urged the Park 51 planners to consider moving the project.[19]

Though the ADL did say that the Muslim community had the "right" to build at the site, the group recommended that the Islamic Center move, out of sensitivity to the pain that would be felt by families of the victims of 9/11. But would the ADL say the same if it were the "rights" of Jews being challenged? Would they have said that the Jewish people should consider carefully whether the exercise of their rights was hurtful or damaging to others? Isn't the whole philosophy of a group like the ADL that the rights of minority groups need to be shielded from the vagaries of the opinions of the majority? As New York City Mayor Michael Bloomberg so eloquently pointed out, that is one of the great things about the United States and its history. It is also a fundamental element of the American Jewish experience.[20]

After the ADL weighed in on the Lower Manhattan controversy, larger establishment organizations took days to stake out their positions. Consider the case of the American Jewish Committee (AJC), which was created in 1906 when "a small group of American Jews deeply concerned about pogroms aimed at Russian Jews determined that the best way to protect Jewish populations in danger would be to work towards a world in which all peoples were accorded respect and dignity."[21] The AJC's official statement on the Islamic Center took an immediate swipe at the "many Muslim countries" where it is difficult, if not impossible, to get a building permit for non-Muslim houses of worship. The statement went on to lay out "hope" that the promises of the project's developers will be fulfilled— while saying it should be shunned if they are not. The AJC called on the developers to both reveal their funding sources and "unconditionally condemn terrorism inspired by Islamist ideology."[22] Not exactly a ringing endorsement of the rights of the community center's developers.

National organizations such the Conference of Presidents of Major Jewish Organizations said nothing at all. Local Jewish groups—the New York Jewish Community Relations Council, for instance—not a word. Thankfully, several days later, the leaders of Reform Judaism in the United

States—Rabbis Eric Yoffie and David Saperstein—did weigh in with a forceful, unconditional response, saying "we affirm our abiding commitment to the principle of religious freedom . . . and to the principle of religious equality that ensures the right of the Muslim community to locate and build its houses of worship like Jewish, Christian or other houses of worship."[23]

Overall, the response from the established American Jewish community to growing intolerance all across the United States toward the Muslim community has been muted at best. Our community would be well advised to remember the words of Pastor Martin Niemöller, variations of which are inscribed, as the indelible lesson of the tragedies of World War II, at both the Holocaust Museum in Washington and at Yad Vashem in Israel: "First they came for the Communists, and I did not speak up because I was not a Communist. Then they came for the trade unionists, and I did not speak up because I was not a trade unionist. Then they came for the Jews, and I did not speak up because I was not a Jew. Then they came for me, and by that time there was no one left to speak for me."

The American Jewish community should be at the forefront of efforts to protect the rights of Muslim Americans in this country. Drawing on our own experience, we should be speaking out clearly to protect the right to immigrate. Voices that claim to promote and protect Israel's interests should be leading the charge against the politics of fear and division that characterize movements like the Tea Party instead of embracing its support when running for office, as Joel Pollak did in running against Representative Jan Schakowsky in Chicago,[24] or lavishing it with praise as some in the right-wing blogosphere do, such as *Washington Post* blogger Jennifer Rubin.[25]

Newer organizations like the Progressive Jewish Alliance did step forward to defend the Islamic Cultural Center. So, too, I add proudly, did J Street. To the majority of younger, more liberal Jews, the issue was a no-brainer: A Muslim community center seeking to style itself after such Jewish institutions as the 92nd Street Y or the West Side Jewish Community Center in New York is exactly the type of project we need more of—not less—at a time of growing religious, racial and ethnic tension.

This is but one example of the growing disconnect between the part of the Jewish community dedicated to social justice and a communal leadership that is far more conservative—in its politics and in its public representation of the community's values. Over this gap hangs a shadow: To what extent is the reluctance of these mainstream leaders to speak out on issues as central as American religious freedom driven by the us-versus-them worldview that dominates the community when it comes to Israel? Have the major established voices of the Jewish community become so focused on the struggles facing Israel that they have lost their ability to recognize broader principles at risk right here in the United States?

What excites many young people I know today about their Jewish identity is its connection to values dating back millennia that compel them to try to make the world a better place, to live out the ideals that they have been taught, to be good stewards of the world that God created, and to treat all God's people equally.

That is why organizations like Progressive Jewish Alliance, Avodah, American Jewish World Service—which are dedicated to fighting for social justice or performing community service in the United States and abroad—are filled with engaged and energetic young people, while the old guard sets up task forces to find out why they aren't connecting with their own children and grandchildren any more.

This divide crosses over into politics as well. In 2008, young people— in and out of the Jewish community—were electrified by the notion of a biracial candidate as harbinger of a truly post-racial era. Support for Barack Obama in what some called the "Obama generation" was at least partly rooted in rejection by younger people of exactly the sort of rigid us-versus-them mindset that drives the communal approach to the Israeli-Palestinian conflict. And Obama is only the beginning of an inexorable trend in the United States toward a longer-term post-racial and post-tribal identity.

To the extent that American Jewish communal institutions hope to reach and relate to the next generation, they must recognize that younger Jewish Americans are growing up in fully integrated communities where they are as likely to be sitting in class next to—and developing meaningful friendships and relationships with—Muslims and descendants of Palestinian refugees as they are with the grandchildren of their neighbors from the old country.

This is modern America. Outside of the confines of ultra-Orthodox and other self-segregated segments of the community who choose to retain their sense of identity by living apart from the rest of us, most American Jews in the twenty-first century are going to blend into the society around them. It is possible for this integration and "assimilation" to take place while retaining a sense of Jewish identity and heritage. But we as a community must help to make that possible, in part by enabling a paradigm that doesn't require an "anti" in order to be pro-Israel.

ENORMOUS CHANGES lie ahead for American Jewry in the twenty-first century. The relationship between Jewish Americans and their identity, their communal institutions and the State of Israel are all in flux. And, as the winds of change are blowing, the torch of leadership is passing from the generation born during or just after World War II to the generations born in the 1960s and later, who lack the same deep, personal connection to the tragedies of the twentieth century and to the thrill of Israel's creation.

The institutions that have dominated organized American Jewry for a century or more are struggling to hold onto their existing donor bases and to attract the next generation of supporters. Though the number of Jewish Americans has held steady or even increased slightly over the past few decades, the number of donors to the community's Federations has been cut in half.[26] Most other major national Jewish organizations are facing similar declines. Only ever larger contributions by a small number of the community's wealthiest members are keeping budgets relatively stable over time and preventing drastic reductions in staff and programming.

The traditional institutions that have led the organized American Jewish community for the better part of the past century need to face the reality that the product they are marketing just isn't selling the way that it used to. This loss of donors, interest and resources has continued over the first decade of the twenty-first century just as the baby boomers and my peers are reaching the stage in their lives when they should have the time and resources to get engaged. Yet membership, participation and donations that should all be going up are not, and more Jewish Americans of all ages are choosing to pursue their activism and charity outside the bounds of the traditional organized Jewish community.

At the same time that the federations and other traditional institutions are facing declines in support, other, newer groups like Jewish Funds for Justice, American Jewish World Service and J Street are growing robustly. They are speaking to the values of disconnected baby boomers and to the younger generation's entrepreneurial spirit, tapping into their commitment to social justice and speaking to their desire to explore their faith and their heritage in nontraditional ways. Neither my peers nor those younger than me are disconnected from our identity and heritage. We are simply dissatisfied with the traditional options the community is offering for connecting to them.

The leadership of established organizations understands the gravity of the moment and is investing enormous time and energy trying to understand what's going on. Unfortunately, they are focusing a great deal of effort on exploring what is wrong with young people today and why they are so disconnected from and ill-informed on Israel. The time has come instead for the establishment to look inward and to examine whether what they're doing and how they operate needs to change and whether it might help their own cause to rewrite the rulebook on Israel.

The conversation this necessitates won't be comfortable. There will be arguments, debate and pain. And, in the end, those who dissent from Israel-right-or-wrong views and approaches will either be welcomed within traditional communal forums, allowed to make their voices heard, or they will be forced out. And with them will go a large segment of the less-affiliated, more progressive Jewish community. Left behind will be those who are both far more politically conservative and more religiously observant.

Whether and how the leaders of established American Jewish institutions deal with this moment of transition is nothing short of an existential challenge. Either they will rewrite the rules governing the Jewish communal conversation on Israel or they will gradually lose touch with important parts of the community. Either they will adapt to a new era and the ways of a new generation, or the central institutions of the American Jewish community will shrink in size and wither in relevance. And new organizations, following new rules and having different approaches, views and policies, will inevitably take their place.

III

FULFILLING THE DREAM

11

WHAT BECOMES OF TEL AVIV IN 2109?

I t took about thirteen hours to fly from Washington to Israel in April 2009 for the centennial celebrations of Tel Aviv's founding. I dozed, I snacked. I flipped through the numerous videos on offer in multiple languages.

I might have been more comfortable making the overnight transatlantic flight in business class, but my journey was, to say the least, less challenging than the one my great-grandparents had made from Russia to Palestine over a century ago. They traveled thousands of arduous miles over a couple of weeks by horse and cart, boat and train.

Tel Aviv made the most of its one-hundredth birthday. As one part of a year-long celebration, the city arranged a reunion of the descendants of its sixty-six founding families and invited us to re-create the famous photo of the lottery where our grandparents and great-grandparents stood on a sand dune, drawing seashells out of a hat to determine where their new homes would be built.

What a hundred years it had been. A century filled with idealism, hope and joy. An improbable dream pursued.

Tel Aviv, built from scratch in a couple of generations, now ranks among the great cities of the world. *Lonely Planet* recently placed it third on its list of the Top Ten Cities for 2011. They call it a "truly diverse 21st century Mediterranean hub . . . a kind of San Francisco in the Middle East. Thanks to its universities and museums, it is also the greenhouse for Israel's growing art, film and music scenes."[1]

As the vibrant, proud standard bearer for the modern Jewish people, Tel Aviv symbolizes the miracle of Herzl's dream come to life. What would my grandparents, born in nineteenth-century Russia, make of the city and country today? Their wonder at twenty-first-century life wouldn't be its high-tech gadgets, wireless Internet and instant communications, but the existence of a strong and independent Israel, a free state of the Jewish people.

When my grandparents arrived in Palestine as children, there were no cars, no paved roads and no planes. The first train from Jaffa to Jerusalem would not run for ten years after their arrival. Their only communication with family and friends back home was through slow and unreliable paper mail. Electric street lamps wouldn't appear for decades. No one spoke Hebrew anywhere.

They and their parents came to Palestine full of hope. Hope of escaping centuries of persecution and fear. Hope that they could create a better life not just for themselves but for their children and future generations. Hope that the long-standing dream of an ancient people could be fulfilled: to return to the land promised to their ancestors and to build there again a home for their people.

There's no denying the progress made toward fulfilling that dream. Despite spending much of its short life in a state of war with its neighbors, Israel has withstood every challenge to its physical survival. Today, with one of the world's strongest militaries, Israel faces little meaningful threat from the conventional armies with which it has fought in the past.

Economically, Israel's success is mind-boggling. The small nation has more start-up companies per capita than any other country in the world (one for every 1,844 Israelis as of 2009),[2] and more listings on the NAS-DAQ stock exchange than any country other than the United States (63, as of 2008).[3] Israel leads the world in the percentage of its economy spent on research and development.[4] In 2008, per capita venture capital investments in Israel were 2.5 times greater than in the United States, more than 30 times greater than in Europe, 80 times greater than in China and 350 times greater than in India.[5]

To walk the streets of Tel Aviv or drive the country's highways is to experience the cutting edge of twenty-first-century life in a modern, first-world country brimming with energy and vitality. It's a far cry from the Israel I first visited in the 1960s, when my oldest cousins barely had running water or electricity in their shack in the overgrown yard where my great-grandparents had made their first home.

As the plane landed, I was filled with joy at the miraculous legacy of my grandparents and pride at the chance to celebrate it. Every visit to Israel is a bit of a homecoming for me. It is the land in which I am rooted, the one place my people can call our own. I was born in the United States, yet my identity is Jewish, and I can't help but feel deeply connected with the country of my people and family. I hope my children and theirs will similarly connect with, love and cherish this amazing country, coming to see it as integral to their family history, people and tradition.

MY JOY AND PRIDE in Israel's present are, however, balanced and at times exceeded by my deep concern for its future. In particular, I worry that all the trappings of success can be washed away in an instant by the failure to achieve a two-state resolution to the Israeli-Palestinian conflict in the near future. Without it, I fear that we will see Israel endure a fate of deeper and bloodier violence, deteriorating democracy and growing international isolation. I worry that, on its present path, Israel will not be there for my grandchildren at Tel Aviv's bicentennial in the year 2109, at least not in a form my family could recognize or relate to.

Israel's failure to address the enormous challenges it faces is due, in no small measure, to a political system characterized by paralysis and a lack of leadership, as well as to friends and allies who enable the country's willful denial of the existential choice it confronts.

Put simply, Israel must choose among three things: the land it has occupied since 1967 beyond the Green Line, its Jewish majority and its democracy. It can only have two of the three. If it chooses to hold on to the land and remain a democracy, then in just a few years the majority of those living there will be non-Jewish and will eventually, through democratic means, assert control and override Israel's Jewish character.

If it hangs onto the land and chooses to remain Jewish in character, it will have to limit the democratic rights of the non-Jewish majority. Only if it gives up the land on which a Palestinian state can be built, can it remain both Jewish and democratic.

One by one, each of Israel's recent prime ministers has come to grips with this reality that looms immediately ahead. Each of them has chosen to pursue—some more assertively than others—a two-state resolution to the conflict. This is the inevitable choice that motivated Yitzhak Rabin to pursue a negotiated resolution with the Palestinians through the Oslo Accords. It is what led Ariel Sharon to pursue a unilateral solution by withdrawing from Gaza.

The current defense minister of Israel, Ehud Barak, warned starkly in early 2010 that failure to make peace with the Palestinians would leave the state of Israel at risk of becoming an "apartheid" regime: "As long as in this territory west of the Jordan there is only one political entity called Israel it is going to be either non-Jewish or non-democratic. If this bloc of millions of Palestinians cannot vote, that will be an apartheid state."[6]

Former prime minister Ehud Olmert came to a similarly bleak conclusion, recognizing that "If the day comes when the two-state solution collapses, and we face a South African-style struggle for equal voting rights (also for the Palestinians in the territories), then, as soon as that happens, the State of Israel is finished."[7]

Dan Meridor is Benjamin Netanyahu's deputy prime minister and the son of one of the leaders of the Irgun, Eliyahu Meridor, a friend and associate of my father's. In November 2010, he summarized the situation for *Ha'aretz* this way:

> It's an illusion to think that the situation can remain as it is. This is not a normal situation. Israel has an interest in creating a border, with Israel on the one side and the Palestinian state on the other. . . . I've reached the painful conclusion that keeping all the territory means a binational state that will endanger the Zionist enterprise. If we have to give up some of the territory or give up the Jewish and democratic character [of the state]—I prefer to give up some of the territory. It is impossible to ignore reality.[8]

These urgent pleas for action to save the future of Israel come not from left-of-center peace organizations or international observers that could be dismissed by Jewish audiences as anti-Israel or anti-Semitic. They come from established leaders of Israel itself, from the center and the right of the Israeli political spectrum, who have nothing but Israel's long-term interests and survival at heart. Their concern that the very future of Israel hangs in the balance is shared by other Israeli political leaders, members of the defense and intelligence establishments and leading Israeli intellectuals.

Their sense of urgency is only likely to grow as the decades-old status quo unravels in the Arab world and the United Nations gets set to recognize an independent Palestinian state. The Middle East is being rocked by change in 2011, with autocratic regimes shaking and crumbling in the face of a democracy movement demanding freedom and dignity. Israelis will soon face the reality that this popular "awakening" against oppression and tyranny is unlikely to stop at the gates of Palestine. Israel's ongoing occupation is perhaps the most poignant symbol of the lack of Arab freedom, and the one instance where Arabs still suffer not at the hands of their own rulers but those of an occupying power.

Additional urgency will be felt when Palestinians call on the United Nations General Assembly to recognize their independence within the 1967 lines. Israel already feels isolated internationally and too easily dismisses any external pressure to change its policies as an effort to delegitimize the right of the Jewish people to their own state. Yet UN action on Palestinian statehood and subsequent efforts to enforce that recognition will inevitably increase pressure on Israel's government to act from Israelis who seek to do business, travel, teach, and perform abroad.

The central challenge to Israel's future and security in the coming years remains that just over five million Jews and nearly five million Palestinians seek to make their home on the same land, and that only through compromise will either find a path to secure peace and true freedom and independence. In fact, according to a leading Israeli demographer, Jews are already only 49.8 percent of the people west of the Jordan, and the trend toward minority status shows no sign of abating.[9]

Some on both ends of the political spectrum are starting to talk of alternatives to the two-state solution, arguing that the two people simply have to learn to live together in a single, peaceful democratic state—something referred to as a "one-state solution." The idea is gaining some traction on the right of Israeli politics. Knesset speaker Reuven Rivlin said in the summer of 2010, "I would prefer the Palestinians become citizens of the state than for us to divide the country."[10] There are those on the left too—Palestinians, Europeans and a limited number of left-wing Jews—who believe this is the ideal answer.

For me, there is no "one-state solution," only a one-state nightmare. To condemn these two peoples to live together in one state is to chain them to a future of never-ending violence and bloodshed. They are like a desperately unhappy married couple living under the same roof for far too long. They need a divorce, and they need it now before they kill each other.

This conflict remains, as ever, a territorial dispute between two peoples seeking to establish their national homeland on the same small property. Like all territorial conflicts, it can be solved, if painfully, through rational compromise. So long as the conflict between the Jewish and the Palestinian peoples remains national and territorial in nature—rather than religious and ideological—a win-win solution can be found. All they need is a good mediator, empowered negotiators and political will.

THE URGENT NEED for Israel to deal with this external challenge is magnified by the serious internal challenges it is failing to address in the absence of peace. As much as Israel's future depends on setting a border, resolving its dispute with the Palestinian people and addressing other security threats, the very nature of Israel itself is also at risk from stresses within Israeli society, mainly religious, economic and social.

Twenty percent of Israel's citizens are Palestinian and another several hundred thousand Israelis are not Jewish by birth. Hundreds of thousands of non-Jews work inside the Green Line, and some of these foreign workers are having children and seek to settle permanently in Israel. One critical test of Israel's character—and its commitment to both Jewish and democratic values—will be how it treats the non-Jews living in the state, in particular the indigenous Palestinian population that considers the land its home as well.

The vision and values of the country's founders on this score were expressed clearly in the State of Israel's Declaration of Independence:

> The State of Israel will be open for Jewish immigration and for the Ingathering of the Exiles; it will foster the development of the country for the benefit of all its inhabitants; it will be based on freedom, justice and peace as envisaged by the prophets of Israel; it will ensure complete equality of social and political rights to all its inhabitants irrespective of religion, race or sex; it will guarantee freedom of religion, conscience, language, education and culture; it will safeguard the Holy Places of all religions; and it will be faithful to the principles of the Charter of the United Nations.

Israel will always—and appropriately—provide preferential immigration to Jews from around the world. After all, one rationale for Israel's creation was to provide a sanctuary for the Jewish people from the persecution and dangers they have faced throughout history and around the world. As the early Zionist thinker Leon Pinsker wrote in 1906, "The Jews are not a living nation; they are everywhere aliens; therefore they are despised . . .The proper, the only remedy, would be the creation of a Jewish nationality, of a people living upon its own soil, the auto-emancipation of the Jews."[11]

It is appropriate and wonderful that the country has developed a culture and language that reflects its identity as the national home of the Jewish people. Hebrew has been brought back to life as the country's primary language, and the flag and the anthem reflect the country's Jewish culture.

However, the fact that the Jewish people can make the rules and exercise power in a country of their own for the first time in nearly two millennia also brings with it the obligation to set an example with their treatment of the non-Jewish citizens in their midst. While ensuring security remains the first responsibility of the state, the state must also be judged by how it puts the values of the Jewish people into practice. We should be particularly mindful of the treatment of minorities in Israel since so much of the Jewish people's moral code derives from our own minority experience and our first-hand knowledge of what it means to be persecuted, mistreated and denied our rights.

The tensions inherent in being both a Jewish homeland and a democratic state for all its citizens are enormous. Achieving an appropriate balance will probably be the foremost internal challenge to Israel's strength and vibrancy in the coming hundred years. It is likely to remain unresolved until the larger fight with the Palestinian people is done.

Israel also faces enormous challenges regarding the role of religion in the state, particularly in light of the large and growing ultra-Orthodox population. Self-described *haredim* (ultra-Orthodox Jews) were 9 percent of Israel's population in 2008, three times more than the 3 percent found in 1990.[12]

Lacking a constitution, Israel has never addressed the need for the separation of religion and state. Even though the country's founders were avowedly secular, they made compromises to secure the political support of the ultra-Orthodox in the early days of the state. They gave rabbis, rather than the state, control over such functions as marriage, divorce and burial, and provided exemptions from military service for religious students as well as special subsidies to support their studies, which even today keep large swaths of the population out of the workforce. Those decisions planted the seeds for deep tensions over religion, not simply within Israel but in the Diaspora, over such questions as conversion and who is recognized legally as a Jew by the state.

These issues cannot be addressed so long as the Israeli right wing needs the votes of ultra-Orthodox factions to maintain a government opposed to territorial compromise. This is a double loss since the same centrist majority that could be built to address the difficult issues related to peacemaking could also sensibly address the country's nagging secular-religious divides.

Israel faces tremendous challenges to its democratic character as well, particularly from new forces on the political right who, unlike traditional Likud leaders such as Dan Meridor and their ideological guides Vladimir Jabotinsky and Menahem Begin, are not deeply committed to the principles of democratic expression and freedoms.

These non-democratic tendencies are found particularly in the politics of Foreign Minister Avigdor Lieberman and his political party Yisrael Beiteinu, as well as some ultra-nationalists who talk of moving non-Jewish citizens out of Israel and stripping them of their citizenship. These factions propose, for instance, loyalty oaths and limiting the freedom of expression of those who oppose the occupation of the Palestinian territories.

There are proposals in the Knesset right now to institutionalize a form of second-class citizenship for non-Jewish Israelis, launch McCarthy-style investigations into organizations that promote civil and human rights and restrict free expression of opinions and criticism. Preserving Israel's democratic character demands that these proposals be defeated, yet the longer the occupation of the Palestinian people goes on, the more momentum builds behind them.

Finally, Israel faces—along with much of the world—deep economic tensions stemming from extraordinarily concentrated wealth existing alongside severe poverty. Despite the country's tremendous economic success, the gap between rich and poor is one of the largest in the developed world—by some measures second only to that of the United States among Western countries.[13] Nearly one in five Israelis lives in poverty, a higher number than in any of the other thirty countries in the Organization for Economic Cooperation and Development.[14]

THE CHALLENGES confronting Israel, both external and internal, in the next hundred years will be different, but no less daunting, than those faced by the families drawing lots on the sand dunes in 1909. At the Tel Aviv centennial, I could not help but wonder just what connection my own young children, and the families I hope that they will have, will develop to Israel. What kind of bonds will they forge to their people and to their national homeland? And, if one day I should be so lucky as to have grandchildren, what sort of country will await them as they journey to Tel Aviv's bicentennial in 2109?

My great-grandparents undoubtedly gave little thought to such questions as they set forth. They certainly could not have conceived of the enormous challenges a free State of Israel would face in its seventh decade. Indeed, for them, it was enough to simply gain freedom from hardship and persecution and to live out the long-standing dream of their people to return home.

The challenges were perhaps simpler in the earlier generations of Israel, at least in the sense of being more literal: planting new crops, building cities and fighting for independence and safety. Today's problems of religious strife, balancing human rights and security needs and income inequality have less straightforward solutions.

The ultimate dream is the same today as it was four generations ago—to be a free people in our own land—yet it has not been fully realized. Only an agreement that ends the conflict with the Palestinian people and establishes recognized borders for the state will grant Israel the full legitimacy it deserves and a permanent place in the community of nations. Until then, violence will fester, regimes like Iran will find it easier to make trouble and Israel's international status will deteriorate.

This problem cannot be ignored. It will not simply go away. Like a train hurtling toward a cliff, Israel must act now to change its current trajectory. The unsustainability of the present course seems clear to just about everyone except the present Israeli government and some of the leadership of the American Jewish community.

It falls to this generation of Jews around the world to sound the alarm and to save the dreams of our ancestors. The Israel that awaits our grandchildren and the relationship they will have to the state depends entirely on finding the courage and the will now to end the occupation and to achieve a two-state resolution to the Israeli-Palestinian conflict.

Only then will those dreams be fulfilled.

12

AMERICA'S STAKE IN ENDING THE CONFLICT

Resolving the Israeli-Palestinian conflict isn't simply in the interest of the parties to the conflict, or even that of the broader international community. It is a fundamental national interest of the United States.

Speaking in part of Israel's conflicts with its neighbors, President Barack Obama has said, "It is a vital national security interest of the United States to reduce these conflicts because whether we like it or not, we remain a dominant superpower, and when conflicts break out, one way or another we get pulled into them. And that ends up costing us significantly in terms of both blood and treasure."[1]

Secretary of State Hillary Clinton regularly argues that the status quo of the past decade between Israel and the Palestinians "doesn't serve the interests of the United States," noting that people around the world draw a closer connection between the United States and the conflict now than they did when she was First Lady. She has observed that, when she traveled the world in the 1990s, "it was rare that people in places far from the Middle East ever mentioned the Israeli-Palestinian conflict. Now . . . it's the first, second, or third issues that countries raised."[2]

Those statements were made before popular uprisings swept across the Arab world in early 2011, rocking the foundations of the Middle East, toppling some of the region's long-standing leaders and redrawing its political map. The Arab "awakening" of 2011 is possibly the most significant political development of this generation, on a par historically with the collapse of communism in Eastern Europe in the early 1990s or the wave of revolutions that swept Europe in 1848.

The uprisings that began in Tunisia and Egypt had nothing to do with Israel or its conflict with the Palestinian people. These were domestic revolts powered by people seeking their freedom and dignity and focused on creating better lives for themselves and their families. They carry tremendous implications for the Israeli-Palestinian conflict, however, as well as for American interests.

Where many decades-old regimes in the Arab world owed allegiance to the United States and its pipeline of military and economic assistance, new, more democratic regimes will be primarily accountable to the will of their peoples. Older regimes could coexist not simply with Israel but with a peace "process" that produced no results. Newer regimes that are more responsive to their people will not be able to indulge the status quo between Israel and the Palestinian people still seeking their basic freedom.

For decades, the United States could have it both ways—providing unwavering support for Israel while maintaining solid relationships with Arab leaders. That juggling act will prove far harder in an era of greater Arab democracy and freedom.

The United States will face countless challenges in the coming years to its status as the world's sole superpower. China and other regional powers are on the rise; ideological extremism is growing; and advanced weaponry and nuclear technology are proliferating. Added to the many twists and turns on the road ahead is now redefining the American relationship with the Arab world.

Ending the Israeli-Palestinian conflict isn't the sole key to navigating the challenging waters ahead for the United States. However, American management of the conflict and the path to its resolution will dramatically impact its stature in the Middle East, in the broader Muslim world and around the globe. Failure to resolve the conflict—or to even try meaningfully—will be widely seen to symbolize the decline of American power. And failure to speak out and act on behalf of freedom and dignity for the people of the Arab world, including the Palestinians, will put the United States on the wrong side of history.

America's strategic interests in the region were apparent well before 2011. Having fought three wars in two decades in the Middle East, the United States is more deeply engaged militarily there than in any other region of the world. Events in the Middle East also resonate around the world, feeding the rising tide of extremism, terror and violence that can erupt at any moment on American soil or elsewhere.

In 2006, the Iraq Study Group (ISG), a bipartisan commission appointed by a Republican-led Congress, was one of the first public bodies to explicitly address the role of the Israeli-Palestinian conflict in the broader Middle East as it looked at ways to improve U.S. strategy in Iraq. Notably, the panel included two people who would go on to assume high-ranking posts on the Obama administration's national security team— Defense Secretary Robert Gates, who resigned from the ISG before the report's completion, and CIA Director Leon Panetta.

The ISG Report stated bluntly: "The United States will not be able to achieve its goals in the Middle East unless the United States deals directly with the Arab-Israeli conflict."[3] The ISG called for a "renewed and sustained commitment by the United States to a comprehensive Arab-Israeli peace on all fronts" as one component of a comprehensive diplomatic offensive, addressing the difficult issues in the Middle East regionally. As the report's authors stated, "all key issues in the Middle East . . . are inextricably linked," and addressing them comprehensively "would help marginalize extremists and terrorists, promote U.S. values and interests, and improve America's global image."[4]

The Israeli-Palestinian conflict is not *the* root cause of extremism and terror around the world, and solving the conflict today wouldn't mean that al-Qaeda would disappear tomorrow. However, American interests are unquestionably being hurt when extremist movements regularly use images of Israel's treatment of the Palestinian people on their websites and videos to recruit and to foment anger and violence.

To the extent that the United States is seen as facilitating the ongoing occupation rather than helping resolve the conflict, America's reputation and image in the Arab world—and, in fact, around the world—suffer. In Shibley Telhami's 2010 Arab Public Opinion Poll, 62 percent of respondents described their views of President Barack Obama and the United States as "negative," and 69 percent described their attitudes toward the Obama administration's policy in the Middle East as "discouraged."[5]

Iran, with its growing power and influence in the Middle East, is another key strategic challenge facing the United States. Iran's apparent pursuit of nuclear weapons capability isn't just a threat to Israeli security, it is a fundamental challenge to American interests, with the potential to set off a regional nuclear arms race, destabilize the region and undermine efforts to halt nuclear proliferation around the world, a cause close to President Obama's heart.

To the extent that Iran's President Mahmoud Ahmadinejad and his regime employ gamesmanship around the conflict and in the region to consolidate power at home and to extend the regime's influence abroad, the ongoing conflict serves Iranian interests and damages American ones. Iranian funding and manipulation of a group like Hamas is less an expression of long-standing concern about the plight of the Palestinians or the occupation of Palestine than a tool the regime uses to extend its regional influence, advance its strategic interests and win supporters on the broader Arab "street."

Resolving the conflict won't end the challenges from Iran or Ahmadinejad, but it would strike a strategic blow against Iran and permit regional alliances to form in order to counter Iran's growing power. Conversely, a comprehensive regional resolution of all issues between Israel and its neighbors could put real pressure on Iran to join the broader consensus so as not to be left alone on the outside.

The United States also has significant economic and resource interests in the Middle East, primarily oil. Energy independence may one day give the United States far greater freedom to disengage from direct involvement in Middle East conflicts, but, until it does, American, and indeed global, economic stability will remain subject to the political situation in the Middle East. Were the Israeli-Palestinian conflict to explode into a larger regional conflict, it would certainly destabilize the supply of oil from the region, roiling global markets not simply for energy but for all sorts of goods, with enormous economic repercussions for a fragile global economy.

The strength of the connection between the ongoing conflict and critical American interests makes it all the more surprising how strongly the link is disputed by key traditional American advocates for Israel. They vociferously object to the merest hint of an American national interest in changing the course of events in the Middle East, as they did regarding testimony submitted to the Senate Armed Services Committee in March 2010 by then head of the United States Central Command (CENTCOM), General David H. Petraeus. His written testimony included the following passage:

> Insufficient progress toward a comprehensive Middle East peace. The enduring hostilities between Israel and some of its neighbors present distinct

challenges to our ability to advance our interests in the AOR [Area of Inter-est—i.e., the area under CENTCOM's purview]. Israeli-Palestinian tensions often flare into violence and large-scale armed confrontations. The conflict foments anti-American sentiment, due to a perception of U.S. favoritism for Israel. Arab anger over the Palestinian question limits the strength and depth of U.S. partnerships with governments and peoples in the AOR and weakens the legitimacy of moderate regimes in the Arab world. Meanwhile, al-Qaeda and other militant groups exploit that anger to mobilize support. The conflict also gives Iran influence in the Arab world through its clients, Lebanese Hizballah and Hamas.[6]

These observations would count for little more than proof of con-sciousness in an introductory foreign policy course at college, yet appear-ing in testimony from the CENTCOM commander, they caused a political firestorm among traditional pro-Israel advocates.

Responding to the Petraeus testimony, the Anti-Defamation League issued a statement saying that the general "has simply erred in linking the challenges faced by the U.S. and coalition forces in the region to a solu-tion of the Israeli-Arab conflict, and blaming extremist activities on the absence of peace, and the perceived U.S. favoritism for Israel. This linkage is dangerous and counterproductive."[7]

According to Alan Dershowitz, talk of an "American interest" in re-solving the conflict is "code" for blaming Israel for the death of American troops in its wars in Iraq and Afghanistan. Writing for the *Huffington Post*, under the headline "J Street Can No Longer Claim to be Pro-Israel,"[8] Der-showitz attacked me for making the "American interest" argument after a *New York Times* analysis noted that President Obama was adopting the Petraeus line in signaling his determination to "reinsert himself into the Israeli-Palestinian dispute."[9]

In a letter to the editor of the *Times,* I had written that the president would garner Jewish support in such a push specifically because "many in the Jewish community recognize that resolving the conflict is not only necessary to secure Israel's future, but also critical to regional stability and American strategic interests."[10] For saying this, I was criticized by Dershowitz, who declared that "J Street has gone over to the dark side."

The Petraeus testimony prompted a public discussion among Middle East observers over the U.S.-Israel strategic relationship. Anthony H. Cordesman at the Center for Strategic and International Studies in Washington wrote, "America's ties to Israel are not based primarily on U.S. strategic interests. . . . [The] real motives behind America's commitment to Israel are moral and ethical." The implication for Israel, says Cordesman, is that the government there should recognize the obligations it has to the United States and act "on the understanding that the long-term nature of the U.S.-Israel strategic relationship will depend on Israel clearly and actively seeking peace with the Palestinians—the kind of peace that is in Israel's own strategic interests."[11]

Commentators and bloggers on the political right pushed back hard against Petraeus, Cordesman and the Obama administration's arguments. Typical of these attacks was that of Caroline Glick, who wrote in the *Jerusalem Post* that Israel is not only "the U.S.'s greatest strategic asset in the Middle East . . . [it] is arguably its greatest asset outside the U.S. military."[12] The argument rests on the notions that Israel acts as a deterrent to prevent the most radical regimes and sub-state actors from acquiring the means to cause catastrophic harm, and that the United States demonstrates its own trustworthiness to others when it stands resolutely with Israel.

The Right is terrified that the public may recognize that the ongoing Israeli-Arab and Israeli-Palestinian conflict runs against American interests because that could lead to meaningful pressure on Israel to cede land on the West Bank. Glick made that linkage explicit in her rebuttal to Cordesman: "The two-state solution, as presently constituted, is antithetical to America's most vital strategic interests in the Middle East" because it "assumes that Israel must contract itself to within the indefensible 1948 cease-fire lines and allow a Palestinian state allied with terrorist organizations to take power in the area it vacates."[13]

In April 2010, Representatives Ron Kind of Wisconsin and Bill Delahunt of Massachusetts circulated to their colleagues a letter to the president expressing support for his Middle East peace efforts, specifically mentioning the Petraeus testimony as evidence of the American interest in resolving the conflict. Members of Congress came under intense pressure from traditional pro-Israel advocacy groups not to sign the letter, and were told that doing so would call their "pro-Israel" credentials into question. To this day, the letter remains a point of contention between J Street and the Israeli government, which maintains that any effort to state that the United States has a national interest in Israeli-Palestinian peace is bad for Israel.

Yet, like it or not, the United States does have a strong national interest in acting immediately and assertively to end the Israeli-Palestinian conflict. What's actually "dangerous and counterproductive," to use the ADL's phrase, is not the analysis of the American defense establishment, but rather the refusal of American Jewish leaders to listen to their own country's intelligence, diplomatic and defense communities when it comes to analyzing the American national interest.

By arguing that a decorated and respected general like David Petraeus is wrong for drawing a simple and logical connection between the festering Israeli-Palestinian conflict and American interests in the region for which he is responsible, American Jewish leaders risk appearing to put their own interests and those of the State of Israel ahead of the interests of the United States.

I understand that leaders of the Jewish community are concerned about what might happen if Americans one day come to believe that their soldiers are being killed or hurt because of Israel. But there's potentially greater cost to standing in the way of American efforts to end the conflict. Traditional Jewish communal lobbies and political organizations should exercise great caution in working through the political process to stop American policy makers from advancing what they view as a fundamental American national interest.

OBAMA AND THE FUTURE

President Obama came into office publicly placing the Israeli-Palestinian conflict high on his foreign policy agenda. The president and his national security team seemed to grasp, even during the campaign, the lessons to be learned from the failed efforts of the prior two administrations. President Obama often spoke, as a candidate, of the need to address the conflict from "day one" of a presidency, not in year seven or eight.

In January 2009, the new president made good on his pledge of early focus by appointing former Senate majority leader George Mitchell as special envoy for Middle East peace on his first full day in office, January 21. He also made his first international phone calls from the Oval Office to the region's leaders, including the Israeli prime minister and the Palestinian president.

The administration's commitment to resolving the conflict through a two-state solution was clear from the start. As the president said in his landmark address to the Muslim world in Cairo, "The only resolution is for the aspirations of both sides to be met through two states, where Israelis and Palestinians each live in peace and security. That is in Israel's interest, Palestine's interest, America's interest, and the world's interest. And that is why I intend to personally pursue this outcome with all the patience and dedication that the task requires."[14]

The president and his team, including Vice President Joe Biden, Secretary of State Hillary Clinton, and Special Envoy Mitchell, have devoted hours of personal attention to the conflict and have defied those who said that, with all the many high-priority crises, there wouldn't be time for a serious push on the Israeli-Palestinian conflict as well.

President Obama's first national security advisor, General James L. Jones, put that level of attention and priority into perspective when he told J Street's national conference in October 2009 that, "If there was one problem I would recommend to the President . . . to solve, this would be it." Why? Because, said Jones, "Finding a solution to this problem has ripples that echo, that would run globally and affect many other problems that we face elsewhere on the globe."[15]

Yet despite the good will and best intentions, the Obama administration has failed in its first two years to bring the underlying conflict any closer to resolution. Errors in strategy and tactics have hampered the effort. For instance, by visiting the Buchenwald concentration camp instead of Israel after the Cairo speech, the president squandered a chance to connect directly with the Israeli people, making his case both for peace and, more narrowly, for the settlement freeze he was demanding. The mistake was costly, and the president was quickly perceived by the Israeli public as favoring the Palestinians over them.

But his early decision to put so much political capital into achieving a total settlement freeze was perhaps the most serious strategic mistake. Opposition to Israeli construction over the Green Line has been American policy for decades, through every recent presidential administration. In May 2009, the administration announced that it was demanding that Israel stop all construction over the Green Line as a condition of moving forward with the peace process. The position was entirely consistent with the Road Map laid out by President George W. Bush, which required the Israelis to halt "all settlement activity," even what is called "natural growth" (building within settlement boundaries to accommodate growing families, etc.). The secretary of state made clear that this meant a total freeze: "a stop to settlements—not some settlements, not outposts, not natural growth exceptions."[16]

The Palestinians were delighted, since throughout the nearly two decades they had been talking about creating their own country, they had also been watching it slip away as the number of Jewish residents over the Green Line passed the half million mark. The rest of the world was pleasantly surprised and supportive. Yet no one in the Obama administration seemed to have thought about what would happen if and when, as was to be expected, the Israelis said no.

Over the next eighteen months, the United States expended enormous capital squeezing a limited ten-month freeze of settlement construction out of the Israelis, and then grudging Palestinian agreement to participate first in indirect and finally direct negotiations. Talks had barely begun before the ten months expired, and by the end of 2010, the strategy lay in shambles. Construction over the Green Line was proceeding again at breakneck speed, the talks had ground to a halt and the credibility of the United States had been badly tarnished.

In a final desperate effort to get an additional ninety-day extension of the limited freeze, the administration offered a package of incentives, including $3.5 billion worth of fighter jets and a host of diplomatic assurances to Israel. Former U.S. ambassador to Israel Dan Kurtzer called the offer "unseemly," a bribe that would reward bad behavior.[17] Analysts had trouble determining what was more shocking, the extent of the offer in return for such a minimal Israeli concession or the Israeli refusal to accept the offer.

The strategic mistake was risking so much political capital on stopping settlement construction in the first place, rather than focusing on resolving issues that would actually end the conflict. Settlements are a symptom of the underlying disease—the lack of a defined border between Israel and the state-to-be of Palestine. For Israelis, building in Jewish neighborhoods of East Jerusalem or in a built-up city over the Green Line like Maale Adumim is different from building in a remote outpost. To the Palestinians—and to much of the rest of the world—there is no difference, as all construction over the Green Line is either illegal or illegitimate.

Defining the border, and the arrangements for securing that border with international help, would put an end to the settlement issue. It would be clear who can build where. Defining and agreeing on a border would also create the atmosphere in which more difficult final status issues, such as Jerusalem's holy sites or the plight of the refugees, could be addressed. Both sides would know the shape of the states they would have under the deal. Putting political capital into a "borders and security first" approach might have helped overcome the block that settlement construction posed to the negotiations.

The question going forward, with the peace process in a shambles, is what the United States can and should do to advance its fundamental interest in resolving the conflict. Some argue that the time has come to walk away from the whole situation. They rely on one of the many well-worn clichés that have emerged around the conflict, this one often attributed to former secretary of state James Baker, that "the United States cannot want peace more than the parties themselves."[18]

Others argue that the time has come to focus less on negotiations and more on pressuring Israel to change its behavior. Some advocate negative measures such as the boycotts, divestment and sanctions mentioned earlier. Others take a more subtle approach, as long-time observer and *New York Times* columnist Tom Friedman did, suggesting that Prime Minister Netanyahu Google the terms "budget cuts and fire departments" or "budget cuts and schools" to understand that there is only one right answer when the country that has given you billions of dollars over several decades, and is now limping along economically itself, asks you to halt settlement building.[19]

I would argue that the time has come for the United States, with broad support from the international community, to publicly put the widely accepted parameters of a peace agreement on the table and then ask the parties publicly to respond. Both sides say that they are ready to deal and that they accept a two-state solution. Let's put them both to the test. Are they really serious about reaching a reasonable resolution of the conflict? If neither party's political leadership can bring itself to say yes to a deal that their publics find acceptable, then let the political process in each of those societies do its work. If one party says yes and the other hesitates, it will be clear where the obstruction lies.

Either way, it is time to end the "peace process" as we know it. The twin mantras that U.S. diplomacy should be geared to "get the parties back to the table" and that "only the parties themselves can reach an agreement" must be discarded. They are canards that allow both sides to avoid facing up to the necessary sacrifices. Nothing helps people avoid tough decisions like a process that demands nothing of substance and is perpetually focused on the date of the next meeting.

The other impetus for American action now is the looming possibility of United Nations action in September 2011 to recognize Palestinian statehood. Frustrated by the lack of a diplomatic horizon offering the possibility of independence through negotiations, the Palestinian leadership is likely to take its case to the annual meeting of the UN General Assembly in September in New York, when the two-year effort by the Palestinian Authority under Prime Minister Salaam Fayyad to build the institutions of statehood comes to an end.

The Palestinians have been pursuing this strategy openly since the breakdown of talks in November 2010, first by rounding up support for a unilateral declaration of independence in South America and, second by seeking a resolution that condemns Israeli settlements from the UN Security Council in February 2011. Security Council action was prevented solely by an American veto, with the other 14 member nations on the Council voting to support the resolution.

While UN action will not itself end the conflict or create a state, it will deepen the sense of Israel's international isolation and could well spark Palestinian action—non-violent or otherwise—to put their newly recognized independence into effect. It is essential that the United States preempt this next move at the UN with an active and ambitious diplomatic initiative to achieve a two-state solution now.

It's been over a decade since President Clinton laid out his parameters for ending the conflict. He made the case then—and it remains true today—that his proposal was fair, that it provided real benefits along with the real pain and sacrifice that are the nature of compromise.

Those most skeptical of the prospects for peace will immediately ask, if the solution is so clear and simple, why Yasser Arafat and the Palestinians said no to President Clinton a decade ago. Isn't that proof that the Palestinians are simply not serious about peace?

Let's remember that President Clinton first outlined his parameters in December 2000, six months after the failure at Camp David. The offer that Arafat declined at Camp David—the one where many claim that Ehud Barak "offered Arafat everything"—had actually improved by the time discussions resumed at Taba in January 2001. The clock simply ran out on the Clinton effort before negotiators could push the deal to the finish line. George W. Bush and his team came into office firmly opposed to Clinton's active diplomacy and refused to reengage until 2007 in Annapolis, by which time his administration had no credibility left to pursue such an effort. Both administrations learned the hard way not to wait until year eight to make a serious push for peace.

Let's remember further that Arafat himself has been dead since 2004. To the extent that failure in 2000 was related to his personal failings or flaws as a leader, it's time to move on.

The Palestinian leaders today—Mahmoud Abbas and Prime Minister Salaam Fayyad—may not be perfect, but they are the best Palestinian leaders Israel is likely to have to work with for quite some time; they are dedicated to diplomacy, negotiation and a two-state solution that recognizes Israel's right to exist. And unlike in 2000, when the Arab League was on the sidelines and disengaged from the peace effort, this time they have their own offer of comprehensive peace on the table. To miss the twin opportunities presented by a Palestinian leadership committed to two states and an Arab League ready to put an end to the broader regional conflict once and for all would be a tragic mistake.

Resolving the conflict now will require a fresh approach to counter the cynicism that has engulfed the Israeli public and so many others around the world. People have simply lost faith that progress is possible. The next step by the United States—together with the broader international community—needs to be a game changer, something that breaks the unhealthy, unproductive patterns of recent years and forces everyone to take a second look.

Ideally, the president should place efforts at resolution into a comprehensive, regional framework—for instance, taking the Arab League up on its Arab Peace Initiative (API), first put forward by Saudi King Abdullah and adopted in 2002 in Beirut and endorsed in subsequent meetings. The API calls for an end to the Arab-Israeli conflict, based on Israeli withdrawal from the territories occupied in 1967, in return for normalization of relations between the entire Arab world and Israel. This would entail not simply an Israeli-Palestinian deal, but agreements with Syria and Lebanon as well.

The API is not a detailed peace plan, but an "offer" to Israel for the regional peace and acceptance it has long sought. It has gained little traction in Israel, surprisingly, although it offers what Israelis have long said they most want—full acceptance into the region and normalization of relations with their neighbors. The Israeli government has never formally responded to the initiative—nor has the United States. President Obama's best bet for progress in the second half of his first term may well be to push forward with a proposal of his own that puts full regional acceptance of Israel squarely on the table as the benefit Israelis will receive in return for their concessions.

A regional approach also offers the possibility of a strategic, diplomatic response to the challenge posed by Iran. The threat of rising Iranian power and increasing extremism in the region could unite Arab moderates and Israel in opposition. It also has the potential to shift Syria out of Iran's orbit and back into a more natural alliance with its fellow Arab countries, while diminishing the power and importance of both Hamas and Hezbollah, who are currently, with Iranian assistance, stirring up trouble in Lebanon and at Egypt's door. Finally, it would encourage a return to more normal and friendly relations between Turkey and Israel, and maintain Turkey as a positive and productive regional gateway for its Arab neighbors to the west.

The potential benefits not only to Israel but to the United States of promoting a comprehensive, regional peace agreement are enormous. With the president likely to find the going far harder in domestic affairs with greater Republican power in Congress, a bold display of international leadership would be one way to score a significant achievement in advance of the 2012 elections.

If history is any guide, however, domestic politics will hold the president back. When the president convenes his advisers to consider approaches to the Middle East, there probably won't be many substantive arguments against taking a lot tougher line with the parties and putting forward the steps that the entire world understands need to be taken to end the conflict. In light of events across the Arab world, there will perhaps be even stronger arguments that now is the time to put forward a new U.S. plan and to place the United States at the forefront of the Arab world's push for freedom.

The main arguments against strong presidential action will be, as always, political. Veterans of prior battles over the Middle East will say that any effort to push both Israel and the Palestinians to make progress will fail under the weight of domestic pressure. The perceived power of traditional pro-Israel lobbies and political forces is still great enough to affect the policy calculus for a White House heading into a tough re-election.

The "loudest eight percent" has been astoundingly effective in shaping the discourse in Washington when it comes to Israel. As with so many issues, a vocal and well-organized special interest, small in number and not necessarily representative at all of the broader community, has harnessed the energy and resources to have a major impact. Even though polls show that broad opinion on the issue is far more moderate and balanced, moderates, by definition, bring less intensity to any struggle. So the vocal, impassioned minority carries the day because the moderate majority can't muster sufficient political energy to counter them.

The key to change, therefore, is to organize this broader pool of "passionate moderates" into a true counterweight to balance the energized minority. Those of us who hope to alter the dynamics of American politics around Israel and the Middle East must build a movement of people with more balanced and nuanced views on the Middle East and support political leaders and solutions that go beyond simplistic Israel-right-or-wrong stands.

Those who believe that peace is essential for Israel, for the United States and for the region must demonstrate to the White House, to members of Congress and to the political world that a sufficient base of political support exists and can be delivered to back them up if they break with the status quo.

And this movement must be significant enough to not only help a White House pursue peace, but to make it politically costly *not* to pursue the end of the conflict aggressively.

The road to Middle East peace starts in the American Jewish community precisely because it is our community's political activism that forms the primary political barrier to a bold American initiative to end the conflict.

Those of us who urge active American leadership to end the conflict don't even need to outweigh the opposition. We simply need to provide sufficient political space for politicians and policy makers to stand up and stake out strong positions without fearing that they are signing their political death warrants. And, given the urgency of the situation, we need to do it swiftly and convincingly.

It's a task that may appear overwhelming and even quixotic. But if we care deeply about fulfilling the dreams of the pioneers, builders and fighters who created the State of Israel, it is nothing less than an existential necessity.

13

GIVING VOICE TO OUR VALUES

Let's get one more thing straight. The ongoing occupation of the West Bank and the blockade of Gaza shouldn't end simply because they are strategically bad for the long-term security and survival of Israel, or because they damage the national interests of the United States. They should end because they are morally wrong, and the treatment of the Palestinian people and the condition in which many of them live should trouble Jews, who, as a people, have themselves experienced far too much discrimination and mistreatment in their history.

I was doing a public radio interview in July 2010 opposite the director of the Washington Institute for Near East Policy, a think tank associated with traditional American Jewish communal views on Israel and the Middle East.[1] The show focused primarily on the prospects for proximity talks between the Israelis and Palestinians, but the listeners who called in were, as is often the case on such shows, less interested in exploring the twists and turns of policy than in venting anger over Israel's treatment of the Palestinians, and America's inability to impact the situation despite the aid and assistance it provides to Israel.

In response to one caller who asked how the difficulties of daily life for Palestinians could be justified in light of Jewish history and experience, I acknowledged that, in my opinion, the ongoing occupation and settlement enterprise are "immoral." I went on to say that, happily, national and moral interests in this case coincide, arguing together for ending both the occupation and settlement expansion.

My counterpart responded that it is wrong to refer to the situation on the West Bank as immoral. He made the case that the occupation was brought on by the 1967 war, that Israel has always tried to make peace and that the occupation would end only when Israel's neighbors accept it and recognize its legitimacy.

I am always taken aback by the argument that there is no moral dimension to the conflict, and it seems that traditional pro-Israel advocates are equally stunned when I assert that there is. Jews—regardless of their politics—take pride in believing that our behavior, individually and communally, is guided by a deep sense of ethics and values.

My father instilled in me the centrality of our communal values by reading every Friday night from the *Pirkei Avot* (Verses of the Fathers), a classic work containing some of the key ethical and moral teachings that have guided the Jewish people for two thousand years. Among the best known are such admonitions as "If not now, when?" and "If I am not for myself, who will be for me?" Shabbat study of these principles, many of which are central to the ethical codes of other, later religions, is a tradition dating back nearly two thousand years.

Perhaps the central precept of Jewish ethical teaching is captured in an anecdote about the great Rabbi Hillel the Elder, who lived in the first century B.C.E., and whose wisdom is central to the *Pirkei Avot*. According to the story, a non-Jew approached Hillel saying he would convert to Judaism if the great rabbi could teach him the whole of the Torah while standing on one foot.

Hillel is reported to have said, "That which is hateful to you, do not unto another. That is the whole Torah; the rest is commentary. Now go and learn." This is an artful rephrasing of the commandment in Leviticus to "love one's neighbor as oneself." The notion that right and wrong are grounded in human conscience and experience and not simply based on rules handed down by God is one of Judaism's seminal contributions to human civilization.

I've always felt that—given our historic experiences—Jews should be especially sensitive to the treatment of minorities and understand intuitively the pain caused when one people oppresses another. Our history in just the past five to six hundred years, from the Inquisition to the pogroms to the Holocaust, has given us more first-hand experience with the dark side of human behavior than nearly any other people. Out of those experiences should come heightened awareness of justice when running our own state, and a sense of responsibility for fair treatment of any minorities living in our midst.

The way Israel treats the Palestinian people over whom it exerts control *is* a test of the moral code we have developed over our history. I believe it is perfectly appropriate to ask whether we are living up to the ideals of Hillel. Are we doing justice to the "teachings of the fathers" about ethics and morality? We teach our young people to "repair the world," to fight prejudice and injustice and to ensure that others are treated as we would want to be treated. We should encourage them as well to apply those principles and standards when it comes to Israel, and to ask whether the treatment of the Palestinian people today accords with our understanding of the principles of our faith.

When Jews visit Israel to celebrate their heritage and their homeland, they should visit the West Bank as well, and see, for instance, the old central market of Hebron, its metal gates shuttered, surrounded by military checkpoints, its streets divided by Jersey barricades to make clear where Jews and non-Jews can walk. They should read the hate-filled graffiti in Hebrew. Witness the chicken wire that provides a roof over the street so the garbage thrown by Jewish settlers won't land on the heads of Palestinians walking below. They should be encouraged to explore the moral dimension of the occupation.

Of course, they should also learn, debate and engage the complex history that has given rise to the conflict. They should understand the Israeli narrative of Arab rejection of the State of Israel, and why the War of Independence had to be fought against Arab nations who didn't accept the division of Palestine into two states for two peoples. They should hear the Palestinian narrative of *naqba* (catastrophe in Arabic), and their agony over the displacement of hundreds of thousands of non-Jews whose descendants are still refugees more than six decades later. They should learn that the occupation of the West Bank and Gaza resulted from a war that Israel fought to ensure its survival, but also see first-hand the impact that four decades of settlement building and expanding Jewish development have had on Palestinian prospects. They should know that the plight of the Palestinian people as refugees for more than sixty years is not the sole responsibility of Israel, and that the refugees have been used for decades as pawns by Israel's Arab neighbors for their own political purposes—domestically and beyond—and that this remains true to this day.

It seems to me the fundamentally Jewish thing to do would be to absorb all of this conflicting information and then to ask a simple question about the treatment of the Palestinian people today: Is this how I wanted to be treated when I was a minority in another people's country? Is this how my people ought to put our magnificent code of ethics into practice when given the chance to exercise power?

Yet, to raise these moral questions opens you to scathing attack and to being labeled "virulently anti-Israel." And what is the charge, if you talk about Israel's human rights record? That you are contributing to the de-legitimization of the state of Israel.[2]

Another response is to insist that any discussion of human rights records begins not with Israel but rather with the worst human rights abusers, as Alan Dershowitz argued in a speech at a conference held by the Committee for Accuracy in Media Reporting in America (CAMERA), as reported in the *Jerusalem Post*.[3] The answer, according to the man who has defined for a generation or more how to make "the case for Israel," is not to permit anyone to have a conversation about Israel's behavior, but to "grab onto the very rhetoric of human rights and turn it against them but also in the direction of truth."

Those making the traditional pro-Israel case argue that Israel should not be criticized because the human rights records of so many other countries are ten times worse. What does Dershowitz say when presented with the notion that Israel's actions might actually be problematic? "China." To the thought that the occupation might be mistreating Palestinians? "Congo."

However, I was never taught that, when it comes to morality, it's good enough to be "better than the worst of them." I don't think that was what my parents had in mind when they showed me how to behave around other people—and it's certainly not what I'm teaching my children.

I cannot bring myself to answer questions about the treatment of Palestinians by saying—like a kid on the playground—"they started it." They attacked in 1948, or they provoked the Six-Day War which led to the occupation. Historical finger-pointing is, to me, simply a way of avoiding dealing with today's reality.

I also question the ethics of those in the Jewish community who cut off the conversation on human rights and morality by personally attacking those who raise the issues. Look, for instance, at the treatment of Richard Goldstone. Goldstone is one of the most respected legal authorities on human rights in the world today. A South African judge, he is credited with working from within the system to help overturn and defeat the country's system of apartheid. His work in the early 1990s, heading a commission that looked into political violence, is credited with keeping the negotiations to effect a peaceful transition from apartheid on track.

Given his tremendous work in South Africa, Judge Goldstone was subsequently asked to play an important role as well in prosecuting war criminals at the International Criminal Court, first regarding Rwanda and then the former Yugoslavia.

Goldstone is also an active member of the South African Jewish community with personal ties to Israel. He served on the international board of governors of the Hebrew University in Jerusalem and headed the board of World ORT (an international Jewish vocational training program). His daughter lived in Israel. He has credited being Jewish—"part of a community that has been persecuted throughout history" as the *Los Angeles Times* puts it—with helping to shape his ethical views.[4] He has referred to the State of Israel itself as the embodiment of the struggle for human rights: "This struggle for human rights has been in the most profound existential sense very much the struggle for ourselves—for our Jewish identity. For the creation of the state of Israel."[5]

Goldstone's contributions to making the world a more just and righteous place should earn him a place of unparalleled respect in the worldwide Jewish community. What he has devoted his life to should inspire us and our children—and represents the best possible way a Jewish person can make the world a better place through the application of Jewish values. He should have been highly sought after by nearly every synagogue in America to be a visiting scholar or speaker. And perhaps he was by those who had heard of him. But then he led the international commission appointed by the United Nations Human Rights Council to investigate the actions of both Israel and Hamas during Operation Cast Lead (Israel's invasion of Gaza in December 2008). The commission's report charged both Israel and Hamas with violations of international law for their conduct during the conflict.

Opposition to the Goldstone Report became a rallying cry in Israel and among right-of-center Israel advocates around the world. Prime Minister Netanyahu labeled it one of the great strategic threats facing Israel. Israel objected on principle to any inquiry that sought to question how it acted in self-defense against a non-state actor (Hamas) firing rockets indiscriminately at civilians, hiding fighters and storing weapons amid civilians and staging its operations from mosques, schools and other civilian locations. Israel's allies asked other legitimate questions about the report itself, from its treatment of the Gaza police force as "noncombatants" to the failure to give sufficient credit to the IDF for warning civilians of impending attack and its other efforts to promote the ethical conduct of its forces.

However, the proper response to the report's charges would be, as Professor Moshe Halbertal (who helped write the Israeli army's ethical guidelines) pointed out in early 2010, to confront the troubling moral questions in defense of Israel's actions, rather than refusing to participate in the inquiry at all. The Goldstone Report can be criticized, as Halbertal effectively does, for refusing to address why Hamas militants would not wear uniforms if not to shelter themselves among civilians. Or why they would launch rockets from crowded urban centers if not to prevent counterattack.[6] But the Israeli response to the Goldstone Report contained no substantive critique. The Israelis did not attempt to engage in an intelligent discussion of the choices Israel could or should have made with respect either to its behavior in Gaza or how to deal with the commission and the subsequent report.

Instead, the Israeli and Jewish establishments unleashed a torrent of personal attacks on the judge that turned his name into a dirty word. No less an icon of peace and co-existence than Israel's President Shimon Peres called Goldstone "a small man, devoid of any sense of justice, a technocrat with no real understanding of jurisprudence. . . . If anyone should be investigated, it should be him."[7] Alan Dershowitz called him an "evil, evil man," a traitor to the Jewish people, and he has repeatedly accused him of using the last name "Goldstone" to give cover to defamation of the Jewish people as a whole.[8]

Now, I'll be the first to acknowledge that the standards to which Israel is held by the international community are not fair. The United Nations Human Rights Council created in 2006 has been far too focused on Israel, to the exclusion of most other significant human rights issues in the world. Israel is, in fact, the only item on the Council's permanent agenda. But that doesn't justify the fact that the default setting of Israel's defenders is to launch into personal attacks. Critics are immediately "anti-Semites" and "Israel-haters," whether individuals like former president Jimmy Carter and Mary Robinson (former president of Ireland and former United Nations high commissioner for human rights), or organizations like Human Rights Watch and Amnesty International. If they are Jewish, they are labeled "self-hating Jews."

With the government of Israel and its defenders labeling any critique off limits and unacceptably anti-Israel, it's not surprising that there's little room for the nuanced position that, despite the disproportionate international focus on Israel, the country still does have human rights issues that need to be addressed.

In Israel, the attacks against human rights organizations are steady, harsh and growing. Operations like the Jerusalem-based NGO Monitor, run by Gerald Steinberg, and the student group Im Tirtzu have launched ads and billboards attacking progressive organizations such as the New Israel Fund for their support of groups that provided critical information on the conduct of the Israeli military in Gaza to international investigators.

The Knesset is considering a range of legislation that would dramatically limit the rights of those promoting human rights in Israel—from imposing onerous reporting requirements on foreign funding in an effort to dry up financial support for the groups, to limits on free speech, to banning entry to Israel by anyone even indirectly associated with the broadly defined range of boycott efforts. The list of pending legislation that would erode the foundations of Israel's democracy is lengthy, much of it designed by Israel's right wing to shut down the country's human rights movement.[9] The ever-increasing proportion of hard-right political parties in the parliament means that proposals once on the far fringes are today on the brink of enactment.

The debate over the appropriate balance between morality and security has been raging since well before Israel's founding. The break between the Political Zionists on the right and the Socialist Zionists on the left in the 1920s and '30s was driven in part by a belief that the Left was putting too great an emphasis on creating a just society when basic survival was at stake. Jabotinsky's disciples rejected the argument that building the national homeland of the Jewish people meant building a model society that applied universal humanist values. They were focused instead on providing a safe haven that could keep the Jewish people secure from their enemies.

Today, the nationalist mindset is fully ascendant. Security and strength are the watchwords of the Israeli political mainstream, if not of the Jewish people as a whole. Given the tragedies of recent history, this is understandable. The Jewish people must be ready to fight our enemies and to defend our existence and freedom. It does no good to be dead and moral, just and enslaved. As we know first-hand, there is evil in the world to fight and there are threats to counter.

However, strength and survival do not require sacrificing the moral core of what it means to be Jewish. One of the most important tenets of Judaism is to help human beings move away from a pure focus on survival to the pursuit of higher good.

So now, as we approach the difficult questions of how to secure the survival and future of the State of Israel, let's not tell ourselves, our children and the rest of the world that it's good enough for us to behave better than the worst human rights violators in the world.

Let's challenge ourselves to do better, to be the "light unto the nations" that we aspire to be, to set a higher standard. Let's find the way to blend the pursuit of security with a commitment to building a more just world. Neither survival without morality nor morality without survival is a satisfactory outcome.

After thousands of years, we do honor to our faith and tradition when we give voice to our values and struggle with the morality of our actions, and we discredit our prophets and teachers when we rule that conversation out of bounds either in the state of our people or in the American Jewish community.

14
WHY NOT?

I did not grow up in Israel, carrying out the mission of Zionism, but in America, deeply steeped in Israel's history and mythology. For most twenty-first-century Jews, where we happen to live is an accident of history. A great-grandparent decided to head to New York rather than Jaffa, or chose the train to Paris rather than the boat to Palestine. Yet we remain bound together as a people, linked by hundreds and thousands of years of shared history and tradition.

Like many others who happened to be born outside Israel, I grew up hanging onto every word of the improbable stories of the brave pioneers who built a great nation, drained the swamps and made the desert bloom. I drank in stories of those who fought war after war against bigger, stronger enemies, and how they won, modern-day Davids taking on Goliath.

We were raised with pride—in our family, our faith and our people. But as children, we also absorbed the dangers. We learned from reading the *Haggadah*, the story of Passover, every year, that "in every generation an enemy will rise up to defeat us." And, of course, in nearly every family, there was a parent or grandparent with a personal story to bring that maxim to life.

The never-ending cycle of war and terror that Israel faced provided ample confirmation of history's lessons, and we knew that our role as American Jews was to be ready and willing to do whatever was necessary to defend our homeland and our people.

This was, of course, unprecedented progress for the relationship between Jews in America and Israel. Where once there had been real skepticism about Zionism and enormous debate within the communal establishment over whether to support Zionism, Israel had now become a centerpiece of Jewish identity in the United States.

For several generations now, Jews in the United States and in other parts of the Diaspora have grown up understanding our role: As our cousins in Israel build the national home of our people, our duty is to answer their calls for help.

And so we have been asked for money—to tame the land and to defend it. And we knew the money was essential, both before and after the founding of the state. Without, for instance, the help of the Rothschilds, my family's own early efforts to settle Petah Tikva would have failed. In the 1930s and 1940s, my father and many others raised money in the United States that was critical both to saving some Jews in Europe and ultimately to the successful fight for independence. And they lamented that they could not raise more.

I remember from my youth the connection we felt as children putting our coins and dollars into the blue *tzedakah* (charity) boxes in Hebrew School for the Jewish National Fund. The fund-raising continues today, with hundreds of millions of dollars still flowing from Jews outside Israel to a wide range of efforts to support the state.

We have been asked to consider making *aliyah* (immigration) to fulfill the vision of Zionism, the ingathering of all the Jewish people back to their traditional, national home. I myself considered it in the 1990s and would again, depending on the course the country follows. Nothing would make me happier than if my children were to develop enough of a connection to the country to consider it themselves one day when they are older. Each year, thousands of new immigrants make the journey my great-grandparents made—and, even today, there are organized efforts to encourage and facilitate Jewish movement to Israel.

We are asked to lobby on Israel's behalf in Washington and with governments around the world. As we've seen, in the United States, those efforts have been spectacularly successful and have been critical to the growth and defense of the state and its integration into the broader world community.

We have been asked to visit as tourists and to establish a personal connection with the country. Recently, we have been asked to send our kids to experience Israel first-hand through programs such as Birthright, in an effort to spark interest and connection with Israel in the younger generation.

In each of these ways, Jews living in the United States have expressed their Zionism—their support of Israel. Each of these actions has reflected the deep emotional and communal bond that exists between Jews who happen to live in Israel and those who do not.

Today, however, Israel needs something much more and far different than it has in the past. Israel is at risk, and the threat is more daunting and more complex than those we are accustomed to facing. It's not simply an external enemy pointing a rocket, building a bomb or proposing a UN resolution.

The threat today to Israel's long-term security and character is its failure to recognize the danger that comes with not achieving a two-state solution, not addressing and resolving the claims of the Palestinian people, not helping them to also achieve their freedom and independence. Without such a resolution—fair, just and immediate—Israel's security, character and international standing will erode quickly, undermining the state itself.

As with so many painful choices, it is far easier to put off till tomorrow the tough choices and sacrifices that need to be made today to ensure the future. It seems to me that the ultimate act of friendship we can offer to the state we have helped to build is to bring these choices and consequences to the center of public debate and attention—both in the United States and in Israel.

If, God forbid, war were to break out tomorrow and Israel's existence were to be threatened, the American Jewish community and Jews worldwide would—without a doubt and appropriately—rally to the flag. The communal alarm bells would ring. The attention of community leadership and members would be focused on the immediate threat. Fund-raising drives would kick into gear; emergency meetings would be called in every community; high-level consultations would be convened in Washington.

American Jews would respond much as they do today in the face of the perceived threat from Iran and its nuclear program, or from "de-legitimization." They would respond in a way, I would argue, that the organized community's leaders did *not* during World War II, in the face of mortal threat to the Jews of Europe.

Yet, today, in the American Jewish community, there is a complete lack of urgency among established leaders and organizations when it comes to the failure to resolve the Israeli-Palestinian conflict.

There is, rather, an eerie quiet. No alarm bells ring; no impassioned appeals arrive from communal leaders to help our cousins in Israel.

Listen carefully and you'll hear even former Israeli prime ministers and many of Israel's military leaders and leading intellectuals begging us to recognize that Israel faces an existential threat. Without a two-state solution, they are warning, Israel will cease to be the Jewish and democratic home that we worked so hard as a global Jewish community to create.

They—not Israel's enemies—tell us that Israel is "finished." They—not Israel's enemies—speak of a future that resembles far too closely an apartheid state.

The leaders of the international community echo these warnings as well. The great statesmen of our generation, of our global community, frantically try to call attention to the consequences of failure.

Yet these dire warnings continue to fall on deaf ears. The loudest voices in the Jewish community condemn those sounding the alarm here as anti-Semites and self-hating Jews. As we seek to build support and consensus around the need to end the occupation and to attain a two-state solution as quickly as possible, they make us out to be worse than the enemies who actually seek Israel's destruction.

Much of the deafening silence from the American Jewish establishment is, I believe, driven by a skepticism shared both in America and in Israel over whether there really is any longer a way to end the conflict peacefully. Fatigue has set in, understandably, after twenty years of failed efforts and unfulfilled promises.

Sometimes the skepticism is driven by opponents of compromise who say there's nothing to be done because there's no partner on the other side: "Can't you see, we offered them everything and they said no; we gave them southern Lebanon, and we got rockets; we gave them Gaza, and we got more rockets."

Sometimes the skepticism is driven by those who are sympathetic to the goal but who think that developments on the ground have progressed so far that they can't be reversed or that the leaders on all sides just can't muster the political will for compromise. Some have given up after twenty years of trying; they say it just can't be done any more. Fatigue has set in; the status quo seems manageable.

What we need right now, however, is a little less "can't"—and a little more "why not?"

Little is more anathema to the spirit that built Israel than to accept the view that a problem isn't solvable, a goal is unattainable or an out-of-the-box idea is too radical to try. This attitude is less reminiscent of the spirit of the Jewish people than of my law school experience where I got credit for spotting issues and problems rather than for creative solutions.

There's also a little too much comfort being taken in reciting the lessons of past failures. I understand Santayana's point that those who don't learn the lessons of history are condemned to repeat them. But it's equally true that the general who spends too much time learning the lessons of prior battles will end up fighting the previous war.

Again, it is not the can-do spirit of a people known for ingenuity and innovation to say that because something didn't work in the past or couldn't quite be done that it therefore can't be done now or in the future. Fifteen years ago, a friend of mine pitched dozens of companies with his design for a slim machine on which you could read books without paper. They laughed. The technical difficulties seemed too great; the notion that people would buy a book without paper too far-fetched.

Where would the world be if our greatest minds hadn't stretched our concept of the feasible? If the Einsteins, the Edisons and the Gates's of the world had taken no for an answer?

Do we let our kids get away with saying they tried and failed, so they're stopping? When they fall off a bike, we tell them to get right back up again; when they swing and miss, we say get right back in the batter's box. Why would we accept anything less as adults—in matters as important as life and death, war and peace?

Too many people these days are taking academic delight in sitting back, folding their arms and saying it can't be done—that it's just not possible to solve the Israeli-Palestinian conflict—so why try?

Too many people are taking the easy way out on this issue—passing the buck, pinning the blame on someone else.

I've heard just about every conceivable argument at this point as to why Middle East peace can't happen. How there are no partners. How everything was tried ten years ago and failed. How these are people doomed by history to hate and kill each other and there's no point in trying to stop it.

I've been told that those of us who believe otherwise are so few and far between that our limited power won't change anything.

But the world can't afford all this "can't."

It's time for a little more "why not?"

There's no reason for us to accept things as they are. There's no reason that—with effort—we can't overcome the daunting status quo.

The conflict has a rational solution. It is still, at the end of the day, a dispute between two people over one piece of land. And it's our choice whether to fight to the death over it or find some way to share it in peace so our children and grandchildren won't have to bleed and die as our parents and grandparents did.

I came face-to-face with this reality in the Mahane Yehuda market in Jerusalem in 1997 as sixteen people lay dead and dying just steps from where I sat.

There, in the space of five minutes, I understood that I cannot wait for someone else to act. Ultimately, this conflict will engulf Israel and all those we care about. We need to overcome the instinct to point fingers and assign blame if we hope to break the cycle of violence.

To "seek peace and pursue it"—in Hebrew *rodeph shalom*—is a central tenet of the Jewish people. All over the world, synagogues are named Rodeph Shalom—including the one in which I was raised, became a bar mitzvah and married. The pursuit of peace for the Jewish people is not a passive undertaking—it's an imperative, a command. Peace will not come on its own. We must actively seek it.

A desire for peace is central to our faith. During every prayer service, we ask God for it. As we mourn, in the kaddish, we pray for it. The priestly blessing, passed from God to Moses to Aaron, and used to this day to bless the Jewish people ends with the fervent hope that God will in fact grant peace to his people.

How is it, then, that any of us can accept in the name of our people, our faith, our history the idea that we must live in a constant state of war? How is it that among those most virulently opposed to the pursuit of peace are some of the most devoutly religious?

My answer to those who say it can't be done is not simply that it can, or that it will make the world a better place for our children. I would argue that we have no choice.

My family wasn't exceedingly religious growing up. My father, the nationalist, was far more a student of politics than of the Bible. But it was in those Friday night sessions as we sat together reading from the *Pirkei Avot* that I first understood the obligation to never give up. In the words of Rabbi Tarfon, "It is not your obligation to complete the task, but neither are you at liberty to desist from it."

I'm not surprised when I look back at my high school yearbook page, to see that I chose to quote Robert Kennedy's adaptation of the George Bernard Shaw line: "Some people see things as they are and say why? I dream things that never were and say, why not?"

The survival of the State of Israel, the interests of the United States, the future of the Jewish people all demand that we dream a far better future than the present-day reality in the Middle East.

This is the great challenge for friends of Israel at this moment in history, to help our cousins in Israel recognize that the path they are on is not sustainable. This is the greatest act of love we can show to the State of Israel—don't sit idly by and watch the country head for a cliff of its own making.

The truest act of friendship today is to ask our Israeli friends and relatives to open their eyes to the critical choices ahead and to the consequences of failing to take these choices seriously.

This is Zionism in the twenty-first century.

Our great-grandparents were Zionist pioneers. They traveled from the four corners of the earth—often running from persecution and imminent threat under the most trying of conditions. Their goal was to ensure the well-being of their families and their people. It was to bring about the survival and rebirth of a nation and a people.

Our grandparents were Zionist builders. Their initiative, drive and innovation turned a land without resources and with few natural assets into a thriving nation on the cutting edge of modernity in a matter of a few decades.

Our parents and theirs as well were Zionist fighters who created an independent state and protected it against a host of enemies who aimed to destroy it.

Now, it falls to this generation to fulfill the dream of Zionism—to see the powerful miracle begun by our forebears through to its conclusion: a state with defined borders, at peace with its neighbors, accepted into the region and the community of nations.

Until this is done, the work of Zionism is not complete. Until this is done, all that has come before—130 years of hard work and fighting since the days when Ze'ev and Batya and Shmuel and Chaya-Frieda set foot in Jaffa—is at risk.

To assist in bringing peace and security to Israel at this moment in its history is the ultimate act of Zionism. It is the final chapter of this installment of the history of the Jewish people.

It is our way to help to ensure that the Jewish people have a home of their own, a state that is safe and secure—and one that lives up to the ideals and principles of the Jewish people.

Our voice must speak the truth as loudly and clearly as possible: The present path that the state of Israel is on is unsustainable. The occupation of another people and the denial of their national aspirations and their rights is not only morally unacceptable, it is a fatal threat to the entire enterprise of the State of Israel.

And a new voice is needed for an American Jewish community, one that is ready to speak these truths and to redefine what it means to be pro-Israel in the twenty-first century. In the process of building that voice, we will rewrite the rules of American politics and of the Jewish communal conversation on Israel.

This is the path that I believe will make it possible for my grandchildren to return to Tel Aviv in 2109 to celebrate the city's bicentennial and to find a safe, secure and thriving twenty-second-century metropolis. Only on this path can we fulfill the dream of Herzl and complete the work of the pioneers, builders and fighters who came before.

NOTES

INTRODUCTION

1. Martin Luther King Jr., "Where Do We Go From Here?" annual report delivered at the 11th Convention of the Southern Christian Leadership Conference, August 16, 1967, Atlanta, GA.

CHAPTER 1: THE PIONEERS AND THE BUILDERS

1. Interestingly, the leading authority of recent times on Abravanel is the Israeli prime minister's father, Ben-Zion Netanyahu, whose biography of Abravanel is considered the definitive modern work on his life and teachings.

CHAPTER 2: THE FIGHTERS

1. Yitshaq Ben-Ami, *Years of Wrath, Days of Glory,* 2nd ed. (New York City: Shengold Publishers, 1983), 80.
2. Shmuel Katz, *Lone Wolf: A Biography of Vladimir (Ze'ev) Jabotinsky* (New York: Barricade Books, 1996), 2:1649.
3. As quoted in Naomi Wiener Cohen, "The Reaction of Reform Judaism in American to Political Zionism (1897–1922)" in *The Jewish Experience in America,* ed. Abraham J. Karp, vol. 5, *At Home in America* (New York: Ktav Publishing House, 1969), 153.
4. Ibid.
5. Jehuda Reinharz, "Zionism: In the United States" in *Encyclopedia Judaica,* ed. Cecil Roth (Jerusalem: Keter Publishing House, 1996), 16:1143.
6. American Jewish Committee, "Who We Are," *American Jewish Committee,* http://www.ajc.org/site/c.ijITI2PHKoG/b.789093/k.124/Who_We_Are.htm.
7. Jonathan D. Sarna and Jonathan J. Golden, "The Twentieth Century through American Jewish Eyes: A History of the *American Jewish Year Book,* 1899–1999," *American Jewish Year Book* 100 (2000): 61.
8. Irving M. Engel, "Report of the Executive Committee: Highlights of 1950," *American Jewish Year Book* 53 (1952): 552.
9. Ben-Ami, *Years of Wrath, Days of Glory,* 318.
10. The Emergency Committee for Israel was established during the 2010 election by well-known neoconservatives William Kristol and Rachel Abrams (wife of Elliot Abrams, Middle East director of President George W. Bush's National Security Council), together with Evangelical Christian leader and former Republican presidential

candidate Gary Bauer. Its activities included attack ads on politicians deemed too critical of Israel for supporting pro-peace positions and the Obama administration's policies. Their staff and spokespeople made clear that an underlying purpose of the ECI was to attack and defeat J Street's effort to organize a new pro-Israel, pro-peace movement.

11. Ben-Ami, *Years of Wrath, Days of Glory,* 318.
12. Ibid., 320.
13. Ibid., 321.
14. Ibid.
15. In 1940, the Emergency Committee for Zionist Affairs issued a twenty-six-page booklet titled "Revisionism—a Destructive Force."
16. Department of Justice memorandum, Nathan M. Cohen to James R. Sharp, JRS/NMC–149–178, September 1, 1942.
17. Department of Justice memorandum, Edgar Hoover to Lawrence M. Smith, April 13, 1943, Division of Records: No. 149–178 and F4173.
18. Ben-Ami, *Years of Wrath, Days of Glory,* 325.
19. Ibid., 521.
20. "Remarks by Prime Minister Yitzhak Rabin on the Occasion of the Signing of the Israeli-Palestinian Declaration of Principles, Washington, September 13, 1993," http://www.mfa.gov.il/MFA/Archive/Peace+Process/1993/Remarks+by+PM+Yitzhak+Rab in+at+Signing+of+DOP+-+13.htm.

CHAPTER 3: BORN IN THE USA

1. *The Sunday Times* (London), June 15, 1969, 12.

CHAPTER 4: SIXTY SECONDS IN SANTA FE

1. Ron Fournier, "Dean Braces for Criticism in First Democratic Presidential Debate," Associated Press, September 4, 2003.
2. Jim VanadeHei, "Rivals Criticize Dean for Mideast Comment," *Washington Post,* September 9, 2003.
3. Ibid.
4. "Face-Off: Democratic Debate," *News Hour with Jim Lehrer,* Public Broadcast Service, September 10, 2003, http://www.pbs.org/newshour/bb/politics/july-dec03/debate _9–10.html.
5. Michael Janofsky, "Some House Democrats Fault Dean on Middle East," *New York Times,* September 11, 2003, http://www.nytimes.com/2003/09/11/us/some-house-democrats-fault-dean-on-mideast.html.
6. Ben Smith, "Mitchell, Swiss?" *Politico,* January 22, 2009, http://www.politico.com/blogs/bensmith/0109/Mitchell_Swiss.html.
7. "Dean Defends Middle East Remarks," CNN Politics, September 10, 2003, http://articles .cnn.com/2003-09-10/politics/elec04.prez.dean.mideast_1_settlements-in-palestinian-territories-israeli-palestinian-dispute-israelis-and-palestinians/2?_s= PM:ALLPOLITICS
8. Michelle Goldberg, "Howard Dean's Israel Problem," *Salon,* September 23, 2003, http://dir.salon.com/story/news/feature/2003/09/23/dean_israel/.
9. Nathan Guttman, "Democrat's Remarks on Israel may lead Jews to cut funds," *Ha'aretz,* September 12, 2003, http://www.haaretz.com/print-edition/news/democrat -s-remarks-on-israel-may-lead-jews-to-cut-funds–1.99894.
10. Michelle Goldberg, "Howard Dean's Israel Problem."

11. Ibid.

12. "Howard Dean on Middle East Policy," http://urbanlegends.about.com/library/bl_howard_dean.htm.

13. Alan Dershowitz, "J Street Can No Longer Claim to be Pro-Israel," *Huffington Post*, April 21, 2010, http://www.huffingtonpost.com/alan-dershowitz/j-street-can-no-longer-cl_b_546841.html.

14. Raphael Ahren, "US politician wants American Jews to buy back West Bank homes," *Ha'aretz*, November 17, 2009, http://www.haaretz.com/print-edition/news/u-s-politician-wants-american-jews-to-buy-west-bank-homes--1.4040.

15. Lisa Colangelo, "Pol Raps Green Donation," *New York Daily News*, April 23, 2001.

CHAPTER 5: THE LOUDEST EIGHT PERCENT

1. They included, among many others, Daniel Levy, a dual British and Israeli citizen, who had been a negotiator for the Israelis at Taba and an architect of the Geneva Accords; Mort Halperin, a veteran of both domestic and international policy in Washington who has a large family in Israel; Davidi Gilo, an Israeli American businessman who played a role in getting the Democracy Alliance off the ground; Sara Ehrman and Debra DeLee, the former executive director of the Democratic Party and the CEO of Americans for Peace Now.

2. American Jewish Committee, "2008 Annual Survey of American Jewish Opinion," American Jewish Committee, September 8–21, 2008, www.ajc.org/site/c.ijTI2PHKoG/b.4540689.

3. All of Jim Gerstein's polls for J Street as well as his analyses of them are available at www.jstreet.org/poll.

4. Joseph Carroll, "Partisanship and Presidential Approval among the Jewish Population," Gallup, May 25, 2004, http://www.gallup.com/poll/11806/partisanship-presidential-approval-among-jewish-population.aspx.

5. Carl Shrag, "Jews Choose," *Slate*, Feb. 10, 2004, http://www.slate.com/id/2095242.

6. See, e.g., Norman Podhoretz interviewed in "Countervailing Trends in American Jewry," put out by the Jerusalem Center for Public Affairs, October 15, 2003, or Fred Barnes looking back at the Bush presidency in the *Weekly Standard*, "Bush's Achievements: Ten Things the President Got Right," January 19, 2009.

7. Jim VandeHei, "Congress Is Giving Israel Vote of Confidence," *Washington Post*, July 19, 2006.

8. The CNN exit poll of roughly 12,000 votes contained only 2 percent Jewish voters, so roughly 240 people. The margin of error on such a small sample is above 5 percent, and the 87 percent figure does seem unusually high.

9. Bryan Schwartzman, "Lieberman Predicts That Sizable Number of Jews Will Vote for McCain," *Jewish Exponent*, October 2, 2008.

10. Charles Blow, "Oy Vey, Obama," *New York Times*, August 20, 2010.

11. Frank Newport, "Muslims Give Obama Highest Job Approval; Mormons Lowest," *Gallup*, August 27, 2010, http://www.gallup.com/poll/142700/muslims-give-obama-highest-job-approval-mormons-lowest.aspx.

12. See AJC Annual Surveys, 1997–2008, which can be found at http://www.ajc.org/site/c.ijITI2PHKoG/b.846741/k.8A33/Publications__Surveys/apps/nl/newsletter3.asp and http://www.ajcarchives.org/main.php.

13. All three of J Street's polls of Jewish Americans can be found on J Street's website, www.jstreet.org/poll. They were conducted in June/July 2008, March 2009 and November 2010.

14. "Mormons Most Conservative Major Religious Group in U.S." Gallup, January 11, 2010, http://www.gallup.com/poll/125021/Mormons-Conservative-Major-Religious-Group.aspx.

15. Andrew Goodman and Michael Schwerner were two young Jewish civil rights activists murdered in Mississippi in the summer of 1964. Goodman, 20, and Schwerner, 24, were in Mississippi helping register African Americans to vote.

CHAPTER 6: ENDING THE CONFLICT

1. Avigdor Lieberman, interview by Martin Doerry and Christoph Schult, "It is a Clash of Civilizations," *Der Spiegel,* March 21, 2010.

2. Gil Hoffman, "Lieberman: We won't have peace for generations," *Jerusalem Post,* September 5, 2010, http://www.jpost.com/Israel/Article.aspx?id=187177.

3. Mark R. Cohen, Professor of Jewish Civilization in the Near East, Princeton University, interview by Mark Bernstein. *Princeton Alumni Weekly,* November 3, 2010.

4. The Balfour Declaration of 1917.

5. The White Paper, 1922.

6. Gershom Gorenberg, *The Accidental Empire: Israel and the Birth of the Settlements, 1967–1977* (New York: Times Books, 2006), 349.

7. Ibid., 51–52.

8. Gershom Gorenberg, "And the Land Was Troubled for 40 Years," *The American Prospect,* May 29, 2007, http://www.prospect.org/cs/articles?article=and_the_land_was_troubled_for_40_years.

9. "Majority of Palestinians and Israelis Prefer Two-state Solution over Binational State or Confederation," Harry S. Truman Institute for the Advancement of Peace, March 2010.

10. The survey presented an agreement incorporating six principles: (1) two-state solution; (2) return of refugees to Palestine only; (3) demilitarized Palestinian state; (4) 1967 lines with an exchange of territory; (5) Jerusalem—Jewish neighborhoods to be in Israel, Arab neighborhoods to be in Palestine; (6) Old City under joint management—sovereignty for both sides and the United States together.

11. "Positions of the Israeli Public and the Political Leadership (MKs) Regarding a Possible Peace Agreement. Poll 2756," Center for Middle East Peace, January 2010, http://www.centerpeace.org/Publicpolljan10.pdf.

12. Akiva Eldar, "Ha'aretz Poll: 64% of Israelis Back Two-State Solution" *Ha'aretz,* June 17, 2009, http://www.haaretz.com/print-edition/news/haaretz-poll–64-percent-of-israelis-back-two-state-solution–1.278220; Dr. Colin Irwin, "One Voice Poll: Israel and Palestine, Public Opinion, Public Diplomacy and Peace Making," April 22, 2009, http://onevoicemovement.org/programs/documents/OneVoiceIrwinReport.pdf.

13. Jonathan Lis, "IDF Intelligence Chief: Israel's Next War Will See Heavy Casualties," *Ha'aretz,* November 2, 2010, http://www.haaretz.com/news/diplomacy-defense/idf-intelligence-chief-israel-s-next-war-will-see-heavy-casualties–1.322484.

14. Sergio Della Pergola, "World Jewish Population, 2010," Berman Institute—North American Jewish Data Bank, University of Connecticut, 2010, p. 60.

15. Remarks of President George W. Bush, White House Rose Garden, June 24, 2002.

CHAPTER 7: THE CROSSROADS OF POLITICS AND POLICY ON ISRAEL

1. Brent Scowcroft and Zbigniew Brzezinski, "Middle East Priorities for Jan. 21," *Washington Post,* November 21, 2008.

2. Chester A. Crocker, Scott B. Lasensky and Samuel W. Lewis. "An American Jolt for the Middle East," *International Herald Tribune,* November 23, 2010.

3. J. J. Goldberg, *Jewish Power* (Reading, MA: Addison Wesley, 1996), 276.

4. See 2007 joint survey of Arab-Americans and Jewish Americans by the Arab-American Institute and Americans for Peace Now at http://peacenow.org/entries/archive3738, and the Anti Defamation League's 2009 Poll "American Jewish Attitudes on Israel and the Middle East Conflict," http://www.adl.org/Israel/poll_2009/.

5. "National Survey of American Jews," Gerstein-Agne Communications, questions 40–41, http://2010.jstreet.org.

6. All of J Street's polls are accessible at www.jstreet.org/poll. In three polls over three years, J Street has asked a series of questions related to the nature of the American role in resolving the Israeli-Palestinian conflict. This time series has explored support for an "active" role, including both criticism of and pressure on one or both of the parties. All three polls have found a similar pattern of support for an active role—with decreasing but still significant support for that role when it includes "criticism" and "pressure."

7. Jeffrey Birnbaum, "Washington's Power 25," *Fortune,* December 8, 1997, http://money.cnn.com/magazines/fortune/fortune_archive/1997/12/08/234927/index.htm; "AARP Tops *Fortune's* List of Most Powerful Lobbying Groups for the Second Consecutive Year," Time Warner, November 16, 1998, http://www.timewarner.com/newsroom/press-releases/1999/11/FORTUNE_Releases_Annual_Survey_Most_Powerful_Lobbying_11–15–1999.php; and Richard E. Cohen and Peter Bell, "Congressional Insiders Poll," *National Journal,* March 5, 2005.

8. The week of April 16, 2010, author, Holocaust survivor and Nobel Laureate Elie Wiesel took out full-page ads in the *New York Times,* the *Washington Post,* the *International Herald Tribune* and the *Wall Street Journal* proclaiming that Jerusalem is "above politics." In these ads, Wiesel was speaking out against the Obama administration, which publicly stated its belief that Israel should not build new homes in East Jerusalem. The ads ran immediately after the restart of final status negotiations.

9. "Pro Israel, PAC Contributions to Federal Candidates" Open Secrets, http://www.opensecrets.org/pacs/industry.php?txt=Q05&cycle=2010.

10. All five ads can be seen at http://www.committeeforisrael.com/.

11. "RJC Launches Major TV Campaign," Republican Jewish Coalition, October 19, 2010, http://www.rjchq.org/Newsroom/newsdetail.aspx?id=7ddde1a3-b2be–471e-b049-cc745a1e55d7.

12. Philip Giraldi, interview by Kourosh Ziabari. "Israeli Policies Are Manifestly Evil: Phil Giraldi," *Veterans Today,* October 15, 2010, http://www.veteranstoday.com/2010/10/15/israeli-policies-are-manifestly-evil-philip-giraldi/.

13. Alex Isenstadt, "Should Edwards Be Shvitzing?" *Politico,* June 1, 2009.

14. Rep. Donna Edwards, Remarks to New Policy PAC, October 16, 2010, http://www.donnaedwardsforcongress.com/2010/10/congresswoman-edwards-speech-at-new-policy-pac-event/.

15. "Lawmaker, AIPAC Feud after Fight over Hamas Bill," *Forward,* May 26, 2006, http://www.forward.com/articles/1009/.

16. Betty McCollum, "A Letter to AIPAC," *New York Review of Books,* June 8, 2006.

17. Uriel Heilman, "In Rare Jewish Appearance, George Soros Says Jews and Israel Cause Anti-Semitism," *Jewish Telegraphic Agency,* November 7, 2003.

18. George Soros, "On Israel, America and AIPAC," *New York Review of Books,* April 12, 2007.

CHAPTER 8: GENERATION OY!

1. Sergio DellaPergola, "World Jewish Population, 2010," Mandell Berman Institute—North American Jewish Data Bank, (Storrs, CT: University of Connecticut, 2010). http://www.jewishdatabank.org/Reports/World_Jewish_Population_2010.pdf.
2. Leonard Saxe, "U.S. Jewry, 2010: Estimates of the Size and Characteristics of the Population," presentation at the Association for Jewish Studies, December 2010, http://www.brandeis.edu/ssri/noteworthy/pop.estimates.html.
3. J Street data from its March 2010 poll; Brandeis data from Theodore Sasson, Benjamin Phillips, Charles Kadushin and Leonard Saxe, *Still Connected: American Jewish Attitudes about Israel* (Waltham, MA: Cohen Center for Modern Jewish Studies at Brandeis University, August 2010), 13.
4. Steven M. Cohen, "Attitudes of American Jews toward Israel and Israelis: The 1983 National Survey of American Jews and Jewish Communal Leaders" (New York: Institute on American Jewish-Israeli Relations of the American Jewish Committee, September 14, 1983), http://www.policyarchive.org/handle/10207/bitstreams/10891.pdf.
5. Ibid.
6. "National Survey of American Jews," Gerstein Agne Strategic Communications, November 2, 2010, http://jstreet.org/wp-content/uploads/images/J_Street_National_Survey_Results.pdf.
7. "Poll: 55% back rabbis' anti-Arab ruling," *Yediot Ahronot (YNET)*, December 15, 2010, http://www.ynetnews.com/articles/0,7340,L-3998010,00.html.
8. Steven M. Cohen and Ari Y. Kelman. "Beyond Distancing: Young Adult American Jews and Their Alienation from Israel," 2007: 8. The Jewish Identity Project of Reboot, Andrea and Charles Bronfman Philanthropies. http://www.acbp.net/About/PDF/Beyond%20Distancing.pdf.
9. Of course, it wouldn't be a Jewish communal discussion if there weren't a contradictory opinion, and that is provided by a group of Brandeis scholars who find "overall stability" in American Jewish attachment to Israel over the past quarter century. Looking at the question of generational attachment, these scholars find that "Respondents under age 45 were less likely to feel connected to Israel but no less likely to regard Israel as important to their Jewish identities." They say that younger American Jews have been feeling less connected to Israel for a generation, but they ascribe "such differences to stages of the lifecycle rather than generational turnover"—i.e., they believe that it's been true for some time that younger Jews are less attached to Israel but that they become more attached as they age (Theodore Sasson et al., *Still Connected*).
10. "Fall 2010 Survey of American Jewish Opinion," American Jewish Committee, October 11, 2010, http://www.ajc.org/site/c.ijITI2PHKoG/b.6328679/k.151A/AJC_Fall_2010_Survey.htm. It is worth noting that there is a vibrant debate among those who study trends in the Jewish population over how and who to count. Specifically, the inclusion or exclusion of those who have Jewish parents and ancestry but do not actively identify or practice the religion is a contentious topic, covered well in Sergio DellaPergola, "World Jewish Population, 2010," *Current Jewish Population Reports*, 2 (Storrs, CT: Mandell Berman Institute-North American Jewish Data Bank, University of Connecticut, 2010), http://www.jewishdatabank.org/Reports/World_Jewish_Population_2010.pdf; and in Steven M. Cohen and Ari Y. Kelman, "Thinking about Distancing from Israel," *Contemporary Jewry* 30 (October 2010): 287–296, http://www.contemporaryjewry.org/resources/2_cohen_kelman.pdf.

11. Fred Massarik, "Intermarriage: Facts for Planning: One of a Series of Reports on the Study Findings," *National Jewish Population Study* (New York: Council of Jewish Federations, 1971), 1.

12. Steven M. Cohen, *A Tale of Two Jewries: The "Inconvenient Truth" for American Jews* (New York: Jewish Life Network/Steinhardt Foundation, November 2006), 6, http:// www.jewishlife.org/pdf/steven_cohen_paper.pdf.

13. Steven M. Cohen and Ari Y. Kelman, "Beyond Distancing," 12.

14. "National Survey of American Jews," Gerstein Agne Strategic Communications, November 2, 2010.

15. Steven M. Cohen, "Attitudes of American Jews toward Israel and Israelis."

16. Michael C. Duke, "We Still Share in the Responsibility: Local Federation Working to Solve 'Next Generation Puzzle,'" *Jewish Herald Voice,* November 18, 2010, http:// jhvonline.com/we-still-share-in-the-responsibility-local-federation-working-to-solve-ne-p10090-96.htm.

17. Theodore Sasson, et al., *Still Connected.*

18. Steven M. Cohen has spent a considerable amount of time examining what he calls "Religious Stability and Ethnic Decline," or "The Tale of Two Jewries." His hypothesis is essentially that American Jews today, especially younger Jews, are "just as religiously committed, God-oriented, and ritually observant as their elders," but that "younger Jews are considerably less ethnically identified than their elders." In a 2006 study, he shows that measures of religiosity ("lit Shabbat candles," "attended Passover Seder," "fasted on Yom Kippur") remained stable between 1990 and 2000, and that synagogue membership has held (with increases in Orthodox and Reform membership making up for the decline in Conservative). However, younger people are less likely to agree with statements connecting them to the Jewish community as a whole or as a people. For example, only 35 percent of Jews aged 35–44 agree with the statement, "Jews in the United States and Jews around the world share a common destiny," compared to 44 percent of those aged 55–64.

19. Jumpstart, The Natan Fund, and The Samuel Bronfman Fund, "The Innovation Ecosystem: Emergence of a New Jewish Landscape" (Los Angeles and New York: Jumpstart, Natan Fund, and Samuel Bronfman Foundation, 2009), http://www.jewish jumpstart.org/documents/InnovationEcosystem_WebVersion.pdf.

20. Frank Luntz, "Israel in the Age of Eminem," Clear Agenda, Inc., 2003: 7, http://www. acbp.net/About/PDF/Report%20-%20Israel%20in%20the%20Age%20of%20Eminem.pdf.

21. Ibid., 3.

22. Anti-Defamation League, "The Top Ten Anti-Israel Groups in America," Anti-Defamation League, October 4, 2010, http://www.adl.org/main_Anti_Israel/top_ten_anti_israel_groups.htm?Multi_page_sections=sHeading_2.

23. Michael Calderone, "Peretz, Investors Buying Back TNR," *Politico,* http://www.politico .com/blogs/michaelcalderone/0309/Peretz_investors_buying_back_TNR_.html.

24. Peter Beinart, "Can the Democrats Fight?," *Washington Post,* December 9, 2004.

25. Peter Beinart, "The Failure of the American Jewish Establishment," *New York Review of Books,* June 10, 2010.

CHAPTER 9: FIVE MILLION JEWS, ONE OPINION?

1. Steven Windmueller, "The New Angry American Jewish Voter," *Jewish Journal,* August 10, 2010.

2. Lisa Wangsness, "Newton Synagogue Cancels Talk by Critic of Israeli Policies," *Boston Globe,* November 17, 2010.

3. Aaron Klein, "'Anti-Israel' group recruiting across nation," *WorldNet Daily,* January 26, 2010.

4. Pam Geller, "Z Street takes on Jihad-loving, Jew-hating J Street: While Hillel Snivels and Stoops," *Atlas Shrugs* (blog), February 4, 2010, http://atlasshrugs2000.typepad .com/atlas_shrugs/2010/02/z-street-takes-on-jihad-loving-jew-hating-j-street-while-hillel-snivels-and-stoops.html.

5. Shazeer Dov, "George Soros and J Street," *Jewish Journal (Boston North),* November 30, 2010.

6. Jennifer Rubin, "Morning Bits," Washingtonpost.com, January 18, 2011.

7. Adam Kredo, "BLOG: Josh Block: J Street's Worst Nightmare," *Washington Jewish Week,* November 4, 2010.

8. The Jewish Council on Public Affairs, the umbrella organization for Jewish Community Relations Councils, announced its Civility Campaign on November 1, 2010, and I was pleased to be among the initial one hundred signatories to a pledge to maintain civility in the community conversation. But without a mechanism for shining the spotlight on those who don't abide by the community's norms, the initiative will not succeed in reining in the troubling vitriol.

9. Abby Backer, "Exclude Me at Your Own Peril," *Jewish Week,* October 26, 2010.

10. "History of the San Francisco Jewish Film Festival, 1980-Present," San Francisco Jewish Film Festival, http://www.sfjff.org/about/history.

11. Stacey Palevsky, "At Festival, Rachel Corrie Film is a Lightning Rod," *Forward,* July 27, 200, http://www.forward.com/articles/110822/.

12. Jay Michaelson, "Peoplehood vs Israel," *Forward,* June 30, 2010, http://www.forward .com/articles/129089/.

13. The advertisement ran in the April 30, 2010 edition of the *Forward.*

14. "N.Y. Rabbis Pull Out of Muslim-Jewish Twinning Project," *Jewish Telegraphic Agency,* November 15, 2010.

15. Robert Bernstein, "Rights Watchdog, Lost in the Middle East," *New York Times,* October 19, 2009.

16. Kenneth Roth, "Human Rights Watch Applies Same Standards to Israel, Hamas," *Ha'aretz,* October 27, 2009.

17. Herb Keinon, "Diplomacy: Israel vs. Human Rights Watch" *Jerusalem Post,* July 16, 2009, http://www.jpost.com/home/article.aspx?id=148966.

18. Josh Block, AIPAC's spokesperson, when asked by Matt Duss of ThinkProgress to comment on the organization's circulating to the press an item that links HRW's criticism of Israel to Saudi funding, said: "HRW has repeatedly demonstrated its anti-Israel bias. . . . Human Rights Watch long ago lost all credibility when it comes to human rights issues in the Middle East." Think Progress (blog), Matt Duss, July 15, 2009, http://wonkroom. thinkprogress.org/2009/07/15/new-israeli-pr-offensive-targets-human-rights-ngos/.

19. Abraham Foxman, "No Accident," *New York Sun,* August 2, 2006.

20. Benjamin Birnbaum, "Minority Report," *New Republic,* April 7, 2010.

21. Lisa Wangsness, "Newton Synagogue Cancels Talk by Critic of Israeli Policies." *Boston Globe,* November 17, 2010.

22. George Soros, "On Israel, America and AIPAC." *New York Review of Books.* April 12, 2007, http://www.nybooks.com/articles/archives/2007/apr/12/on-israel-america-and-aipac/.

23. Stephen M. Walt, "Settling for Failure in the Middle East," *Washington Post,* September 20, 2009.

24. Jeffrey Goldberg, "A Poisonous Endorsement for J Street," *Atlantic* online, September 20, 2009, http://www.theatlantic.com/international/archive/2009/09/a-poisonous-endorsement-for-j-street/26875/.

25. Jeremy Ben-Ami, interview by Jeffrey Goldberg, "J Street's Ben-Ami on Zionism and Aid to Israel," *Atlantic*, October 23, 2009, http://www.theatlantic.com/international/archive/2009/10/j-streets-ben-ami-on-zionism-and-military-aid-to-israel/28935/.

26. Philip Weiss, "J Street Leader compares Walt and Mearsheimer to 'Protocols,'" Mondoweiss, October 23, 2009, http://mondoweiss.net/2009/10/j-street-leader-compares-walt-and-mearsheimer-to-protocols.html.

CHAPTER 10: REWRITING THE RULES

1. I should say, in the interest of full disclosure, that Rabbi Jonathan Roos made my synagogue, Temple Sinai, a welcome place for open discussion of Israel and hosted an event sponsored by J Street within months of his installation as our senior rabbi.

2. *Miskan T'Filah: A Reform Siddur*, ed. Elyse D. Frishman (New York: Central Conference of American Rabbis Press, 2007), 40.

3. Many American security experts have argued that resolving the Israeli-Palestinian conflict is an American national interest. For examples, see General David Petraeus's statement to the Senate Armed Services Committee on March 16, 2010, http://armed-services.senate.gov/statemnt/2010/03%20March/Petraeus%2003–16–10.pdf, or Anthony Cordesman's June 2010 piece, "Israel as a Strategic Liability?," http://csis.org/publication/israel-strategic-liability.

4. Benjamin Netanyahu, keynote delivery at the General Assembly of the Jewish Federations of North America, November 9, 2010, http://www.youtube.com/user/IsraeliPM#p/u/2/ysyZe9fOa1Q.

5. The Reut Institute, "Building a Political Firewall Against Israel's Delegitimization Conceptual Framework," The Reut Institute, March 2010, 25, http://reut-institute.org/data/uploads/PDFVer/20100310%20Delegitimacy%20Eng.pdf.

6. Michael Kotzin, "Introducing the Israel Action Network," *Jerusalem Post*, October 26, 2010.

7. See, for example, the website of the Global BDS Movement at www.bdsmovement.net.

8. Akiva Eldar, "For Israel, 'Delegitimization' Is Becoming an Excuse," *Ha'aretz*, November 29, 2010, http://www.haaretz.com/print-edition/opinion/for-israel-delegitimization-is-becoming-an-excuse–1.327551.

9. Michael C. Duke, "We Still Share in the Responsibility: Local Federation Working to Solve 'Next Generation Puzzle,'" *Jewish Herald Voice*, November 18, 2010, http://jhvonline.com/we-still-share-in-the-responsibility-local-federation-working-to-solve-ne-p10090-96.htm.

10. John Hagee, "Jerusalem Countdown Sermon Series," 2005, as cited in Rachel Tabachnick, "Hagee vs. Hagee—in his own words," *Talk To Action*, May 21, 2010, http://www.talk2action.org/story/2010/5/21/162959/223/Front_Page/Hagee_vs_Hagee_In_His_Own_Words.

11. John Hagee, "Sermon #1: 'Jerusalem and the Roadmap to Peace,'" *Jerusalem Countdown Sermon Series*, 2005, as cited in Rachel Tabachnick, "Hagee in His Own Words—Part Two," *Talk To Action*, May 25, 2010, http://www.talk2action.org/story/2010/5/25/124234/555/Front_Page/Hagee_in_His_Own_Words_Part_Two.

12. Footage of Joe Lieberman at CUFI 2008 Conference. "Don't Go, Joe!" video, *J Street*, http://www.youtube.com/watch?v=Tk_ihPV1TMg.

13. "Pastor Hagee and Benjamin Netanyahu in Jerusalem 3/8/10," http://www.youtube.com/watch?v=tYW9pAZfKLE.

14. Gary Bauer, "Gary Bauer on Foreign Policy: January 26, 2000: GOP Debate in Manchester, NH," *Gary Bauer on the Issues*, http://web.archive.org/web/20050206025635/http://www.issues2000.org/2000/Gary_Bauer.htm#Foreign_Policy_0.

15. Gary Bauer, "'Two-state Solution' Not Synonym for Peace," *Politico,* September 3, 2010, http://www.politico.com/news/stories/0910/41739.html.

16. In Steven Gutkin, "Huckabee Says 2 States in Holy Land 'Unrealistic,'" *Breitbart* via *Associated Press,* August 18, 2009, http://www.breitbart.com/article.php?id=D9A5BQ 482&show_article=1&catnum=2.

17. "Poll: American Support for Israel Remains Solid; Increase in Support for Action to Prevent Iran from Going Nuclear," Anti-Defamation League, October 26, 2009, http://www.adl.org/PresRele/IslME_62/5631_62.htm.

18. "Bipartisan Poll Shows Voters Want America to Stand with Israel," The Israel Project, November 3, 2010, http://www.theisraelproject.org/site/apps/nlnet/content2.aspx?c= hsJPK0PIJpH&b=5708939&ct=8856649.

19. "Statement on Islamic Community Center near Ground Zero, Anti-Defamation League," Anti-Defamation League, July 28, 2010, http://www.adl.org/PresRele/CvlRt _32/5820_32.htm.

20. "Bloomberg on Mosque Vote," *Wall Street Journal,* August 3, 2010, http://online.wsj. com/article/NA_WSJ_PUB:SB10001424052748703545604575407673221908474.html.

21. "Who We Are," American Jewish Committee, http://www.ajc.org/site/c.ijITI2PHKoG/ b.789093/k.124/Who_We_Are.htm.

22. "AJC Speaks Out on Controversial Downtown New York Islamic Center," American Jewish Committee, August 2, 2010. http://www.ajc.org/site/apps/nlnet/content2.asp x?c=ijITI2PHKoG&b=849241&ct=8552057.

23. "Reform Jewish Movement Welcomes Approval of Cordoba House Mosque and Community Center," Religious Action Center of Reform Judaism, August 4, 2010. http://rac.org/Articles/index.cfm?id=21580.

24. See, for example, a vigorous defense of the Tea Party by Joel Pollack, who ran for Congress in 2010 in Illinois' 9th Congressional District, linking his Jewish roots and history to his support for the Tea Party's agenda, http://www.pollakforcongress. com/2010/09/12/tea-party-freedom-fest-speech-by-joel-pollak/.

25. See, for example, "The Myth of the Anti-Israel Tea Party," Jennifer Rubin, *Washington Post* blog, and "The Tea Party is Great for the U.S.-Israel Relationship," *Israel Matzav,* December 7, 2010.

26. "For Jewish Federations, Decline in Donors Dwarfs Recession Woes," Jacob Berkman, Jewish Telegraphic Agency, November 9, 2010, reporting on a study released by the Jewish Federations of North America, http://jta.org/news/article/2010/11/09/2741673/ federations-leave-behind-serious-questions-in-new-orleans.

CHAPTER 11: WHAT BECOMES OF TEL AVIV IN 2109?

1. Lonely Planet's Top Ten Cities for 2011, http://www.lonelyplanet.com/usa/new-york-city/travel-tips-and-articles/76165.

2. Dan Senor and Saul Singer, *Start-up Nation: The Story of Israel's Economic Miracle* (New York: Grand Central Publishing, 2009), 11.

3. Ibid., 12.

4. Ibid., 13.

5. Ibid.

6. Rory McCarthy, "Barak: Make Peace with Palestinians or Face Apartheid," *Jerusalem Post,* February 3, 2010, http://www.guardian.co.uk/world/2010/feb/03/barak-apart-heid-palestine-peace.

7. Barak Ravid, David Landu, Aluf Benn, Shmuel Rosner, "Olmert to Haaretz: Two State Solution, or Israel Is Done For," *Ha'aretz,* November 29, 2007, http://www.haaretz. com/news/olmert-to-haaretz-two-state-solution-or-israel-is-done-for-1.234201.

8. Barak Ravid, "Deputy PM: Israel Must Cede Land to Remain Jewish and Democratic," *Ha'aretz*, November 15, 2010.

9. Sergio DellaPergola, "World Jewish Population, 2010," Berman Institute—North American Jewish Data Bank, University of Connecticut, 2010.

10. Leslie Susser, "Is One-State Solution an Answer to Greater Israel Dreams?," Jewish Telegraphic Agency, August 2, 2010.

11. Leon Pinsker, *Auto-Emancipation* (New York: Maccabean Publishing Company, 1906), 15–16.

12. Uzi Rebhun and Gilad Malach, "Demographic Trends in Israel," The Metzilah Center for Zionist, Jewish, Liberal and Humanist Thought (Jerusalem, 2009), 27, http://www.metzilah.org.il/webfiles/fck/Demo%20eng%20final.pdf%281%29.pdf.

13. The United Nations Development Program provides one measure of income inequality for all nations, and Israel ranks second among the thirty-one member nations of the Organization for Economic Cooperation and Development, http://hdrstats.undp.org/en/indicators/161.html.

14. Organization for Economic Cooperation and Development, *Israel: A Divided Society. Results of a Review of Labour-Market and Social Policy,* http://www.oecd.org/dataoecd/0/40/44394444.pdf.

CHAPTER 12: AMERICA'S STAKE IN ENDING THE CONFLICT

1. Remarks of President Barack Obama, press conference at the Nuclear Security Summit, April 13, 2010.

2. Secretary of State Hillary Clinton, from remarks at AIPAC, March 22, 2010, http://www.state.gov/secretary/rm/2010/03/138722.htm

3. The Iraq Study Group Report, 39, http://media.usip.org/reports/iraq_study_group_report.pdf.

4. Ibid., 33.

5. Shibley Telhami, "2010 Arab Public Opinion Poll," University of Maryland in conjunction with Zogby International (August 5, 2010), 6, http://www.politico.com/static/PPM170_100804_arabpublic.html.

6. Statement of General David H. Petraeus, U.S. Army Commander, U.S. Central Command, Before the Senate Armed Services Committee on the Posture of U.S. Central Command, March 16, 2010, http://armed-services.senate.gov/statemnt/2010/03%20March/Petraeus%2003–16–10.pdf.

7. Abraham Foxman, press statement in response to March 16, 2010, testimony from General David Petraeus, March 18, 2010, http://www.adl.org/PresRele/IslME_62/5721_62.htm.

8. Alan Dershowitz, "J Street Can No Longer Claim to be Pro-Israel," *Huffington Post*, April 21, 2010, http://www.huffingtonpost.com/alan-dershowitz/j-street-can-no-longer-cl_b_546841.html.

9. Peter Baker, "Obama Puts His Own Mark on Foreign Policy Issues," *New York Times*, April 13, 2010.

10. Jeremy Ben-Ami, Letter to the Editor, *New York Times*, April 21, 2010.

11. Anthony Cordesman, "Israel as a Strategic Liability?" Center for Strategic and International Studies, June 2, 2010, http://csis.org/publication/israel-strategic-liability.

12. Caroline Glick, "Our World: The Plain Truth about Israel," *Jerusalem Post*, June 7, 2010.

13. Ibid.

14. Remarks by President Barack Obama, Cairo, Egypt, June 4, 2009.
15. National Security Advisor James L. Jones, remarks from J Street's 2009 National Conference, http://conference.jstreet.org/conference_2009.
16. Mark Landler and Isabel Kershner, "Israeli Settlement Growth Must Stop," *New York Times,* May 27, 2009.
17. Daniel Kurtzer, "With Settlement Deal, U.S. Will Be Rewarding Israel's Bad Behavior," *Washington Post,* November 21, 2010.
18. Thomas L. Friedman, "Reality Check," *New York Times,* December 11, 2010.
19. Ibid.

CHAPTER 13: GIVING VOICE TO OUR VALUES

1. A recording of the interview on the *Diane Rehm Show* from July 7, 2010, can be found on the show's website, http://thedianerehmshow.org/shows/2010–07–07/us-israeli-relations.
2. See, for instance, the campaign against the New Israel Fund launched by the Israeli organization Im Tirtzu in 2010, or visit the website of NGO Monitor, a project designed to catalogue the misdeeds of the human rights community in Israel.
3. Hilary Leila Kreiger, "Dershowitz Spars over How to Defend Israel in the U.S.," *Jerusalem Post,* October 12, 2010.
4. Sudarsan Raghavan, "World Report Profile: Richard Goldstone; A South African Jurist Takes on Balkan and Rwanda Conflicts, Seeking to Punish War Criminals," *Los Angeles Times,* March 14, 1995.
5. Claudia Braude, "Goldstone's Gambit: The Man behind the U.N. Report," *Forward,* September 16, 2009.
6. Moshe Halbertal, "The Goldstone Illusion," *New Republic,* November 6, 2009.
7. Shuki Sadeh, "Peres: Goldstone is a Small Man Out to Hurt Israel," *Ha'aretz,* November 11, 2009.
8. Ha'aretz News Service, "Dershowitz: Goldstone Is a Traitor to the Jewish People," *Ha'aretz,* January 31, 2010, http://www.haaretz.com/news/dershowitz-goldstone-is-a-traitor-to-the-jewish-people–1.265833.
9. Debbie Gild-Hayo, "Harming Democracy in the Heart of Democracy," Association for Civil Rights in Israel position paper, October 2010, http://www.acri.org.il/eng/story.aspx?id=769.

INDEX